Praise for *Two Spirits, One Heart*

"Marsha Aizumi's *Two Spirits, One Heart* is a moving memoir of facing one's fears while traveling down unknown, fearsome paths. We recommend this book to all parents. Each of us can enrich our lives by learning about this remarkable story of courage, fear, and understanding. This author's eloquence allowed us to share in her great adventure by walking in her shoes with her son, Aiden. You will experience, as we did, her triumphs and tears."

Harold and Ellen Kameya, Founders
L.A. Asian Pacific Islander
Parents, Families, and Friends of Lesbians and Gays (PFLAG)

"*Two Spirits, One Heart* is a powerful account of a mother's love during the transition of her daughter's sexual transformation into a beloved son. This marvelously written autobiography captures the personal anguish and triumphs of their journey together and allows the reader to experience and understand the bravery, pain and acceptance gender change requires. Thank you, Marsha, you touched my heart."

Karen Jorgensen Burstein, Author
What a Woman Wants and *Pay for Results*

"It's not a story about losing a daughter or gaining a son; it's about a mother's unconditional love and acceptance of her child. It's about a mother and child's journey together towards understanding and embracing truth beyond society's boundaries and expectations regarding gender identity and expression. It will make you feel empowered to be yourself, to be an ally, and to be a supportive mother, father, parent, or guardian to your transgender child who is most importantly, still your child."

Phoenix Schneider
MSW, Mentor, Activist, Program Director
The Trevor Project

"*Two Spirits, One Heart* is an honest and open look into a mother's heart and mind on the journey with her child's transition from female to male. Marsha and Aiden's story is one of struggle, compassion and the real meaning of unconditional love."

Terry Stone, Executive Director
Centerlink: The Community of LGBT Centers

"All too often, we see appalling cases of LGBTQ youth who suffer immensely because they have been marginalized or rejected by their own family members. Marsha's personal account of providing unconditional love and support to her trans son before, during and after his transition is truly inspiring. A must read for any loving parent who is struggling with the gender identity or sexual orientation of their own child."

Darrin Wilstead
Mentoring & Alumni Program Director
Point Foundation

"Since I met Marsha, I have been astounded by the love she feels for Aiden. I can only think how fortunate Aiden's spirits are to have a mother that so nurtured them and instilled the courage to be himself. They are beautiful together, their family is beautiful, and this book is so important at a time of such polarization in our society around identity. I wish this were required reading for every parent as it is a roadmap to acceptance, compassion, and unconditional love for one's child no matter who or what they turn out to be."

Michael Ferrera, Director
LifeWorks at the L.A. Gay & Lesbian Center

"This is Marsha and Aiden's courageous story of inspiration, tenacity and hope. It provided us with a deeper understanding about the spirit of a boy who never gave up and a mother whose unwavering love and acceptance provided the ability for that spirit to take flight. This book also illustrates the passion it takes to find your way and the compassion it takes to support that journey."

John and Joan Hall, Founders
Opportunities for Learning Public Charter Schools

"As a physician, I was so deeply moved by Aiden's 'coming out' letter to his family and friends that I asked his permission to share it with another patient unable to express himself so elegantly. As a mother, I was once again moved to tears by the eloquence of Marsha's raw emotions and unconditional love for her son. This is an inspirational book that should be mandatory reading for all high school, college, and medical students."

M. Kathleen Jones, M.D.

"Marsha Aizumi's candid account of her journey toward acceptance and eventual celebration of her transgender child is a spiritual odyssey that has universal resonance. It is one that speaks to the human desire for wholeness and authenticity. Her story poignantly illustrates the spiritual wisdom that beyond the labels 'lesbian,' 'FTM,' and 'Asian' lies a child that longs for the unconditional love of a mother."

Rev. Dr. Jonipher Kwong
First Unitarian Church of Hawaii

Two Spirits, One Heart

Two Spirits, One Heart

A Mother, Her Transgender Son,
and Their Journey to Love and Acceptance

MARSHA AIZUMI
WITH AIDEN AIZUMI

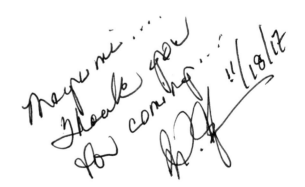

MAGNUS
BOOKS

This book is dedicated to the four people who have been an integral part of my incredible journey: my son Aiden, who courageously asked me to stand by his side and travel down this amazing road together; my son Stefen, whose unconditional love for his brother serves as a model for me of what true acceptance can be; my future daughter, Mary, who brought love back into Aiden's life; and to my husband, Tad, the rock of our family and the love of my life.

M.A.

To Mary, my best friend and the one I love the most; to my brother, Stefen, for always taking the Little Mermaid sleeping bag; to Uncle Bob and Auntie Bonnie, for just loving me; and to Papa and Momma, for first loving Ashley, then loving me even more.

A.A.

Table of Contents

Introduction

For as long as I can remember, my life has been grounded in the concept of living the life you dream. I pursued my dream when I adopted my two children from Japan. I retired to live my dream when I sold my insurance business and became a stay-at-home mother. And as I began to write this book, I dreamed of creating a safer world for both of my sons.

When I talk to my children about their future, I always tell them to follow their dreams. Even if the dream may not be realized, I believe that they are being led in the direction of their heart's desire. Perhaps they will meet someone who will teach them a valuable lesson or introduce them to an individual who will impact them in a positive way. I no longer ignore signs that appear more frequently and grow in intensity. I listen to the voice inside my head that feels in alignment with my heart. This is how I strive to live my life and this is how I have raised my children.

My oldest child was born female, but today he lives as a man. According to Native American belief, he has two spirits. His dream was to live in alignment with how he thinks and feels as a man. For years, this was his ongoing struggle.

Together, my son and I represent two separate spirits: a mother and her child. Aiden has faced his journey as he reconciled who he was meant to be. I faced a journey as well, choosing to be the mother I was meant to be. And we have faced a journey together as he traveled down the road of transition and became the person that lives inside of him. It has been a difficult journey for both of us and for our family. We have had to confront more fear and doubt than each of us thought possible. But someone once told me that fear backs down when standing in the face of love, and no truer words were ever spoken with respect to our journey.

We have walked down some dark paths with very little light to guide our way. Aiden feared rejection and though it still haunts him, he chooses to focus on the positive things in his life. I feared for his safety, acceptance, and future happiness, but now choose to focus on how he has attracted a sense of worthiness, opportunities for leadership and love for what he does. The rewards for our courage and our determination to set aside personal fears and step into the light of love have brought us more awareness and more joy than I could ever imagine. We developed a deeper understanding of ourselves and others, grew in confidence to tackle the unknown, and experienced fear take flight as we stood together fearless on the outside, but often trembling on the inside. Throughout this journey we have chosen to travel together. And we have been guided by only one heart, and that heart was love.

What is now so evident is that Aiden lives in the best of both worlds. As female for twenty years, he has acquired the sensitivity, intuitive nature, and compassionate qualities often valued in women. As a man, he is more objective, rational, and focused—qualities stereotypically male. Most of us strive over our lifetime to balance the "yin and yang" of our existence. At age twenty-four, Aiden has integrated both into his life.

For those who are struggling with their child's sexual orientation, gender identity, or any perceived difference, I hope this story gives you hope, information, and a vision of what your love and support can mean to your child. I didn't foresee that this path would bring me so much joy and provide me with such rich and rewarding experiences. I did not believe that I could summon up such courage to speak up and speak out. I would never have known how profusely my love could flow or how far my love could reach. All of these things have been gifts of this path I have chosen to walk with my son.

When I first sat down to write this book, my fingers positioned over the keyboard, my heart beat with excitement. My words were flying off the page as the memories spilled out naturally and effortlessly. In a short period of time, I had written several pages, when usually it took hours to compose the same length of material. I was motivated by the speed of my book's creation.

Months later, my mood shifted. Writing about the difficult times my son and I experienced, I hesitated and began to filter and analyze what I was going to say or what I had already written. My fingers no longer flew over the keyboard, not only as I relived the painful events from my past, but also projected into the future, speculating who might read this book and how they would judge me.

In the end, I have chosen to write as much of the truth as I could possibly write, while protecting those sensitive areas of my son's personal journey. Some names in this book have been changed to respect the privacy of others. But most of the names are real family, friends, and allies who have nurtured, accepted, and loved us through this journey.

I want Asian-American Pacific Islander families to know that I, too, wrestled with the honor of my family name and the dignity of my ancestors. But I have chosen to honor my family by telling the truth to all who will listen.

I want mothers to know that I began writing this book for LGBT individuals and their families, and now realize I was writing a book about a mother's love. I believe any mother can relate to my story. We all want the best for our children, we all face times of uncertainty, wondering if we are doing the right thing, and we all want to be the best mothers we can possibly be, although there are times we may stumble and fall.

I also want parents to know that I, too, faltered and denied what seemed to be such clear and obvious signs about my son's identity. Sometimes the guilt of this avoidance makes me so sad that I wish I could rewind those years and make different decisions. But I can't. I did the best I could at the time and must forgive myself for anything I did out of not knowing or not being ready to face the journey that lay before me. I hope this book brings peace to parents who may share similar regrets or remorse.

I have chosen to write this book for lesbian, gay, bisexual, and transgender (LGBT) individuals and their families as a tribute to all who have decided to love their children in spite of their fears and as a message of hope to all who are still fighting the fear that this journey has brought into their lives. May the thoughts I am sharing encourage you to continue to love your child no matter what and may this book serve to inspire you to release the fear and embrace the love you have for your child.

Finally, the most important reason that I have written this book is to serve as evidence of the fact that although this road we chose to take was not easy, it is filled with amazing experiences that I would never have been able to behold had I cowered in shame, fear, or anger. This journey has been healing. It has lifted my awareness and has opened my eyes to the wonders that were always around me, but I had failed to recognize. I walk in the world taking beauty and acts of love less for granted. I walk in the world recognizing acts of courage, compassion, and acceptance more often where once I moved through that world unconsciously. I may not notice every one of these incredible moments, but I certainly recognize and appreciate more of them than ever before.

This journey with Aiden has made my life so much richer. It has deepened my appreciation for my husband and brought me closer to my younger son, Stefen. I am living the life I dream, and I am living it because Aiden had the courage to say, "This is who I am."

Marsha Aizumi

May 2012

Ashley

"And the day came when the risk it took to remain tight inside the bud was more painful than the risk it took to blossom."

—Anais Nin

CHAPTER ONE

Marching to a Different Beat

We marched side-by-side, my daughter and I, the smile on her face stretching almost as long as the band that was playing around us in the parade. I missed that smile. Where had it been all these years? At last, at long last, Ashley seemed to be finding herself, five years after coming out as a lesbian. She was turning the corner after some very difficult intermediary years—for both of us. I could see it in her face, her movement. She marched with her head held high, part of a drum corps comprised of predominately gay and lesbian musicians. She felt happy. She played her music, and played it with people marching to the beat of the same drum—literally and figuratively.

It was a day worthy of celebration: Ashley and her drum corps band mates won first place. After the hugging and cheering were over, most of the group decided to continue the celebration by having dinner together. Initially, Ashley and I waited with the group for a large table to open up. But, eventually, we decided to skip the victory dinner and head home.

I was tired from marching as an unofficial photographer, and Ashley's mood clearly showed her preference. Happy a short while ago, she moped around, a black cloud hanging over her head now. Anyone within ten feet could sense her irritability. How could an interior storm blow in so quickly on such a triumphant day, after a victorious performance?

"I was binding all day; it was really getting uncomfortable," Ashley remembers, referring to the often painful way she tied down her breasts with an extremely tight vest fashioned out of nylon and spandex. She learned this from other lesbians who identified with their masculine side. This binder reminded me of the spandex bodysuit I wore once under a form fitting garment to erase my bulges. The binder made me feel hot, unable to breathe, and I remember I couldn't wait to get home and take it off. It made me appear thinner, but I never wore it again because it was so uncomfortable.

The pressure of the binding seemed to increase something else: Ashley's suppressed feelings. She recalls, "I felt frustrated, anxious, and just stuck." She paced the restaurant lobby. Her face took on a scowl and she retreated from conversation and interaction with others. A bubble of discontent formed around her.

Like summer race riots partially attributable to the heat that percolates and boils already deep-seated resentments, her binding created a similar inability to hold back thoughts and feelings she had bottled up for years. She could restrain herself from expressing this resentment, but could not hide her unhappiness.

Totally baffled, I shook my head. Wasn't this the same girl I'd seen marching, smiling, and celebrating a couple of hours before? I see myself as observant and every bit as sensitive as any other mother, but the vast ocean of mystery known as the emotions of a young girl developing into a young woman had me totally perplexed that day.

We drove home in silence. My introvert nature recharged the way all introverts do: by withdrawing into my own quiet world. Ashley brooded beside me, also withdrawn and quiet, but for different reasons. We found a restaurant close to home and stopped for a quick dinner. Her mood was still surly, but I reasoned we could make it through the meal. This wasn't the first time, nor would it be the last time, I would have to be patient with my daughter.

It had been a long day for both of us. We'd eat dinner and drive the short distance home. I envisioned each of us walking into our separate bedrooms, she to find a happy place, me to read and crash on a Sunday night.

As we ate, I tried to make pleasant conversation, picking at my dinner as I feigned being happy and involved. But Ashley grew more ill tempered by the moment. I swallowed back my own frustration, not wanting this wonderful day to end in an argument with my daughter. Finally, I couldn't take it anymore. I looked at her and calmly tried to speak as I felt my teeth begin to clench, "We have had the most wonderful day together. Your band performed so well and you took first place. And you have become grouchier by the minute. What is your problem?"

My exasperation now released like a spent geyser, I braced myself for a harsh response. Any number of possibilities could be heading my way: something I did, said, didn't do, or didn't say. While my friends and colleagues know me well for sensing others accurately through verbal and non-verbal cues, my "A" game deserted me in this important moment: reading my daughter. I waited for her to tell me what new boundaries I'd apparently crossed.

Instead her voice softly said, "Momma, you promise you're not going to get mad..."

My brow furled and my body stiffened. I didn't expect that response.

Since they were young, both of my children learned one of my cardinal rules of communication: use this phrase before confiding something that they know will provoke a reaction from me. "If you warn Momma, then I can prepare myself not to get mad," I'd said. "If you don't warn Momma and tell me something that will make me mad, I will probably get mad." My message was clear: if you blindside me, you will receive a negative reaction. If you prepare me, I can ground myself to hear the bad news. A couple of times, they'd failed to use the "promise" phrase, and felt the after effects. After that, my children, especially Ashley, grew very good at giving me a heads-up.

I responded in my usual way, my voice calm and gentle: "I promise, Ash." My energy settled into a tender and loving place as I watched her forehead crinkle and her eyes draw upward, formulating the words she'd say. Her body sank ever so slightly into a position of uncertainty, hesitation. I picked up deep fear. She later told me she felt like dinosaurs were running between her stomach and heart, big, loud, and thumpy. "In that moment the restaurant around us disappeared, and all I could hear was my heart pounding like a drum." Ashley recalls.

My daughter stared at the table between us. I waited—my own uneasiness building with each silent second.

Finally, the words tumbled out of her mouth like boulders down a mountainside: "I'm uncomfortable in my body now, and I want to transition to a guy."

She glanced up at me warily, waiting for a response. Some eternities can be measured in seconds. Ashley looked like she was experiencing one of those moments without end.

My mind froze. I stopped breathing for what seemed like a minute; all extraneous noises and people disappeared from my consciousness. We gazed across the table at each other. Ashley's eyes searched mine for an answer: when I told her I loved her, did I mean "forever, no matter what, and no matter whom you are?" Her face wore her deepest fear; that I was two seconds away from rejecting her and throwing her out of the house, adding to the sad and disturbing collection of horror stories that often accompany these types of revealing moments.

But I wasn't thinking about rejection, transgender kids, uncomfortable bodies, or anything of the sort. Instead, the enormous missing scenes of a movie dropped into place: a two-year-old refusing to wear dresses and bows; a first grader announcing she was in love with a girl named Allie; a middle school student who didn't feel like she fit in anywhere; a high school cutter and binder; a withdrawn, emotional, and angry teenager; and a high school senior who refused to wear the traditional black drape for senior pictures and opted to don a tuxedo like all the boys.

Often, I tried to grasp what my daughter's choices meant. "Do you feel like you want to be a boy?" I once asked her.

"No, Momma."

"But you dress like a boy, want to wear your hair like a boy, and you don't like anything girlie."

"I am a butch lesbian. I just like boy things."

Now I realized she had finally come to terms with the truth: she could no longer masquerade as someone she was not. She wasn't a butch lesbian.

She was a boy in a girl's body.

Immediately, the voices in my head rushed to center stage. They fought for the microphone and began to speak all at once:

What does 'transition to a guy' really mean?

Does she want to change into a boy physically?

What does THAT mean?

What will we call her?

How will I keep her safe?

HOW WILL I KEEP HER SAFE!

The only thing I remember *not* hearing? An answer.

As these and other questions grappled for my spinning mind's attention, Ashley called herself "transgender," more specifically, a female-to-male transgender person or "FTM." Within her calm description, my academic mind picked up signs of contemplation, research, and investigation. She'd thought this through. Conversely, although the word transgender was not a foreign word to me, I didn't use it. Or understand it fully. I was still learning how to be the mother of a lesbian.

Finally, I spoke. "How many people know about this decision?"

"No one, Momma, but you." Flags of fear shot up. When Ashley came out as a lesbian, many knew before Tad and I were told. She felt some sense of acceptance. This time it was different. I felt afraid for her because she was uncertain—not about her direction, but about whether people would accept her. Family members and friends still loved her when she came out as a lesbian, but she was also still a girl. Would they love her as a boy?

I had no answers. I didn't know what it truly meant to be a transgender person. When Ashley came out as lesbian, I knew this meant she was attracted to girls, I learned that her masculine inclination made her a "butch" lesbian, and she always reminded me that there was no risk of pregnancy, like being in a heterosexual relationship. During her lesbian years, I could hide behind the fact that she was still considered a girl, and the topic of being lesbian rarely came up. But being transgender would be a whole different issue. The only thing I knew about being transgender came through my observations of a male to female young person who I met through Parents, Families, and Friends for Lesbians and Gays (PFLAG) and some casual conversations with the mother of a transgender teenager whom I didn't know very well. This unsettled me as much as Ashley's revelation. I felt completely unprepared, out of control. As I sat in the restaurant, trying to pull myself together, my scurrying thoughts vacillated between several things: fear for Ashley's personal safety, fear I wouldn't have the answers to support her, fear of Ashley never finding love and social acceptance.

I didn't know the process of becoming a transgender person. I didn't know where to turn to or whom to ask for advice. I couldn't think of a single person with whom I was comfortable turning to for answers. I don't have to know the answers to something, but my comfort level relies on knowing where to turn. In business and in education, I developed proficiency for creating both a "Plan A" and a back-up "Plan B."

This time I had neither.

However, I did know one thing beyond the shadow of a doubt: since I was the first person to whom she'd announced this life-changing decision, I held a responsibility they didn't exactly write about in all those parenting books I'd read—setting the course to prepare my family before my child's transition. It felt no less solemn and imposing than the day I stood before a judge, promising I would love and guide this little girl, adopted from Japan, as my own. Little did I know on that day what that promise would mean.

I flashed back to Ashley's last shocking announcement: the day she declared herself a lesbian. She did so dramatically, mixing in the news during a heated and tearful conversation about repeated lies unrelated to her sexual orientation. I didn't handle the revelation well. I was upset with the way she'd broken the trust of her father and me. She had been lying about so many things. I wanted to cry every time I saw her. I retreated to analyze my shortcomings as a parent, which ran in opposition to the open, communicative, upfront mother everyone else knew. In my eyes, her dishonesty represented a personal failure on my part as a mother to teach my children the importance of honesty and being trustworthy. I was crushed.

But there was a problem. Ashley thought my reaction was about *whom* she had chosen to love.

Things will be different this time, I vowed as I sat in the restaurant. Ashley would know without question that I was on her side. She would never be alone on this journey, regardless if everyone else in the family rejected her. I would be her rock, as well as her sounding board. As I grounded myself into this decision, resolve poured deep within me and commitment centered within my soul. A sense of peace flooded my body and settled into my heart. I loved my daughter; that was the only thing that ultimately mattered. To the core of my being, I would stand by her side.

I often wonder why I wasn't more bowled over by the news that my child wanted to transition to be a man. Yes, I had fears and concerns, but I never said to her, "Are you sure?" or protest "You're too young to make a decision like this." I realized that for three years I watched my child continue to be depressed, withdrawn, and unhappy, even after coming out as a lesbian. So, somewhere deep within, this declaration gave me hope that perhaps this could be the answer to Ashley feeling whole, complete, and happy.

But as strong and committed as I appeared for Ashley on the outside, a part of me still felt uncertain and scared that I would say the wrong thing, support a decision that was irreversible, and not be able to protect my daughter from a world that would ridicule, condemn, and want to hurt her. One moment I was filled with determination, the next moment a frightening thought would enter my mind and I would feel my resolve begin to wither. I would then have to gather my courage and not succumb to the negativity, but look for the positive, the hope, and the good in what I was facing. I struggled, but I persevered. I would not lose this battle. My child's future depended on my optimism and my resilient spirit.

"When are you going to tell Papa?" I asked. Being married for thirty-six years to Tad, I didn't believe he would flip out or respond angrily. He was a calm, accepting, and forgiving man from whom I had learned much from over the years we were together. But I also knew he could feel hurt being left out of this life changing decision. On top of hurting my husband, the dishonesty of keeping a secret from him made me feel like I was sleeping on a bed of cracker crumbs. I would never feel comfortable until my husband knew all that was going on with Ashley.

My husband and I didn't have any secrets—and I wasn't going to hold hers from him for long. Tad needed to know as soon as possible, along with our son, Stefen. In time of crisis, my family is one that will rise up, band together, and share our strength with one another. United we had faced challenges in the past. More than ever, we needed to give Ashley our solid support. First, she had to tell Tad, then Stefen.

She cringed and shook her head. "I don't know."

"How do you want to tell Papa? We have to figure out a way to let him know."

"I think I will write him a letter."

I nodded. "That sounds like a good plan." I expected that Tad, being a rational thinker and needing time to process information, would read the letter, take a few hours or perhaps a day, to ponder what he read, then approach me to talk about what all this meant. It felt like a good approach.

"And what about Stefen?"

"I will give him a letter, too."

I wasn't worried about Stefen. His kind heart and unwavering admiration of his sister, I expected, would allow him to readily accept Ashley's new gender identity.

We left the restaurant silently, agreed on the next step. Ashley's face showed her relief: I wasn't mad, and I was in her corner. Still, her body tensed with a fear only those in her position could ever truly appreciate: she still had to tell her dad. As I looked at her, I wanted to tell her he'd be good with it, that there was nothing to worry about ... but I couldn't. I could hope that I knew my husband well enough to predict his response, but I honestly didn't know how Tad would take the news. He loved his little girl so much.

Tad also dreamed of a life where Ashley could do extremely well as a professional golfer. This dream faded in and out with Ashley, but her father never lost hope. Tad saw the two of them walking the golf courses together in the future, sharing memories of that perfect shot or the shot that got away. Golf had become a way for Tad to bond with both Ashley and Stefen. And even though Ashley could still golf as a guy, she would never be as competitive due to her relatively short height and lesser strength when hitting the ball. Without her ability to compete at a high level against other guys, she would lose her motivation to keep playing. And Tad would lose bonding time with his daughter as well as his dream that she would play college golf, and perhaps go on to a professional career.

As I drove home, my mind launched into high gear, a two-sided conversation working through future concerns.

"I wonder how Tad will take this?"

He'll be okay, because all he wants is for Ashley to be happy.

"What about Stefen? Will he be ridiculed and rejected because of this new situation?"

I have to stay positive and not think that way. Stefen has good friends who come from good families. The ones who won't accept Ashley aren't friends we'd be comfortable staying in contact with.

"It will be okay."

Our family will be okay. I just have to see that picture.

* * *

I got through each day guarding Ashley's secret until she was ready to tell more people. In the meantime, to whom was I going to talk? I didn't know anyone who had already journeyed down this road. And I didn't feel comfortable talking to others before Tad knew.

Anxious and often edgy on the inside, I resorted to my normal course of action when there is nowhere else to turn: I ordered some books online. I would read as much as I could to understand what being a transgender person meant, along with the way in which my world would change as Ashley's world changed. While waiting for the books to arrive, I spent countless hours on the computer reading everything I could find about this new word in my vocabulary, a word that would become central to my life. This research deflected me away from my fears and uneasy thoughts because my mind was preoccupied with learning. Studying also made me feel I could come up with a plan, so I felt less out of control.

The more I researched, however, the more I realized just how challenging my future was going to be. But despite the adversity that lay ahead, this was about my daughter's life. So reminding myself of that, I felt my courage return even with my concern, and I began to integrate the information I read into my mind, then into my heart.

A few days later, Ashley told me that she delivered a letter to both her papa and younger brother. She had begun writing the letter months ago, but only finished it after revealing to me her plans to transition.

To all my Family and Friends:

It has taken me over a year to be able to sit down and finally write this letter. It is one that has taken place late at night because I can't sleep with my thoughts being pulled at by these unspoken words. What I am hoping is that no matter what this letter contains that you will just love me for me. I am still the same person you picked up from school, or hugged on Christmas. I am the same friend that you had lunch with or studied with, cramming in information late into the night. The only difference will be how you will see me physically.

When I came out as a lesbian, years ago, you all stood by me and showed me nothing but support and love. I know that it may have been hard for you, but none of you left my side...and none of you loved me any less. You learned and you grew with me. I am more than grateful every day to have such accepting people in my life.

I have spent this last year looking at myself and asking, "Who am I?" Or rather "What am I?" I rarely ever refer to myself as a lesbian, and when I am called miss or ma'am it makes me cringe. When I look into the future I do not see myself being someone's wife, but rather someone's husband. I don't see myself being a mother, but a father. I have come to believe myself to be a female to male transgender person...a boy trapped in a girl's body and unable to fully embrace my life without accepting that fact. And what I want is to transition into the boy I am on the inside; to let my body match my brain.

If I could paint the perfect picture, this letter will not affect my relationship with you in a negative way. What I wish for is that you will still accept me for who I am, and understand that the person inside is still the same. I would love to see you all on this journey with me and supporting me along the way. I know this is a process that will take time and adjustment. You will be losing your daughter, your niece, your female friend and cousin, and your sister, and in return be gaining another son, another nephew, another male cousin and friend, a brother... It will be mourning the death of a person you have come to know on the outside, but I remain the same person on the inside. I know that it may take you all some time to adjust. All I hope for is that you will still love me no matter what the person on the outside looks like.

I hope that you will start to use only the male pronoun when referring to me, even though that will take some time. I have yet to pick a name to represent this new person that I am transitioning to. I hope that when that time comes you will all be willing to call me by that name with a sense of love that you do when you talk to

me now. I hope that when you refer to me that it is not with shame, but with pride.
I pray that this is not something that will change the closeness that we share as a
family, or the ability that we have to talk as friends.

    I love you all with every ounce of my being.
    The transman formerly,
    Ashley Akemi Aizumi

It took Ashley a week to complete the letter she began months ago. She worked on it a little bit every night. Again, her ability to think through and research her choices paid off: she got the idea from a 20/20 TV special on transgender kids and their families, because the older female to male transgender (FTM) teenager wrote a letter to his parents. Ashley felt most secure delivering the news by letter, because she could express exactly how she felt and not stumble over the words. "Also, I knew I would chicken out if I had to tell someone in person," she later confided to me. "I was nervous."

Ashley walked through the house, strategically placing the letters where her brother and father would find them: in front of the television screen for Stefen, near the computer for Tad.

Stefen found his letter when he returned from school. Thinking it was a note from me; he opened it and read the words. His reaction was both nonchalant and deeply relieving: "It doesn't matter. I already guessed. Either way, we get along." Although his response may seem blasé and lack emotion, those words hold within them a deep loyalty and respect for his older sister. Stefen's unconditional love and acceptance of Ashley has never wavered. And it is just one of the many wonderful things I cherish about him.

Tad found his letter when he sat down at the computer. As he read her words, sadness filled his heart. He saw the last remnants of his little girl walking out the door. In some ways Ashley being a lesbian rested more comfortably with Tad. He would still have a daughter.

Although I couldn't guess what Tad would say, I knew how he would process the news. To the outside world, not a lot of emotion or discussion would be visible. Tad would process this new information privately. Sometimes he might drop a remark or two about how he felt about something that concerned him, but Tad was a man of few words, possessing an accepting, unpretentious personality, and known as a generous friend and family member.

As it turned out Tad didn't feel that Ashley was making a lifestyle choice. He believed her desire to become male rested within her genetic makeup. However, she was such an outstanding golfer as a female and she was his little girl. No longer would they have golf to bond them every weekend, no longer could he dream of a golf career for her, and no longer would she be the daughter he loved so much. He grieved for the loss of it all.

When I read Ashley's letter, her honesty stunned me. However, my tears flowed when I felt optimism and hope rise from her words—hope that her physical transformation would not overshadow her core being, her most intrinsic values as a young adult. She asked that her friends and family recognize that no matter what gender she presented to the world, who she remained within would be unchanged. And isn't that what mattered most? I could not have felt more proud as I read the depth of courage within Ashley's statement of truth and her request to be acknowledged on her own terms.

Despite this, fear stirred inside me. *Who would accept her? Who would not?*

I already had one answer close to my heart. Tad, in the face of losing his daughter, put his sadness aside and vowed whether male or female, Ashley was his child. And Stefen had already shared that whether brother or sister, it did not matter to him. Our family never sat down, had a discussion, or made a plan regarding Ashley's desire to transition. I only remember telling Tad what the costs would be for the actions Ashley planned to take, and meeting no resistance from him. I only remember the times when I stumbled and felt I couldn't get up, and my husband reached out his hand. Or Stefen sensing my emotional reserve hovered near empty, came up behind me, wrapped his arms around my neck, and gave me a much-needed hug.

So, with Tad, Stefen, and I firmly planted around Ashley, we would journey down this unknown road. We didn't know what this journey would look like and we didn't know how we would manage, but we knew why we would walk by Ashley's side. We were a family and this was not just Ashley's journey but our journey as well. Her circle of love and acceptance had grown from one to three. It was a beginning.

CHAPTER TWO

The Early Signs

For the first twelve years of our marriage, Tad and I thought we would never have children. To begin with, my chances of bearing a biological child were bleak. It seemed my body didn't want to carry one. Those chances sank further thanks to multiple medical issues that included surgical removal of an ovary with a cyst the size of a grapefruit, along with a case of endometriosis (a painful condition resulting from the presence of mucous membrane outside the uterus).

As for adoption. I wasn't ready to consider it. I still dreamed of holding a baby I had carried after nine months of lovingly nurturing its growth. I even bought a soft, gray corduroy maternity jumper and white blouse that hung in my closet waiting for that day to come when I would announce, "I'm having a baby!"

But, until I became pregnant, Tad and I focused our attention on our businesses—his hair salon, my insurance agency—and happily lived the life of a married couple without the responsibilities of children. We traveled with friends, took disco dancing lessons, and thoroughly enjoyed our fun-filled, carefree life, complete with success symbols like sports cars, designer clothes, and expensive jewelry.

Yet, these material signs of success could not replace a void that continued to pull at my heart. I didn't despair, but I felt the absence of something deeper, something that would provide more meaning and purpose to my existence. For months, I denied the feelings growing stronger each day. When my husband bought me another diamond necklace, ring, or bracelet, I pushed away the longing for a moment, but the moment passed. I bought a fancier sports car, but driving my newest toy of distraction around the city never erased the barren feeling that lay within me.

In time, I came to grips with the source of the emptiness: all I really wanted to be was a mother. The yearning overtook me like a winter storm, especially during the holidays. Sitting by the fireplace wrapping gifts for my family, I still felt cold inside. My arms ached to hold my baby, breathe in his or her innocence, and let the rest of the world pass me by. As a woman who grew up with two brothers and held many happy family memories, I longed to have children with whom I could share my love, with whom I could build memories of my own. This became my hope.

However, Tad didn't want children. He'd lost a younger brother unexpectedly to heart failure, a father not yet sixty to lung cancer, and a young aunt to a brain aneurysm. And those losses hurt him so deeply that, as I saw it, he simply did not want to risk losing another person he loved. What if he lost this child too? He felt too vulnerable to love a child. On the other hand, I had not lost any family members except for elderly grandparents, so I did not share his feeling of vulnerability.

At this time, I was heavily involved in a seminar program that encouraged each individual to become a "dream machine," with the belief that whatever you pursued with unwavering passion and confidence would become reality. I bought into the philosophy of this program and began to follow my tugging desires. Soon, two challenges presented themselves and stood face to face with me: How would I convince Tad to have children? How would I overcome my fertility issues?

The short answer: I had no idea.

But a deep commitment filled me with an unstoppable belief that my dream would come true. I released any expectations of how my dream would appear. I just saw a picture of me holding a baby. Once I surrendered into the possibilities, miracles began to happen.

I followed my intuition, which said, "While you are waiting for your baby to find her way to you, look for chances to be a mother." One of the first opportunities that arose was to take care of my young niece Stephie. Little by little, she became my weekend daughter. I loved spending time with her; I called her my angel. She filled that empty space in my heart, and gave my maternal instinct something to wrap its arms around. Stephie would arrive on Friday and stay until Sunday. We read books, took walks, played in the park, and visited children's museums. I loved her as if she were my own. She would say, "I love you so much, Auntie Mimi, that when we aren't together I feel like crying...and then I do." Stephie's words resonated with me, as I experienced an emptiness that could only be filled when she returned to visit me again.

Tad also fell in love with Stephie. He enjoyed the way her joyful spirit and melodic voice filled our home with love and laughter. Eventually, he began to envision life with a child.

Then, one night, I decided I would approach the subject and see how he felt. I wasn't sure what his response would be, but he seemed as open as he was ever going to be, so I decided to nudge him lightly towards fatherhood.

"Honey," I slowly inched into the conversation, "I know you have told me that you don't want children. But having Stephie around us has been such a joy. I really want a child. Would you consider having just one?" Without much elaboration or emotion, Tad responded, "Okay." Although it might have appeared to others that Tad's lack of emotion or discussion meant he didn't care, I knew that he would never consent to having children if he adamantly opposed it. Tad's agreement signaled his readiness to be a father. My heart soared to the moon and back hearing that one word.

I laid out a plan that, if I were fortunate enough to give birth to only one child, I wanted a girl; someone with whom I could shop, and have intimate mother/daughter conversations over tea and scones, and teach to cook, knit or crochet. Of course, I knew that the right child would come to me, be it a girl or a boy, but deep inside I wanted a daughter.

Overcoming Tad's resistance, I now had to face my fertility issues. We turned to a specialist who poked, prodded, and tested both of us. "You need to have surgery on your fallopian tubes," I was told. I moved forward without hesitation. After surgery, there were more tests. Finally, my doctors determined that my only option was expensive in vitro fertilization, which cost five thousand dollars per procedure.

Regular injections to encourage more eggs to develop from my one good ovary became part of my morning ritual. Each morning after kissing my husband goodbye, I drove to my friend Bob's dental office, got my daily injection of fertility medication, hugged him with gratitude, and then drove off to work. The daily routine wove its way comfortably into my morning schedule, but the emotional impact ended up being more that I could bear. Each failed procedure overwhelmed me with sadness. In a matter of weeks, I plummeted from the sheer elation of having my fertilized eggs placed inside of me and hearing, "Congratulations, Mrs. Aizumi, you are pregnant!" to utter despair when a nurse phoned me with blood results: "I am sorry, Mrs. Aizumi, the eggs did not implant."

I laid the phone back in its cradle gently, then sat and cried, letting the devastation of the news consume me.

After nearly two years of fertility testing, surgery, blood tests, injections to produce multiple eggs, a medical procedure to harvest, fertilize, and replant eggs in my uterus, and two failed implantations, I couldn't take the heartbreak of a third failed procedure. While riding back from the doctor's office with Tad, I burst into tears. My head exploded with painful, plaintive, pulsing thoughts—the kind that loop through your mind as though they live there:

"I can't take another day of shots to produce multiple eggs."

"I can't take another day of someone sticking me with a needle to take my blood."

"I can't take waking up hoping that today will be the day I am told I will have a baby and then finding out that I am not pregnant."

"I just want to be a mother."

Tad drove silently, not knowing what to say or how to console me. Finally, he turned to me and said, "I think you're hungry. I'm going to find a drive through restaurant and get you something to eat right away."

Food? You think my tears are about being hungry? Could you misread me any more?

After a few minutes, I calmed down. I realized it was Tad's way of comforting me and showing his love. He didn't know what else to do. Neither did I. My tears stopped. My melancholy warmed into gratitude. My husband cared so much for me. Together we would work this out.

At that point, adoption became a viable option. I didn't care if the child was my biological offspring or not. I just wanted to love a child that would call me "Momma." I turned to Tad. "Honey, we have spent ten thousand dollars trying to have a baby and we still don't have a child. We can either spend another five thousand dollars to try in vitro again, or we can take that money and use it for the cost of adopting a child overseas. I am ready to pursue the adoption route if you are okay with it."

Tad only cared for my happiness. He could see the joy a child brought into our lives through Stephie, so he would have supported either course of action. In addition, most of our beginning years as husband and wife went towards supporting Tad's new career as a hairdresser, opening up his own salon, acquiring commercial property, and constructing a two story commercial building where he operated In Vogue Hair Design. He said he wanted to support my dream to have a baby, as I had stood by him for so many years as he achieved his dreams. If I had any uncertainty about my direction, my dentist friend Bob erased any doubt about adoption when he said to me, "If you want to be a mother, it doesn't matter where the baby comes from." His words further confirmed that I needed to move forward with adoption.

We began the search for our baby girl. We chose to work with a Japanese adoption agency because I wanted a child that shared our heritage. Furthermore, I knew that I couldn't risk having a child taken away from me with a stateside adoption that allowed biological parents to change their minds within six months. The thought of falling in love with a child, only to have her taken away, was incomprehensible. My two failed in vitro procedures already gave me the sense I had lost two children. I could not risk losing a third.

My father's cousin, who lived in Japan, referred us to one of that country's organizations, Agency to Rescue Children. I contacted a Southern California mother who adopted two children through this agency and served as a liaison between adopting families and Japan. This mother connected me to the agency director who devoted her life to saving children born out of wedlock. She was a wonderful, fearless advocate. With traditional Japanese family honor at stake, many desperate unwed mothers often disposed of their newborn babies, sometimes in the trash. Agency to Rescue Children provided pregnant mothers with the funds to have their babies in a hospital, and assured them that their babies would be placed in good homes in the U.S. We felt safe that these biological mothers would not be able to reclaim their babies, and we knew Japan was removed from the U.S. by a very wide Pacific Ocean. Tad and I went through the lengthy process of filing the paperwork with a local adoption agency, Immigration and Naturalization Services, and an attorney in Hawaii who translated paperwork from Japanese to English. A social worker, in addition, interviewed us and conducted a couple of home visits. The adoption agency easily deemed us fit parents with a good home.

Now the wait for our new baby girl began.

In late May 1988, I received the call: our baby had been born! In June, a photo arrived in the mail. She was adorable. I showed my new baby girl to anyone who asked. And those who didn't ask, I showed them anyway. The picture became my hope, but I agonized over the continuing wait to see her in person and hold her in my arms. I muted the agony by busying myself with expectant mother activities: decorating her nursery, lining the dresser drawers, and folding and refolding the baby clothes I bought. I spent hours in the room. I cradled an imaginary baby in my arms, telling myself that soon I would have my daughter to hold. I envisioned her deep-set eyes looking into mine and knowing that I loved her with all my heart.

On Labor Day 1988, after sixteen and a half years of marriage, Tad and I welcomed Ashley Akemi Aizumi into our lives and we became a family. I chose her name because Ashley meant peace and harmony, and Akemi meant bright and beautiful. Her name symbolized all I wished for her life.

When Ashley arrived at Los Angeles International Airport, more than twenty people turned out on a sunny afternoon to greet her. Quite a receiving party for an infant! As we waited for Ashley to clear customs, my heart beat in anticipation. I couldn't sit still, pacing back and forth between family and friends, hoping to distract myself from the minutes that trudged excruciatingly slow.

As usual, my mind raced: *She's almost here. I wonder what she looks like now. She is three months old. Will I love her the minute I see her? Or will it take days for us to bond, because she was born to another?*

My thoughts flowed endlessly until I saw a Japanese woman walking out of customs, cuddling a little baby to her chest.

There she is! A lump formed in my throat.

My family and friends exclaimed at once: "Ashley's here!"

They circled around the Japanese woman, cooing and craning their necks to get a first glimpse. One mother realized that I was on the outside of the circle. "Get in there. This is your baby," she said, pushing me forward.

I pushed through the crowd and received my first look at the baby I had dreamed about for years. She was beautiful. After the Japanese woman placed Ashley in my arms, my father snapped a picture of mother and child, my face red from the tears. Every time I see that picture, I travel back to that moment and remember how complete I felt when I held her in my arms for the first time. She was my child, not biologically, but spiritually and emotionally. And somehow I felt we had chosen each other.

Ashley was everything I dreamed: animated, playful, and physically affectionate, with a spirit of wonder and joy. She filled our lives with love and delight. After waiting for so many years to love this child, I often laid her on a blanket on the ground and just watched her coo while taking in all the new sights and sounds. She followed my voice, which amazed my girlfriends since she'd not been part of my life for her first three months. Even though my girlfriends weren't mothers, Ashley's connection to me was dramatic and apparent. She seemed to already know instinctively that I loved her completely, even though she had only been with me for two days. I felt such deep contentment and bliss; what could possibly match this happiness? I loved everything about being a mother; the smell of her baby shampoo when I gave her a bath, the smell of her baby powder when I changed her diaper, and the feel of her soft skin as I dressed her. Most of all, I adored the way she looked deep into my eyes as I cradled her while she drank her bottle.

However, within just thirty days, my other life crept in. As much as I loved being a stay-at-home mother, the family insurance business beckoned me to return. My younger brother had recently joined the business and ran the day-to-day affairs, but he needed me back sooner than I anticipated. As president of the small company, a position I accepted after my parent's semi-retirement, I felt obligated to come back. My mother's prompting sealed the decision. I knew she would never encourage me to return so soon if she didn't feel a pressing need.

My mother volunteered to watch Ashley when I returned to work. Hollowness crept into my heart when I dropped her off at my mother's house in the morning and it lingered within until I picked her up at the end of the day. My mother observed that Ashley was more listless when I was gone, "like losing a part of her heart when I wasn't around." When I returned, Ashley grew happier and more animated. She missed me terribly. I missed her even more.

I struggled for weeks. Then the universe responded to the debate inside my head, causing me to re-think my priorities. My brother, who kept his life insurance office at my parent's home, approached me and said, "I don't think Mom should be babysitting Ashley." My mother had been diagnosed with Parkinson's disease a few years earlier. Although she functioned well with medication, the responsibilities of caring for a baby wore on her, though she loved watching Ashley. My brother sensed that it was too much with her current condition.

I sat down with Tad. "My mom can't watch Ashley any longer, and I don't want to leave her with another babysitter. Part of me wants to retire and stay at home with Ashley, but my brother isn't ready to run the business without me."

"What if we turn the vacant suite at our building into a nursery for Ashley?" he asked. "This way you can still work and Ashley will be next door."

That's one of the many reasons why I love my husband so much. When I get stuck, he always finds a wonderful solution. Tad's recommendation became our plan. I hired an *au pair* from Switzerland on a friend's referral. Sylvie came with me to the office and watched Ashley in the nursery. After about six months, Sylvie accepted another position and I hired an older Japanese bachan —grandmother—to watch over Ashley. Within six months, I knew Bachan was the perfect babysitter when I dropped into the nursery one day to find her sitting in the playpen with Ashley; not an easy task—

Bachan was not petite like some Japanese women. I delighted in imagining the conversation between her and my expressive child:

"Bachan, here!"

"No, Ash-a-ree, Bachan too big."

"No, Bachan, here."

"Playpen will break, Ash-a-ree."

"Bachan, play...Bachan, sit here."

As Bachan climbed inside the playpen, I could envision her thinking, I hope nobody sees me!

Well, I saw her—and I loved it! This woman would do anything for my daughter and proved it by sitting in that playpen. I'm still smiling about it.

Now we were one happy family. I handled insurance in suite 210, Tad cut hair in suite 104, and Ashley played in suite 211—a 700-square-foot, three-room play area with bath and shower. At lunchtime, Ashley and Bachan would walk into the insurance agency and I would have lunch with her. Then Bachan would return Ashley to the nursery for a nap, walk in the park, or take her to the library, finally giving her a bath before making the trip home with me. Once home, I would cook dinner, we would eat, then we'd play with her toys, read a book, or watch a video. Ashley received her final bottle, as I swayed her back and forth in a white wicker rocker. I was living my dream.

Tad came home late most evenings, since his clientele included predominately professional women who made evening appointments. But on Mondays when I worked, Tad took care of Ashley, so he had special time with her at least once a week. I felt blessed to be able to work, spend time with my child and watch her grow. I also was happy for Tad, since he could enjoy the full experience of feeding, bathing, diapering and playing with his child, even if only once a week. He was —and is—a wonderful father.

For two years, I dressed Ashley in the cutest soft pink clothes with bows and matching shoes and socks. Although my little baby girl didn't like scratchy, uncomfortable clothes, she allowed me to put any outfit on her that provided space to run and play. When we would go out in public, people would comment on how adorable Ashley was. With big observant eyes, an animated smile, and coordinated outfits, she caught the attention of many a passerby.

Between the ages of two and three, things began to change. Ashley started to assert herself and adamantly voice what she wanted to wear. Must be the "terrible twos or trying threes," I thought. She was learning to make decisions, to be her own person. Encouraging her independence, I let her choose between two pretty outfits, which seemed to satisfy her for a while.

Soon, she didn't like any of my choices. She only wanted to wear pants and T-shirts, and I'm not talking about the matching *Little Mermaid* sets. Our dressing time conversations started sounding like tug-a-war:

"Let's put on this nice top and skirt, Ashley."

"NO, I don't like it."

"Okay, then do you want to pick, Pumpkin Pie?"

"Yes"

"Here are two outfits. Which one do you want?"

"None. *Ninja Turtle.*"

"But you just wore that yesterday and these are so cute."

"I don't like them, yucky."

I resigned myself to the lost battle. "Okay, honey, pick the one you want."

I walked away thinking, *Gosh, people are going to think Ashley doesn't have very many clothes, since she wears the same outfit all the time.* I began not washing her clothes as often, so I could tell her, "Oh, honey, that outfit is in the laundry." At least this limited her to wearing the outfit weekly and not daily.

I found ways to give Ashley what she wanted while keeping her in feminine apparel for a while. She loved the male superheroes and boyish themes, but I always made sure the outfits were softly colored, so she didn't seem like such a tomboy. Her favorite outfit was a soft pink and green short and T-shirt set, with dinosaurs on the front. She loved the fierce, teeth snarling T-Rex on the shirt. I focused on the muted pink and mint green shorts that seemed so feminine.

Brushing Ashley's hair wasn't much easier. She barely sat still for a simple brushing, and she wouldn't allow me to put any kind of ribbon or decoration in her hair. However, she liked to wear baseball caps—dark or beige-colored caps. Pink was a color that, more and more, she refused to wear. Fortunately, her straight hair fell nicely in place. To my relief, she did not ask us to cut it short.

When Ashley was three years of age, Tad and I adopted a second child from the same organization in Japan. This time Tad, Ashley and I flew to Japan to pick up Ashley's baby brother. In the beginning she adored him. When the novelty wore off, she announced that we could send him back to Japan now.

It became clear to me that Ashley disliked anything she considered girlish. Initially, the jealousy between Ashley and Stefen over his toys was not apparent, because he was a baby; she didn't covet his rattles and mobiles. But as he grew older, she seemed to be resentful of his clothes and his toys. We didn't conclude a jealousy of gender at the time, but thought it signaled the beginnings of sibling rivalry. I went out and located a book called *Sibling Rivalry*, written by Adele Faber and Elaine Mazlish, not wanting resentment in any form to disrupt their relationship. I loved their philosophy and it definitely influenced my perspective as a mother in a positive way.

During birthdays and Christmas, I seemed to repeat the same lecture each year about the green-eyed monster that arose out of Ashley. And I didn't understand her destructiveness and disinterest when playing with her toys. When she received a doll for Christmas, she tossed it in the corner of her closet. Once she got a Barbie doll for her birthday, she played so roughly with it, Barbie's head broke off.

In later years, when she had a choice between a *Little Mermaid* or *Ninja Turtle* sleeping bag, guess which one she convinced her baby brother he should have? Looking back we now realize that her jealousy was less about him and his gifts, but more centered around her receiving Barbie dolls and Little Mermaid things, while he received the "cool" Batman, Ninja Turtle, and Power Ranger toys. Eventually we relented and both kids received the popular action figures, videos, and trading cards, instead of the feminine items that we had lovingly purchased for Ashley in the past.

Then there was her vivid imagination. She would pretend to be a spy or Batman or a Ninja Turtle. People told me that girls sometimes gravitated to male heroes because they were primary characters in stories and depicted as more powerful. This held true throughout the twentieth century—Superman, Power Rangers, Batman. That gave me some relief. I would throw out names like Wonder Woman or Super Girl and she would stare at me like, "Who is that?" Even the most popular Power Rangers on that show were all boys. The female Power Rangers dressed in pink and yellow seemed secondary characters, in Ashley's eyes, less powerful and interesting to her. The most powerful female was a crazy Asian villain, Rita, who cackled and pumped her fist towards the heavens in triumph when she thought she was defeating the Mighty Morphin Power Rangers. *Great*, I thought. *The antagonist is an Asian woman.* In a way, I could see why Ashley didn't want anything to do with being a girl. The few available role models did not appear to be strong, sane, or heroic at all.

I remember one day at an outing with a group of families, a sports coach watched Ashley run and play. "She is going to be a good athlete, you can see it in her walk," he told me. She didn't walk like a dainty girl, and although she appeared very graceful, nothing feminine attracted her. Her talents revealed themselves in all things physical, especially when hand-eye coordination was involved. By the time she was four, she already showed a fondness for golf. She hit the ball so well that Tad began to fashion miniature golf clubs in our garage—metal clubs, not plastic. Papa and Ashley became Sunday buddies, hitting balls in Grandma Mary's yard and later at the driving range.

Halloween revealed another early sign of Ashley's proclivity. After age three, she no longer allowed me to dress her in anything feminine. Her early years as a ballerina or fairy were finished. She opted to be a cowboy (rather than a cowgirl), then Zorro, then one of the male Power Rangers. Halloween was her favorite holiday. I thought she loved this day because she collected a bagful of candy. In reality, she loved it because it was the one day out of the year when she could dress like the boy that lived inside of her.

Ashley wanted to take karate lessons and play golf with her papa. She took piano lessons, although she would have preferred drums. I swayed her to the piano. After working all day, the thought of coming home to hear my daughter banging on the drums did not fit well with my introvert's need for peace and quiet. I missed the ballet lessons, cute little ponytail ribbons, and dresses that I thought were synonymous with mothering a little girl.

When Ashley began preschool, I didn't seek her out among the other girls, but with the boys. She'd run, climb trees, or jump out of swings with them. I watched her, both bemused and a bit forlorn: my little girl years had involved playing house or school, dressing up and playing with dolls. Ashley liked to golf, roller skate, and pretend she was a Power Ranger.

In elementary school, Ashley's best friend was a girl named Sara. Ashley and I met Sara and her family at kindergarten orientation, and we've been friends since. Her mother was also named Marsha. Like me, she was Japanese, with a girl and boy the exact same ages as my children. From the beginning, we noticed a big difference between our two girls, but Ashley and Sara grew close, more like cousins than friends. Since Sara was a typical girl, Ashley played with the two younger brothers.

Around this time, Tad and I enjoyed a popular TV show, Picket Fences, about a small town sheriff, his wife, and their three children. The one-hour weekly drama interwove family-oriented themes in its storylines, through the eyes of a sheriff, his family, and the townsfolk. One week, the show would cover responsibility and demonstrate how people take or don't take responsibility; the next, it would tackle prejudice, honesty, or loyalty. We liked Picket Fences because of the themes and "kooky" ways in which they were depicted.

One week, a very bizarre episode aired: a cow gave birth to a human baby. Tad and I talked about how strange that program was, but on some level, how plausible the story was. Cloning children outside the womb was not so foreign to us, since we had gone through in vitro fertilization; plus, cloning of animals was the rage in the scientific community and the media.

Ashley always knew she was adopted. The adoption social worker encouraged us to use the word when we spoke with her, even as a baby. The social worker explained that this word would become part of our natural conversation and Ashley wouldn't feel like there was something negative about being adopted. But after hearing Tad and I talk about a cow giving birth to a baby, Ashley came up to me visibly upset. "Tell me the truth, Momma: was my mother a cow?"

I scooped her into my arms and assured her that her biological mother was not a cow but a human being. As much as Tad and I loved Ashley, there remained a part of her afraid of being abandoned, afraid of not being accepted. It struck me, hard: even at this young age, Ashley felt different. I looked into her eyes and sensed the thoughts swirling in her little mind: if her mother were a cow, it would explain her strange feelings and her inability to be like all the other girls. I thought these feelings were related to being adopted. Years later I would understand that was only a part of her discomfort.

When Ashley was in first grade, I began to notice the sheer strength of her preferences. One day, she came home and talked about a classmate named Allison. Ashley loved Allison. How strange, at this pure and honest age, to be talking about *loving a girl*. What a difference from my first grade year! I felt like I was in love with a boy named Gary. I also remember he kissed me, concerning my mother so much that she called the school to talk with the teacher. I thought, *What was so wrong with him kissing me?* I know he received a stern lecture, because he never tried to kiss me again.

How ironic that, at the same age, both Ashley and I were "in love." However, Ashley loved a girl and I loved a boy. The observation moved through my consciousness, but didn't cause me concern. In hindsight, the signs were quite clear: Ashley was walking a different path.

Later that year, something happened that really disturbed Ashley. At recess, she was in one of the bathroom stalls when two girls entered the stall next to her. The next thing she knew the two girls had popped their heads over the top of her stall and were peering down on her. As if it wasn't embarrassing enough to be infringing on her privacy, they boldly asked, "Are you a boy or a girl?" At the time, Ashley didn't understand why, but she remembers the question sent a ripple of uncomfortable feelings through her.

After that incident, Ashley would rush home to the bathroom after school, her bladder ready to explode. I could tell she hadn't gone all day. "Ashley, it's not a good idea to wait all day to go to the bathroom," I told her. "You could get a bladder infection."

"Bathrooms are so awful at school. They are really yucky."

"Well, just put toilet paper on the seat after you wipe it off, so it is not so yucky."

"But I don't like to sit on the toilet seat."

"You won't be sitting on the toilet seat," I said. "You will be sitting on the toilet paper, honey."

"Okay, maybe I'll try that."

"Good, because I don't want you to get a bladder infection from not going to the bathroom."

Also in first grade, Ashley attended Sara's sixth birthday party. Something happened before the majority of kids arrived that again stood out for Ashley. "There was one other girl and Sara," Ashley recalls. "Sara and this girl went into Sara's bedroom and they locked me out. I couldn't get in and I was knocking and trying to get in. All of a sudden, they opened the door, threw naked Barbies at me and both gave me a kiss on the cheek. I think the next week I tried to get the other girl (not Sara, she was like family) to kiss me again."

When Ashley was in second grade, I prevailed upon her to wear a beautiful dress with a velvet top for school pictures. Any little girl would feel pretty in this dress. When I saw the pictures, I was stunned: the oddest smile had crossed Ashley's face, in fact not really a smile, but a combination of embarrassment and resignation. I was already having funny feelings about her sexual orientation, but I thought the photographer must have clicked her photo when she wasn't ready. I threw the school photos in her memory box and didn't give it a second thought until I began gathering information for this book.

When Ashley was in third or fourth grade, I also made her wear a dress for picture day. She came home and shared a story about a boy taking a look at her and commenting, "Oh my God, you're a girl!" At that early age, she passed for a boy because she competed with the best of them and dressed very much like them. She informed me that she would not wear a dress ever again for picture day.

I remember so many other subtle signs of what our lives were to become. Ashley wanted to buy dark-colored clothes and boy's black tennis shoes. "You can buy boys tennis shoes as long as they aren't black, and any type of T-shirt and pants, as long as you don't look like a boy," I told her. Conversely, I encouraged her younger brother to buy black tennis shoes and wear darker clothes because they didn't show the dirt as readily. When Ashley's elementary school decided to switch to uniforms, my little girl would only wear the boy's collared shirts or sweatshirts, shorts or long pants. She refused skirts, skorts (a short culotte), or cardigan sweaters. I rationalized her attire by concluding that Ashley liked boy clothes so she could pass them down to her younger brother. Lucky me; I didn't have to buy as many outfits.

After I took a picture of her with a fellow fifth-grade girl, I more strongly suspected that Ashley straddled the line of sexual orientation. Both wore long hair with beads braided into their straight-flowing locks. Her friend's soft face, warm smile, feminine hair and clothes matched the way she stood. On the other hand, Ashley appeared soft and feminine in her face and hair, but her clothes and stance did not match. If you covered up Ashley's face, the headless picture looked like that of a boy by the way she leaned into her girlfriend, hands on hips, conveying protective, masculine energy. I realized my daughter's masculine tendencies and preferences would not change in subsequent years. However, I am good at avoiding what I don't want to face: *You are reading things into a picture. Ash will be fine*, I told myself.

I occasionally shared my concerns casually with a couple of mothers. I would say something like, "I hope that Ashley outgrows this tomboy stage." I didn't want to give away my feeling that I might be facing sexual orientation issues concerning my daughter. One mother or the other invariably replied with something comforting, such as, "I was a tomboy when I was young, then I noticed boys and that is when I changed," or "When she gets to the age that she likes boys, she'll be different. Don't worry; this is just a phase."

I wanted to believe these mothers, because the thought of Ashley being a lesbian made me shudder. My trepidation did not stem so much from the fact that she would love someone of the same gender, but rather the prejudice and hatred she would face in our not-so-tolerant society—especially in the schools. I breathed a sigh of relief when these mothers gave me answers that I could believe. My fear faded.

Once in a while I would drop a comment or two to Tad. He reacted very objectively about her sexual orientation, expressing his acceptance no matter whom she loved. I wished I could have been more accepting of the idea of her being a lesbian, but I remember growing up in a conservative town and being the only Asian person in my class. I still recall the shame when others taunted me because I was different. I still feel the daggers that stabbed at my heart when people called me names, pulled at their eyes to make them slanted while chanting some Asian sounding words. Kids could be so cruel to those perceived unlike them.

Around this time, I also talked to Auntie Bonnie, who was Uncle Bob's wife, expressing my concerns. She replied, "If she ends up being a lesbian, you will just have to love her more." Such simple advice, filled with so much wisdom.

Ashley seemed to maneuver successfully through uncomfortable situations. The only time she recalled feeling extremely awkward in elementary school occurred in fifth grade, when the teacher showed a human reproduction video. The boys and girls were sent to different rooms; each watching a puberty video relating to their gender. As Ashley sat and watched the girl's video, she saw the changes that would take place in her body, like starting her period and developing breasts. A wave of discomfort crept throughout her body. And when the girls were given a bag of sample products, rather than modestly putting them in her backpack like all the other girls, Ashley took the panty liner, ripped off the paper protecting the sticky backing, slapped it on a boy, and ran away.

Her actions were so typical of young boys. Even though the anatomies of the individuals on the screen matched the anatomy she possessed, the video unsettled her. Her uneasiness centered on many of the upcoming physical changes. To her, breasts and menstrual periods seemed so wrong, and Ashley didn't understand why she felt this way. She just felt like something was off.

Ashley's elementary days passed with only a few more of these uncomfortable moments. Everyone accepted her as a tomboy. She was joyful, spontaneous, and good at sports, so she always had lots of friends. Plenty of boys wanted her to play on their teams.

Since she was a tomboy, Ashley blended in well in school and especially in golf circles, with only occasional moments of judgment or curiosity. Conversely, as she and I both learned over the years, boys headed on a path in which they yearn to live as a girl face great cruelty—even in elementary school. Children often hurl hurtful comments at effeminate boys that are not tough or athletic by nature.

All in all, the elementary years were wonderful for Ashley and me. She did well in school, excelled in golf, showed early signs of musical talent, and took up plenty of invitations to hang out at friend's houses, sleepovers, and birthday parties. Much of my happiness hinged on how well my children were doing academically and socially. I was very happy. I sensed very little that would suggest difficult times ahead. I am grateful for that ignorance, because any foreknowledge would have robbed Ashley and me of those happy moments that took place in her early school years.

When Ashley left elementary school and started middle school, she experienced the usual combination of apprehension and excitement. She changed classrooms during the school day, dressed for physical education, and endured the uncomfortable changes to her body that she learned about in fifth grade. Most girls looked forward to leaving that little girl period of their lives and becoming young women. However, my daughter was uneasy for reasons that, I thought, pertained to transitioning to middle school. That was a large part of it.

But there was a much larger part, as I soon learned.

CHAPTER THREE

Middle and High School Days

Middle school arrived—a tough and anxious time for any parent. We took extra steps to prepare Ashley during the summer for her new school by joining her on walks around the campus. I really wasn't worried about her social transition; by the time she left elementary school, she moved among circles of boys and girls with ease. As long as I helped her get comfortable with her new school site, I believed she could acclimate well to her new surroundings.

I couldn't have been more wrong. From the first weeks of school, she suffered adjustment problems. One day, after she came home with sadness on her face yet again, I asked her what was wrong.

"All my friends are talking about boys, drill team, and girlie stuff," she said. "And everyone is so loud and there are so many people. It's just hard."

"Well, it is a new school with more kids, so it will be noisier. Maybe it will take a few days to get used to everything."

"Yeah, maybe."

Day after day, I continued asking her the same question, to closely monitor her feelings: "How was school today?" Most times, I received similar glum answers. I knew from her past that a combination of time and the space to establish her own routine would eventually alleviate her discomfort. Once she made new friends and found kids with whom she had something in common with, she would be fine . . . right?

"In elementary school, nobody cared about gender, what I wore or what I looked like," Ashley recalls. "When middle school rolled around, appearance became an issue. Boys started paying attention to what girls wore or what they looked like, and I didn't fit in. I suddenly felt like a black sheep. All the girls who were tomboys like me returned to school with girlie clothes, talking about boys and makeup. I returned the same, with shorts and T-shirts, all from the boys' section of department stores. All the girls hung out with other girls and all the boys hung out with other boys. Most of the boys were still my friends, but they wanted to sit with other boys. People would tell me that I had to start changing into more girlie clothes; that I was supposed to like boys now and talk about boys, makeup, and other girl stuff. I felt stuck in the middle; trapped between girls who I didn't relate to and boys who I related to more, but no longer felt as welcome in their circles. I felt so lost and alone."

I sensed Ashley's struggles, but I didn't know what to do—not exactly how I envisioned the middle-school years as a parent.

By the third week of school, Ashley started to describe her emotional breakdowns. She wanted to cry in her fifth period class because there were so many people and too much noise. Naturally, my tendency to clearly define problems and arrive at solutions kicked in, and I found a solid, legitimate reason to explain her reactions: her hormones were affecting how she felt. One moment, she was happy as a clam, because she did well on a test, project, or made a new friend. The next moment, she became angry as a hornet, because an old friend had chosen to try out for drill team and started hanging out with other drill team hopefuls. Then her pendulum would swing not only into another emotion, but another level altogether— sadness that her life and friends were changing and she wanted things to stay the same.

I empathized with her. I remember in middle school how I was rejected by old friends for new friends, how I liked a boy from afar while fearing others would tease me, how I tried to adapt to the myriad of new feelings and physical changes that were part of adolescence. You don't hear very many people speak of middle school in glowing terms. My daughter was growing up. I knew she wouldn't be immune to struggle.

On the other hand, Ashley's problems felt more to me than normal teenage angst. I decided to talk with her fifth period teacher, Ms. Chang, and see what was truly happening. At Back to School Night, I pulled Ms. Chang aside to get the full story.

"Mrs. Aizumi, I have wanted to talk to you about Ashley," she said. "She is having trouble, and I don't know how to help her."

"What do you mean she is having trouble?" I responded cautiously.

"Well, most days she comes into my room very upset. Usually before class ends, she is crying."

I was shocked. "This is happening every day?"

"Almost every day."

I realized how badly the situation had deteriorated. Ashley's daily portrayals seemed far less miserable, and she never refused to go to school. However, I moved on the situation after that short interaction with Ms. Chang: first, I was determined to find a way to change this pattern; secondly, the meeting bonded me with this teacher, who seemed to genuinely care about my child. I kept in regular contact with Ms. Chang to monitor Ashley's emotional state.

"I remember each day was the same. I felt stuck in a repeating cycle that began right around PE (fourth period Physical Education). It felt weird that we were all changing in the locker room. Then I would be okay around lunchtime, mainly because I was hungry. But I felt isolated. I didn't fit in anywhere. At the end of the day in Ms. Chang's class, I had a panic attack regularly. They were always the worst. I felt like I was going to fall over and die from not breathing. My lungs and throat closed up, and I couldn't get enough air. My hands would get really sweaty and my heart would race in my chest. I would wait them out and hope that the panic would stop. If that didn't happen, the only way I learned to stop them was to force myself to cry, because it would open up my lungs. I don't know what it was . . . if it was the end of the day and all the stress, worrying, and being uncomfortable just built up, or if it was the timing of the day. All I know is every day at fifth period, I would have a panic attack."

Ashley's panic attacks were terrifying. Not feeling like she could catch her breath, her mind raced with fear that she would suffocate. I know the feeling myself, so I never doubted how horrifying the experience could be. Once I woke up with a panic attack at 3:00 A.M. and all I could think about was getting some fresh air so I could breathe. I ran to our bedroom sliding glass door knowing I would trigger the alarm when I opened it, but I didn't care. My heart pounded violently and my head screamed, *AIR, GET SOME AIR!* All I could think about was getting my head outside the bedroom door and breathing in fresh air. As the alarmed blared and my husband groggily sat up to see what was going on, my heart began to calm as I felt I could now breathe. I can't imagine having a panic attack almost every day. That would have not only been horrendous, but also exhausting and depressing.

Ms. Chang and I made arrangements for Ashley to see a school psychologist. That seemed to help. She visited a safe and quiet place every week, and knew she could ask her psychologist for support if she ran into trouble. With both Ms. Chang and a school psychologist solidly on her side, Ashley calmed down. Except for an occasional meltdown, she appeared to be headed in a positive direction.

Socially, though, her life was declining. This happy, spontaneous child who filled her days with friends in elementary school became more and more alone. I felt powerless to help—what could I do? Find friends for her? She still had some friends, but many had moved physically and emotionally away from her. Now her girlfriends gravitated towards drill team and boys. The now-pubescent boys grew more and more enthralled with girls, along with organized sports programs, separated by gender, such as girls basketball and boys football. Ashley shared nothing in common with either group.

Being a tomboy no longer afforded Ashley the advantage of moving between her male and female friends. She attempted to find a place where she belonged, but after sitting with different groups and feeling like the fifth wheel, she withdrew. The connection she so desperately longed for at this time began to unravel with old friends and made it difficult to bond with new ones. Unable to find a place to belong, her self-esteem plummeted. There was no comfortable place where she could be herself and feel accepted.

"It would have been so awesome to just be who I wanted to be without the social pressure to assimilate and conform," she reflects many years later. "To feel like I was accepted no matter what I looked like or how I dressed."

Unfortunately, in an effort to come up with solutions for Ashley, I did not contribute positively to any of her feelings of acceptance. When she came home complaining about the social rejection she was experiencing, I suggested she shed some of her tomboy ways in dress and attitude. "After all," I reasoned with her, "you are approaching your teens." That made her increasingly angry, while she simultaneously pulled away from me—not a good combination. I only wanted her to feel accepted at school. Instead, I unknowingly added to the social pressure she felt.

I struggled with being a supportive parent. I didn't know how to help her without feeling I was taking away lessons that would prepare her for the future. I grappled with how much I should protect Ashley from heartache. On one hand, she had extra baggage due to her adoption. Should I do as much as possible to shield her from despair? Yet, I believed that occasional struggle was important to properly prepare her for the world. She needed to find her own value and worth so she could contribute to the world with confidence and humility. I believed Ashley would become more resilient and stronger as she encountered adversity, sought support, and developed skills to move through obstacles. I made myself available to listen and empathize how difficult this time was for her, but I encouraged her to seek out the positive in every situation and persevere.

Somehow, we made it through the first year of middle school. We both hoped that the difficulties of that year were behind us.

That was not the case.

On the first day of seventh grade, the horror of horrors began: Ashley started her period. It happened in her fifth period class, thankfully near the end of the day. She thought she needed to go to the bathroom. Her stomach hurt, but she waited. She still had an aversion to school restrooms. When she came home, Ashley went to the bathroom and saw blood. "I had watched the video, so I knew. I was like 'Oh, no.'"

On top of this monthly reminder of Ashley's femininity, her breasts began to grow. She wasn't destined for small breasts like me, but a large bust, a constant reminder of her gender. When Ash and I went shopping for a bra, a mother/daughter rite of passage, we bought both a sports bra and a regular bra. She never wore the regular bra. She put it in the Goodwill bag soon after this trip. I only found out about it years later.

Throughout seventh grade Ashley continued to struggle socially. Having no close friends, she began to hang out in Ms. Chang's room, knowing she would find a safe and nurturing environment with a popular teacher. Soon, Ashley's former teacher became her best friend.

Grace Chang is a fun-loving, intelligent, and dedicated teacher who returned to the school district from which she graduated. "You're killing me, so and so!" I would hear her shout with feigned frustration as a student left her room. The young boy laughed. Students loved her animated and humorous ways of interacting with them. Ashley connected to her kind, caring, and easygoing sense of humor as well, while admiring her success and effortlessness with fellow teachers and students. Ms. Chang taught science and math while also coaching the girls basketball team. "She was athletic, successful, and friends with everybody," Ashley remembers, "so I figured I could grow up, be athletic, and everything would be okay. She would let me shoot hoops with the basketball team after school even though I wasn't on the team. She basically took me under her wing, never judging me, and letting me be who I was."

The bond between Ashley and Ms. Chang strengthened when it came to sports, especially golf. I observed this, and I loved it. They spent many weekends at the driving range, providing Ashley with hours of laughter and bonding. Since Ashley started playing golf at a very young age and possessed talent for the game, her skills were more refined than Ms. Chang's. They turned this disparity into a point of competition and amusement.

"My ball just won't go where I want it to go!" Ms. Chang would exclaim with annoyance.

"Don't think about it or care so much," Ashley would reply. "You try too hard and think too much. Just hit the ball."

"Okay." Ms. Chang would then set up to hit her ball without thinking too much or trying too hard, as Ashley directed.

"Now, Ms. Chang, don't care so much. Just hit the ball!"

The club would descend, strike the ball, and Ms. Chang and Ashley would visually follow its wayward flight. Ashley would then glance at her former teacher and declare knowingly, "You cared!"

Looking at each other, they would break out in laughter. What an endearing moment—a twelve year-old child giving her sixth grade teacher golf tips, the grown adult realizing the advice came from a child wise beyond her years. Their bond was special then, as it is today.

I thought their strong bond would help lift Ashley out of her struggles, except it didn't. Even though Ashley counted Ms. Chang as her friend, she still moped around, saddened by her old school friends turning toward other activities and different sets of friends. I tried to raise her spirits by saying, "Who else has a best friend who can drive?"

The act of forming close relationships with teachers wasn't unusual for my children and me. I encouraged it. I always believed that Ashley and Stefen needed to understand gratitude at a very deep level. To model gratitude and support in elementary school, I would volunteer to help my children's teacher a few hours per week, grading spelling tests, photocopying pages, and stapling math practice sheets to form workbooks. In addition, when Ashley began first grade, I started the Guardian Angels Project to include my children in this demonstration of gratitude. Every month, a designated family secretly slipped something small into their teacher's box to thank her for the loving spirit she brought to work each day: a favorite magazine, a homemade goodie, or even a simple card. For eight months the teacher would randomly find a surprise in her box. Then, on the last day of school, I created a floral presentation where all the students sang a song or wrote notes of appreciation while presenting a flower individually to his or her teacher. My children, along with others, expressed their gratitude for a year of academic, social, and emotional growth. It was like a final hug. In the background, a song would softly play, like "Wind Beneath My Wings," "Hero," or "Because You Loved Me."

Initially, only students participated but later, parents were included. Most of the teachers cried. All of the teachers walked away from this memorable, heartwarming moment feeling appreciated and recognized for their yearlong work.

As a result of these acts of gratitude, I became close to most of my children's elementary school teachers and a few of their middle school teachers. I'm also very comfortable associating with teachers because I've been an educator for many years myself. More than fifteen years later, some of the Guardian Angel mothers and I still have breakfast with one teacher when schedules permit. We have exchanged Christmas cards for years with a few teachers, and we attended yet another's wedding. Our family has been invited to many teacher retirement parties, and every summer we have a potluck reunion with two other teachers. Yesterday's educators are today's dear friends.

Grace Chang unknowingly became Ashley's saving grace and one of our valued friends. When she wasn't Ashley's teacher any longer, she sat as an honored guest at our dinner table. I loved her openly expressive ways and the manner in which she easily got along with our family. I would ask, "Grace, do you want to come back after you and Ash play golf and have dinner with us?" Her face would light up with a smile and her body would perk up. "Okay!"

Like a young child, Grace often seemed untouched by the world around her and radiated a spirit of hope and wonder. Ashley saw a woman comfortable with herself who excelled in sports, kept lots of friends, and lived life on her terms. Ashley gravitated even more to her. Grace became the embodiment of everything Ashley wanted to be. The benefits were mutual. We provided Grace a place to feel at home and a family she could join when her own parents were busy with their lives. Her father was a top corporate executive, and until his retirement, he and Grace's mother traveled back and forth between Asia and the United States. In addition, we all loved to play games, so when Grace didn't go out with her adult friends, she hung out with me playing *Trivial Pursuit* on the computer, plopped herself on the floor in front of the TV with Ashley and Stefen playing video games, or joined our family for board games and a lot of laughs.

Later, when Grace needed a helping hand in her classroom at the beginning or end of the school year, Ashley eagerly jumped in. As Grace's friend, Ashley could cross the line between student and teacher. This made her feel special. Middle school students still hold teachers in high regard, and Ashley hung out with one of the most popular. This kept Ashley from feeling totally alienated and alone, plus it provided her with some bragging rights while others talked about their full weekends with friends.

In seventh grade, another guardian angel entered Ashley's life in the form of her science and math teacher, Judy Kearns. This teacher had family members who experienced panic attacks, so she knew the debilitation that these attacks brought into one's life. Judy had genuine empathy and concern for Ashley. Throughout the school year, she monitored how Ashley was doing, encouraged her with a reassuring smile or pat on the back, and watched over her in times of higher stress like the seventh grade science fair. Later when Ashley moved to the high school and Ms. Kearns took a job at the District Office, located adjacent to the high school campus, she made sure that Ashley had access to her. Today, Ashley and I are still friends with Judy.

Besides some of the physical changes of puberty, Ashley started gaining weight the summer between seventh and eighth grade. In seventh grade, she was slender and willowy, with tomboyish ways. When eighth grade rolled around, she wore oversized T-shirts to cover her developing breasts, and baggy pants. The weight gain along with the loose clothing masked her growing curves. In spite of the physical changes, she definitely appeared more masculine. She never wore pink or white—pink for obvious reasons, white because her sports bra would show through. Ashley always selected boy's athletic shoes.

She also began cutting her long, straight hair. This led to a bit of friction. Her father offered to trim it slightly, but she wanted to chop it off. With her masculine attire, the short hair promised to take away all vestiges of femininity. That's what she wanted. However, Papa didn't want to lose his baby girl. I feared that, by appearing so masculine, Ashley would become a target for taunts and bullying. Somewhere along the way, we compromised, Ashley more than Tad and me. He persuaded her to keep it a little bit longer. We were taking baby steps, being pulled every step of the way. She wanted to take giant leaps forward and grew more and more impatient.

Then there was the matter of sexual orientation. By middle school, Ashley knew she liked girls, but she tried to change. She remembered sermons at church condemning homosexuality. I also felt conflicted by the teachings of our church. I wanted my children to know a higher power existed, but I felt uncomfortable with their condemnation of gay and lesbian individuals. At one Bible study session, I remember a church member standing up and saying, "We must not tolerate homosexuality any longer. It is an abomination." After that session, I felt sick. I no longer went to Bible study, but dropped my children off at Sunday school and waited for them in the car, reading my Bible or some other religious book. I didn't want to hear their judgment and homophobic feelings, but I wanted my children to have the comfort of knowing when we died we would meet again in heaven.

When Ashley was in eighth grade, girls started telling me that she liked a boy in her science class. I remember feeling somewhat relieved. But it couldn't have been further from the truth, as Ashley shared years later. "I met Daniel in science. We were kind of buddies. Sara thought that I liked him, but I think *I wanted to be him*. He was dating this cute girl. I didn't think I necessarily knew I wanted to be a guy, but I knew that he was a good athlete. I wanted to be a good athlete. These are the guys that girls liked. I even tried to write like him by holding my pencil the same way."

My daughter lived vicariously through her science classmate. She began to observe how the opposite sex did things—and she copied them. Ashley says, "I still had no idea what the root cause of all my issues were at the time. I just thought I was different or a late bloomer, but definitely not a transgender person. I wasn't even aware that there were options or that people could change genders to become the one they were meant to be. I had barely become aware of the gay and lesbian population."

The fluctuations of Ashley's emotions and her concealment of her physical changes perplexed me. One day, she seemed happy; the next, she languished in sadness. Her golf skills brought her recognition, and this spotlight boosted her self-esteem, but she remained forlorn. When Tad and I heard the high school might introduce a girls golf team the following year, we celebrated the fact that Ashley could showcase her talents with other females, rather than compete with the stronger male golfers. She would finally find a place to belong.

Little did I know that she was hoping to play for the *boys* golf team. She could hang out and be one of the guys, just like in elementary school. The creation of the girls golf team dashed those hopes.

Today, I understand the emotions that ran rampant through my daughter. When she showed happiness about something that evoked feminine energy or feelings, the male side of her felt out of alignment and pulled her into a confused state. That brought on the anger or sadness. On the other hand, when her masculine side predominated and she felt happy, her female body questioned and fought those thoughts and tendencies, bewildering her. She lived for so many years in unresolved conflict of her identity. When I reflect on these years, I wish I could have done more to comfort, guide, and support what she went through. I still hold guilt for those times.

We survived eighth grade seemingly without much drama. At the end of the year, the middle school threw their traditional promotion party to honor its students' advancement to high school. Girls dressed in semi-formal attire, while boys dressed in their shirts and ties. Yards and yards of material hung over the well-worn cafeteria walls, transforming its appearance. Other decorations matched the theme of the event. Parents worked long and hard to convert an ordinary room into a special place for students to end their middle school days and enter the final four years of their mandatory education.

I bought Ashley a simple black dress with lace on the bodice and a straight line of crepe forming the bottom. It wasn't showy, but it was a dress. Her father fashioned her hair into a shoulder-length, flipped-up hairstyle. She looked nice and sweet, but I couldn't help but notice how awkward she appeared. When she walked, she clomped around, not with delicate steps but more of a flat-footed boy's walk. With her wide shoulders, built up from all her golf practice, she now seemed more out of place in a dress than ever.

After the party, she came home and told me she danced with a guy. She seemed happy that someone would find her a worthy partner. Then she talked about a girl asking her to join a group of girls on the dance floor. As she told me, I heard giddiness in her voice; this request was even more special to her. I could sense she was happy to get attention from either gender. Interest from guys flattered her, but interest from girls made her heart flutter. Her attraction to other girls and the thrill of being noticed by them were signs that were growing stronger.

When I return back to my middle school days, my happiest memories are of drill team, dances, and having crushes on boys. How different from my daughter! Although I understand that each child is unique, a feeling grew inside me that Ashley and I were different in more than our choices of extracurricular activities. I never heard her talk about boys; the only people who seemed to pique her interest were other girls. And the girls to whom she gravitated shared the same type of quality: a need to be cared for and protected. She liked being someone else's hero and told me it came from the simple knowledge that men were heroes and they always saved the girl. Sounds like the kind of story lines kids see in Disney movies and cartoons. Even in elementary school, she wanted to be the hero. She once shared a story about a day when it started to rain at recess, and she gave another girl her jacket so the girl wouldn't get wet. Ashley ended up soaked. Normally, elementary school girls can't run fast enough from the rain. My daughter threw all those cares aside and gallantly rode to the rescue.

These memories take me back to Ashley's early childhood years, to Halloween where she always chose to be a character that saved people—Batman, Zorro, and Power Rangers. Although I didn't want to admit that Ashley could be a lesbian, the signs grew increasingly obvious.

One day, she broached the subject with me, subtly. "Momma, what would you think if one of my friends was gay?"

"Well, Ashley if they were a good person that wouldn't matter to me. Do you have a friend who is gay?"

"No, I was just wondering what you would think."

"I look at people's hearts and that is the most important thing to me. If your friend has a good heart, then I know I would like them."

Although I wouldn't depict middle school as intolerable, these three years brought some very trying and uncertain times. Ashley's confidence continued to slip. Everyone could see it. Her uncertainty about her sexual orientation cast doubts about herself in general. She seemed slowly and inexorably to withdraw into a secretive world that held no place for me. I told Tad, "I think she is in trouble." However, we remained unwilling to probe into her sexual orientation for fear of opening up Pandora's Box. Consequently, I vacillated between avoidance and worry when she seemed to move further and further away from me.

My mind unleashed a pack of thoughts no less fearsome than wild dogs: *What is causing Ashley so much turmoil? Could she be into drugs or alcohol? I hear kids are experimenting earlier and earlier. No, I would be able to see those signs... Could Ashley be struggling with issues about her adoption? Adoption could be part of her problem, but when we talk about it, she doesn't seem so angry anymore. Are we putting too much pressure on her to golf competitively? Now that could be a cause for her withdrawal and sadness, but she loves to golf. She says she wants to go professional and gets along so well with everyone on the course, but she hates the pressure of practicing and having no social life. Maybe we should see a family therapist.*

Meanwhile, I began to consider that her problems centered around sexual orientation issues. I don't remember asking myself, *Is my daughter a lesbian?* I don't remember Tad and I having lengthy conversations about Ashley's orientation during this time. I think my heart knew the answer, but my head was not ready to ask the question.

Since Ashley didn't have a lot of close friends, girls rarely came over. So, she spent many hours practicing on the golf course. In retrospect, it was a paradox. She didn't have many friends, so practicing golf filled that void. Yet she didn't want to practice, so she could have a social life. But whom could she relate to and what would she do socially? Most girls spent time at the mall, shopping and hanging out with their girlfriends, or meeting each other at the movies. Ashley didn't like to shop for girl clothes, her anxiety attacks made attending movies a potentially negative experience, and she held no interest in talking to other girls about makeup and boys. In the end golf became her social life with Ms. Chang and Papa.

After school, she usually joined her father on the driving range and played tournaments on the weekends. The golf course became her second home, and her dad and Grace Chang became her closest friends.

Ashley moved on to high school, hoping that she would find a place where she could finally belong. As her mother, I prayed for the same. Ashley's freshman year featured her prominence on the girls varsity golf team—a source of pride for any parent. She stood at the top of the six-girl starting roster and received the limelight on many occasions. One outspoken, returning senior golfer walked into the coach's office and asked,

"Okay, who's the new hot chick golfer?" I could only imagine how Ashley cowered with intimidation as she also stood there. Later, Ashley grew to adore this senior and tried to emulate her level of confidence and perfection.

Outside of golf, Ashley's freshmen year felt like a continuation of middle school for me—she was lonely, withdrawn, often sullen, and rarely happy. She could no longer retreat to Grace's room to feel accepted. Furthermore, Grace believed it was time for Ashley to find friends her own age. So Grace intentionally kept her distance. At dinnertime, Ashley often recalled her day of sitting in the halls of the high school, eating lunch alone. As she replayed her isolation, food stuck in my throat because I sympathized so deeply with my daughter's loneliness. I wanted to cry. I visualized her sitting by herself, chewing on a sandwich that tasted like cardboard, and feeling like she was nothing. A nobody.

I managed to withhold my tears. I just smiled weakly and said, "I know you will find some friends, Ashley. You are a good person with a kind heart. Anyone would be lucky to have you as their friend."

For the first two years of high school, Ashley tried to fit in. We talked about cute boys at school, golf, and teachers she liked—and those she didn't. She didn't want to be different. She wanted to feel and act like the other girls. She fought so hard to change so she could fit in, but in the end, it brought her more sorrow and depression.

When Ashley was a sophomore, we attended a high school football game. I know she would have preferred to go with a classmate. I felt sick that my daughter had to see a football game with her mother, because she had no one else to go with. I pretended to be honored that she wanted to take her mother to a high school event, but inside, I was heavy with melancholy. *Why can't Ashley find some friends? Out of 3,600 students at the high school, there's not one person who she can connect with?* Not one to wallow in this negative place, I threw on a warm coat and replaced my inner gloom with a happy face. At the game, I tried to keep my distance as she sought to connect with others. One boy who interested her hung around and finally asked if she wanted to grab a bite to eat after the game. Her happiness stretched across her smiling face. Maybe he wasn't going to be her boyfriend, but for tonight one boy wanted to spend time with her.

A few hours later, she called me and asked to be picked up from the restaurant. "Can you drive James home?" she added. After we dropped off James, she told me the bigger news: James had asked her to go with him to homecoming! This was a big deal for any girl, but for Ashley, it was monumental.

In spite of this exciting news, doubts spun through my head. When Ashley emerged from the restaurant, she held James' hand. For some reason, it felt wrong. Why should it? Wasn't it natural for high school boys and girls to hold hands? Of course—but that's not what hit my thoughts as I watched them. Instead, I envisioned two *boys* holding hands. Ashley said that, while their fingers interlocked, each tried to be dominant, leading to a sense of discomfort for both of them. "His hands were rough, felt sticky, and dirty," she said, "not like holding soft, smooth hands with a girl."

However, it took nothing away from her happiness at being invited to homecoming, a happiness I openly shared.

Ironically, if I saw two boys or two girls holding hands today, I silently applaud them for their courage and if I can catch their eye, I give them the biggest smile I can to convey my approval and acceptance of their relationship.

A couple days later, James retracted his invitation. The rebuff angered Ashley, but she didn't seem too broken up. If a boy dumped me for homecoming, I would have been devastated, then enraged. She was mildly angry—and relieved? I didn't expect that. When I observed Ashley holding James' hand, it marked the first time I truly accepted that my daughter might be a lesbian.

Also during Ashley's sophomore year, a huge wake-up call charged into our lives: Ashley started cutting herself. Cutting, also known as self-mutilation, is a condition where individuals who are emotionally debilitated by current events cut parts of their body, like wrists, arms, or legs. Generally, people do not intend to kill themselves. Instead, it is a way to release pain—or feel pain—for those numbed by depression. Ashley started with a safety pin, so it was not very deep. Her cutting progressed to using a knife. Sam, a police officer neighbor and wonderful friend, noticed the telltale marks on her wrists when her shirt cuff pulled up unexpectedly.

I asked Ashley about the onset of the cutting. "By my sophomore year in high school, I was so depressed and so socially isolated, I started to cut," she recalls. "I felt trapped, completely at the mercy of my emotions. At a certain point, I was so full of emotional pain that the only way to release the pain was to physically cut myself. I would think, 'I'll just do this once and then I'll be good.' But it wasn't like that. It was very temporary. Once the cut healed or started to heal, the pain wasn't there anymore, but I still felt so much pain emotionally. I kept cutting until one day, someone caught me and told me I had to tell my parents or he would do it for me."

When Ashley finally admitted her self-mutilation to us, I thought, *How could that be?* Just a few years ago, she was so happy that I thought myself the best mother in the world. I loved my child with all my heart. Shouldn't that be enough for her to make it through those years of "why did my biological mother give me up for adoption?" Now I saw a morose, withdrawn child who listened to angry, head-throbbing music fronted by lyrics that spoke of inner rage and being misunderstood. If the pain felt either too great or not great enough, she cut herself.

I lived in denial for so many years. With every obstacle we overcame I hoped our struggles were over, that the course of Ashley's life would change directions and our uphill battle would end happily. When it didn't, I used my work as a temporary distraction so I could gather strength to face the next challenge. But some challenges could not be deflected. Cutting was one of them. I sprang into action immediately.

Tad and I sat at the kitchen table with Ashley to broach the topic. She said things like, "I wanted to feel physically the pain that I felt inside." I didn't understand what she was talking about. I asked her if it helped to cut. "At the moment it helps, but then it doesn't, so you have to cut more," she said.

Numbed by her honesty and declaration of guilt, I didn't know what to say. With a quivering voice, my husband softly pleaded with her, "Please stop doing this, Ashley. It is breaking my heart."

Knowing that my usual go-to resource, books, would not be enough, I sought a good therapist for Ashley and our family. In my desire to help her feel comfortable, I let her interview and choose the therapist. We found one that reminded Ash of her Grandpa Tak, my father who had died when she was eleven. She said, "I want to meet with him."

I knew that Tad needed to attend these therapy sessions with Ashley and me. However, Tad had heard what he considered a horror story about a family that entered therapy together. At the end of each session, family members were dismissed from future sessions—but the father ended up continuing sessions alone. Tad feared that would happen to him. Talking about feelings did not top his priority list. I'm sure most men can relate to that. In the past, I had floated the idea of therapy as a means to encourage him to talk to me, rather than brushing things off. If I would say, "Let's sit down and talk about our differences in parenting and how to be more united" and he would say, "Whatever you want to do is fine with me," I'd reply, "Let's find a therapist who could help us talk through this." Immediately, he would respond, "Tell me where and when you want to talk and I'll be there." We used to laugh about it, because I knew he was so afraid of becoming the last man standing in a therapist's office, he would do anything to avoid counseling.

This time, Tad knew his little girl was in trouble. Although fearful of the never-ending therapy sessions, Tad agreed to participate in the meetings. I didn't want our son, Stefen, to feel excluded, so I invited him to the group session—his choice. It relieved me when he declined to participate. I thought the rest of us could be more open and honest without Stefen there. His presence would have prompted all of us to hold back from speaking our deepest truths for the same reason: a desire to protect his gentle spirit.

As we walked into the therapy office, Ashley felt apprehensive, I felt hopeful, and Tad vowed to "spill his guts" so he wouldn't be landlocked in therapy for the next year. The therapist gave each of us an opportunity to share. Through our sharing, we discovered Ashley's cutting had nothing to do with her sexual orientation, but rather her desire to cut back on golf. That surprised both of us. She wanted to play for the high school team, but did not want to spend her weekends competing in tournaments that would give her visibility for college scholarships. Ashley's cutting resulted from feeling Tad's pressure to practice and compete so prestigious colleges might recruit her. Ashley admitted that it was partially "feeling the pressure to be someone and fulfilling all these expectations—go to college, play golf, be this scholarship winning and successful golfer, daughter, and student" but there were other pressures she wasn't quite willing to face yet.

Tad was disappointed. If she kept playing, both he and her high school coach felt an NCAA Division One school would sign her. But I could see it in Ashley's eyes: she didn't want the pressure that came with the full-ride scholarship. She enjoyed golf and competed with the best in her age group, but she never dreamed of playing at the highest collegiate level, which required hours of daily practice and travel around the United States.

However, this was her papa's dream. And she knew it.

The therapy sessions gave Ashley a safe place to speak her truth: she did not want to live and breathe golf. Tad admitted that he loved watching Ashley on the golf course, and he believed she could excel in college golf. But, in keeping with his stature as a wonderful father, Tad said he would support whatever she wanted to do if she would agree to one thing—*stop cutting.* I also told her that whatever choice she made regarding her golf was fine with me. Golf was my husband's passion. I would share that passion only if it reflected Ashley's wishes.

At our second therapy session, the hour sped by, each of us participating vigorously, opening up, laughing, and speaking with complete honesty. I felt encouraged. How therapeutic! The usually quiet, reserved Tad grew animated. His words spilled out without restraint. Known among family and friends as having a dry sense of humor, my husband transformed into a stand-up comic, finding his stride in the middle of therapy as he expressed his feelings openly. The therapist and I were laughing so hard that tears streamed down our cheeks. I added my own brand of comedy in between his riffs.

Ashley watched us in amazement, wondering who really needed the therapy. She kept saying, "My parents are so weird."

By the end of the second session, the therapist said that our family exhibited such openness and love for each other that we didn't have to come back unless we felt it necessary.

Ashley said that she didn't need any more sessions. She walked out of therapy with less pressure to play golf on the weekends and a new sense of freedom. Most of all she felt heard. I didn't see any reason for us to return, either, because she was in a better place. I was happy.

Meanwhile, my husband felt like he had just been paroled from a year of therapy sessions. He wore a mile-wide grin. Normally a very subdued man, he let out an enthusiastic "Woo-hoo!" with a little fist pumping as we walked to the parking lot. He also noted that we had just paid the therapist one hundred and fifty dollars to laugh for one hour. Each of us felt lighter and filled with more hope. Those two sessions were worth every dollar and then some.

For weeks, we lived in a blissful state. All our problems seemed to disappear. I felt like I was walking on a cloud. When my child is flying high, so am I. I felt like a wonderful mother again! I saw a glow return to Ashley's cheeks, a sparkle to her eyes. We nipped the cutting problem before it could grow and fester. Suddenly, her weekends filled with relaxation and time to cultivate friendships. Happy music filled our home; our family felt connected and laughed more readily. We started to put our cares behind us. The mood swings in our home vanished, except for an outburst here and there—normal behavior for a teen and a preteen. Lightness and optimism replaced the sadness and anger. Tad stopped pressuring Ashley to play golf, this time without my nagging. Consequently, our relationship relaxed. We had just faced a family crisis head on—and won. I felt rejuvenated by the promise of more peaceful and untroubled days.

Back at school, Ashley began to struggle academically, but it didn't last long. A blessing dropped from the sky in the form of the Health Academy, a small learning community that Arcadia High School was starting. The city of Arcadia lay east of Pasadena, California, known for the New Year's Tournament of Roses Parade and the Rose Bowl football game. Arcadia is a quiet, conservative city that attracts residents due to their highly regarded school district. It became a selling point to us when we moved into the city as our children neared kindergarten.

The academy and its block schedule at the high school were designed for students who wanted to go into health-oriented professions. This block format allowed kids more time to obtain instruction and support from their teachers. For example, Ashley took a history class twice a week for two hours instead of five times a week for one hour. The missing hour was made up through a night class or on Fridays. The innovative teachers dedicated themselves to the non-advanced placement (AP) students who might struggle in school. The Health Academy was a groundbreaking and creative way to support and focus on these non-AP students. I thought this was perfect for Ashley's learning style.

However, she was reluctant to sign up. I asked her to trust my judgment on this one, and she did. She enrolled, and immediately loved the program. She found more time to do her homework. The longer blocks allowed teachers to fully introduce concepts, assign homework, and check student comprehension prior to the student leaving class. Students like Ashley then left with greater confidence that they could complete their homework successfully. Teachers really got to know their students and gave them a lot more individual attention. Most teens love added attention, and Ashley was no exception. She flourished in this environment. When the high school tried to eliminate the program her senior year, a few parents and I fought to keep it going. Arcadia extended it one more year.

The Health Academy finally gave Ashley a sense of belonging. She began to make a few friends. She connected with her teachers in a way that reminded me of Grace Chang. That's when I began to see another paradox within Ashley. She felt quite at ease with adults, a testament to her inner spirit, which always stretched beyond her years. However, a small child also resided within her teenage body and soul, one that loved to be nurtured by her mother, like a toddler seeking adoration. As a young child, Ashley used to say to me, "I want to be your favorite child. Tell me the truth: who do you love the most?" I would diplomatically tell her, "I love you so much."

Then she would ask, "What about Stefen?"

Naturally, I would say that I loved him, too.

Hmmph! She'd stomp away, not happy with my answer.

The Health Academy fed both sides of Ashley. Her adult side loved interacting with her teachers. Her child side loved the individualized nurturing. On top of these two areas, her athletic ability also grew. Since Ashley was the Most Valuable Player on the Arcadia High golf team all four years in high school, her teachers followed her success each season. She received many accolades for her accomplishments. More importantly, though, the Academy cared about her as an individual. She had a supportive environment during a time when there were few places for her to belong. Everybody needs a place, a community, to which they can attach themselves. Ashley found her place in the Health Academy.

During her adolescence, Ashley's other community was the church, which seemed to fill her longing for spirituality. I think the thought of heaven suited her and the thought of a loving God comforted her. She understood lessons learned from the Bible at a very deep level. "She is a wise person, living in the body of a young child," her Uncle Paul used to say.

When Ashley was very young, thoughts of me dying overwhelmed her. "Momma, if you die, when you start going up to heaven, I am going to grab your legs and go up with you," she told me. It didn't feel like an empty promise; she loved me that much. Her first grade teacher intimated that she never saw a child that openly expressed so much love for her mother. The implication: I held an immense responsibility as her mother. Ashley didn't eat well when I had to take business trips. I tried not to leave for long, otherwise, when I returned, I felt guilty over any weight she lost. Although I know her love was deep and true, I also sensed that her reality as an adopted child created an ingrained fear of abandonment. Technically, it had happened once before—when she was born. She always feared I would leave her. Sometimes, it worried me so much that I told Tad, "If anything happens to me and I am placed on life support, please give Ashley time to prepare for my death before you pull the tubes."

Ashley begged me to promise that I would never die. Although I wanted to promise her, I couldn't grant her wish because I knew that life offers no guarantees—except *dying*. I didn't want her to suffer, but I also didn't want to tell her something that wasn't true. If I experienced an untimely death, a broken promise would be more detrimental to her already low trust level and self-esteem. "I want to be here for a long time," I told her, "but I can't promise." I also explained to her that no matter what happened, she would always see signs that I was near. If the time came that she needed to look for me in the world around her, I told her she would find me in a butterfly landing on her shoulder, a hummingbird hovering in a flower, or a rainbow that appeared after a storm. It was all I could offer within the church's promise that we would meet in heaven one day.

Right in the middle of the increasingly smooth period with the Health Academy, a visiting pastor at the church we were attending betrayed Ashley. Originally believing she was a boy, he treated her fine. But when he found out she was a girl, he asked her to leave the church until she found herself. Translation: "Erase all of your homosexual feelings." This man of

God judged my child and sent her away, implying that she was not worthy of God's love. I feel an anger begin to grow even today as I think about this man.

That conflicted directly with what I teach my children: God loves each of them. Perhaps this is not the message all churches would preach to lesbian, gay, bisexual, and transgender (LGBT) individuals, but I believe in an all-loving God. Never did I see an edition of the Bible that quoted John 3:16 as, "For God so loved the world, *except for LGBT individuals*, that he gave his one and only son, that whoever believes in him shall not perish but have eternal life, *except for LGBT individuals*." Nor did I see in Romans 13:9, "Love thy neighbor, *except for LGBT individuals*, as thyself." Finally, I know that Matthew 7:12, the Golden Rule, does not say, "So in everything, do to others, *except for LGBT individuals*, what you would have them do to you for this sums up the Law and the Prophets."

If there is an area in which I still need to develop acceptance, it involves churches whose rigid doctrines prohibit love of all people. I know that in judging the judgmental, their sin is also mine. I must be accepting of those who still travel the journey of acceptance, as I am still traveling that journey myself. While I want to be all accepting, there still resides within me a part that wishes to lash out at an institution that preaches about love, yet acts quite differently. "Why would you condemn my child who loves God so much, just because she was born into the wrong body?" I want to ask. "Would you condemn a child with red hair or freckles?"

Even as I write these words, years after the incident, it hurts me that a *preacher* found Ashley unworthy of God's love. At a time when she needed acceptance and love so desperately, a church minister asked her to leave her own church because he questioned whether she deserved to be loved in the eyes of God. The truth of the matter: physically, emotionally, and spiritually, my child was rejected.

Then I remembered something: *not all churches operate like this*. Not all church-going people condemned others in the way this visiting minister condemned Ashley.

Years later, I talked to the pastor's wife about this incident and why we left the church. She was appalled and apologetic. "We all love Ashley, and nothing changes how we feel about her," she said. Upon hearing about the incident, the pastor went to his elders and the assistant minister and asked if they knew anything about this. They did not. He personally spoke to both my husband and me, informing us that he had checked into this matter and could not identify the visiting minister who had spoken to Ashley. We did not know the visiting pastor's name, so no further action was taken. I told both the pastor and his wife, "It is not your fault. I could have come to you, but I didn't. We were going through too much at the time."

In reality I couldn't go back to the church and face the same rejection that Ashley had suffered. I could be mad at this visiting minister with whom I had no ties, but I didn't possess the emotional or mental energy to fight this church. I had heard other church members condemn homosexuality. I chose to withdraw, not wishing to face a situation over which I was unsure of a positive outcome. Like my child, I wanted to be accepted and loved for who I was, not what the church thought I should be.

Presently, we're not active or attached to any religious institution. I know churches that would welcome our family with open arms. I have visited some and talked to some of their wonderful ministers. I have chosen not to go back and become a member. I have a very private relationship with God. At a church near my work, I sometimes take my lunch breaks by sitting in the quiet and peaceful sanctuary. These few moments fill my soul and give me an opportunity to connect with one who I see as all loving and all accepting. For now, this is all I need.

We all need places to belong. However, the church brought Ashley great shame and emotional pain. So did high school. For all of its many positive aspects, such as the Health Academy and the golf team, the school couldn't completely oversee how students treated each other. Although Ashley was beginning to make some friends, when it came to sexual orientation and gender identity, this high school campus was just as intolerant as any other. There were so many incidences of cruelty that I don't know how Ashley made it to her senior year without falling apart sooner. When she walked down the halls in school alone, fellow students would sling taunts, insults, and other derogatory names at her, such as "fag" and "queer." Even today my child is very reluctant to travel back to those days. I've broached the subject with him cautiously, only to see the pain flare quickly in his eyes. His shoulders slump down, reliving the sheer weight of the misery and pain of that time. When I ask what people said to him, he shrugs his shoulders and says, "I don't remember." When I throw out derogatory comments, his eyes drop down to the floor and he tells me, "Yeah, they said that."

During these times of intimate sharing, I feel so guilty that I didn't do more during those high school days. *But what could I have done? Could I have been more vigilant with my child? Could I have talked more with the school or teachers?* The same inner voice that asks those questions answers with, *No, that would have made him feel even more powerless, having his mother advocate for him in that way.*

I'm left with no other choice but to continue releasing these feelings of guilt as they arise. It hasn't been easy, but it is getting better. I truly believe that these days of struggle made my child the committed advocate and compassionate human being the world knows today. But even that awareness and belief does not completely erase the pain I feel for what my son went through.

As Ashley continued high school, I didn't know about the cruelty. She chose to shield me from all of the hurtful things that were part and parcel of her daily existence. I focused on her success in golf and the Health Academy. Admired for her skills on her high school golf team, she strove to become more of a leader. When she became a co-captain her junior year, she was proud of her accomplishment. So were we. When she was promoted to captain her senior year, she seemed to find a place of leadership and admiration.

A couple of important things happened during Ashley's junior year. First of all, the parents of one of Ashley's friends asked to meet us. They wanted to talk about Ashley's relationship with their daughter. They felt like this relationship was moving in a dangerous direction, because their son had caught the two girls kissing. They didn't speak English well, so they brought their daughter, Ashley's friend, as an interpreter. I don't even remember what we talked about, or what we resolved. I did not take a position on Ashley's sexual orientation, because she had not yet come out. The other parents said they were not in favor of their daughter and Ashley hanging out together. We said we would talk to our daughter.

At the end of the day, we got through the meeting and nothing basically changed. I dealt with the matter in my normal way when faced with an overwhelming challenge—I put it aside hoping it would go away.

In some ways I felt guilty about Ashley's sexual orientation leaning towards liking other girls. Part of me believed that her attraction to other girls could be inborn. Another part of me felt that I might have encouraged her attraction to girls. The reason? She loved me so much. I also considered a host of other possible reasons: Was her adoption the reason she loved me so intensely? She lost her first mother. Was she afraid to lose me? Or did I love her so much because I had waited for her for sixteen years? Did I love her too much? Was our love for each other being transferred to her love for other females?

During middle school, I would often see a large number of missed calls from Ashley when I went away on business. She said she would sneak the phone into her room because Papa wouldn't have wanted her to call me so much. When I didn't answer my phone, she thought something happened to me. She would plead for me not to walk alone, in case someone snatched me away. She asked that I call her every day when I left for any reason, which I did. In fact, until recently, whenever I traveled, her face would look sad and concerned, or she would say, "You didn't tell me you were leaving!" and abruptly turn away with a *humph!*

With Stefen, our love flowed differently. His love was not so desperate and fragile. He never threatened to kill himself if anything happened to me. He hugged me openly in front of friends and said "I love you," regardless of who was with him, and when I traveled and asked him if he missed me, I would receive a "not really." He just loved me and I felt it. And I loved him so deeply in return.

With two adopted children, I made every effort to be the perfect mother. I knew they both felt a deep sense of loss. Ashley's loss manifested into rage and torment when she was in elementary school. Pacing and fuming, she would scream, "My mother was a dirty, filthy animal." I always believed this was her way of justifying her mother's choice to put her up for adoption. A human being couldn't give up a child she loved, but an animal could. When Ashley was even younger, about three or four, there were nights she didn't want to be alone and would literally roll around in her bed as if in pain. I remember seeing this and thinking, *Is she trying to get out of going to bed?* But the torment seemed so real and so deep that I would enter her room, take her in my arms and just hold her. Somehow this reassurance of my love calmed her down and allowed her to fall asleep.

Stefen's loss turned into sadness. I remember going into his bedroom one night when he was about four years old, and seeing him whimper I asked, "What's wrong, honey?"

"I miss my mother in Japan," he said softly.

I ached for his loss. Even though his honest words stabbed at my heart, making me feel I wasn't enough, I somehow understood the void he felt.

I prepared myself for these moments by sitting and imagining my parents telling me I was adopted. At times, when I convinced myself that I could have been adopted, a cold, steel-like emptiness entered my body. I felt my connection to my parents snap and my heart focus dejectedly on the missing link. It was that loss I hoped to overcome whenever I saw my children's rage or grief. I wanted them to know I would never abandon them, no matter what they did. I constantly hugged them and told them how much I loved them. But had I unknowingly pushed Ashley into becoming a lesbian because I had encouraged this emotional and passionate child who loved me so much?

After being raised in an Asian household, where feelings were not always acknowledged, I wanted both of my children to feel something quite different—comfort when they came to me no matter how they felt. This is not to give the impression that my parents were not loving and kind. People called my mother "the sweetest, kindest person they had ever met" and my father "such a nice and caring man." However, they were not raised to express their feelings openly. I knew they loved me, even though they did not express this love often in words. In their later years, my parents learned to be expressive of their love and it was wonderful.

I wanted to be loving and kind like my parents. I also strived to be much more open to my children's feelings. I listened to them, encouraged them to acknowledge their feelings, and express both their positive and negative thoughts openly and honestly. If they made a mistake, I wanted them to know I would listen and not react. I gave them tools like the "Promise You

Won't Get Mad" phrase to help me respond more calmly.

Was my connection to and acceptance of them too much? Had I overly protected my children to the extent that I encouraged Ashley to be a lesbian?

As I studied more about sexual orientation, I became assured that I hadn't done anything wrong. Ashley's sexual orientation rested within her core being, not in how much or how little she loved me. Already filled with guilt in so many other areas, I managed to release any culpability about how much I loved my child and how much she loved me. I was far from the perfect mother, but I was a good mother.

Later in Ashley's junior year, my reliance on denial was no longer an option. She began to lie about her whereabouts and activities. My denial and avoidance had forced her not to face what she knew in her heart. When Tad and I finally confronted her, she flung back what she thought would divert our attention away from her lying. "I am a lesbian, and Linda is my girlfriend that I am taking to the prom."

Our meeting had been with Linda's parents. I was furious: not about her sexuality, which I could understand her concealing, but about her lies and deceit.

Looking back, the truth about her sexual orientation and lies were meshed together. But I only saw the lies, and Ashley only saw my reaction to her coming out. It was messy and I didn't handle it well. Whenever I walked by her, I couldn't look her in the eye. I believed her shortcomings were the result of my inadequacy as a mother. I felt such immense responsibility that anger filled me. I believed the most important aspect of parenting was to instill strong core values into our children: honesty, compassion, responsibility, respect, and trust topped my list. Knowing my daughter had disregarded these highest values made me feel like I had failed in my duty to my children.

As a result, our communication was very superficial for months. Tad and I grounded her from the prom. She was furious. Linda went to the prom without Ashley.

Just when things couldn't get worse, they did: Ashley found out that Linda was lying to her, flirting with and kissing boys. No tolerance existed in Ashley's heart for unfaithfulness. She valued trust above all else. Ironically, the trust that she broke with us was broken with her by Linda. Ashley cut Linda off, not only as her girlfriend, but as a friend at any level.

Ashley's trust issue, I believe, stemmed from her adoption. She needed to feel that people would be there for her no matter what, because her biological parents had chosen otherwise. The minute anyone acted in a way to shatter that trust, the relationship was irreparably damaged. She wrote off friends, teachers, girlfriends, and her biological mother when they failed to pass the trust test. As much as I tried to impress on her that it took an act of love for Ashley's frightened sixteen-year-old biological mother to put her up for adoption, Ashley always felt that keeping her would have shown greater love. All my love couldn't fill that hole in her heart. Even today, trust remains a huge issue, especially in close relationships.

At the beginning of Ashley's senior year, in spite of the rocky junior year, excitement permeated the air, as the soon-to-be graduates began applying to colleges and universities. Ashley applied to schools in the University of California system, as well as state colleges. When she tore open her first acceptance letter, immense pride shone in her eyes. Most of the colleges accepted her; furthermore, some of their golf coaches talked to her about walking on the golf team. Walking on the team is a term used for individuals who wanted to try out for a position on the golf team. If the coach thought they had the skills to strengthen the team and a space was available, individuals were invited to try out. Without the pressure of receiving a scholarship and having to live up to the expectations of that honor, Ashley began to consider playing college golf. If she didn't like it after the first season, she could walk away because she didn't have a financial obligation that tied her down. We submitted videos of her swing and information about her accomplishments. Coaches responded with interest.

When the final seven months of Ashley's high school days began, great anticipation filled our home: which college would she choose? Would the college golf coach invite her to walk on the team? However, more emotional outbursts bubbled below the surface, ready to explode. These weren't little outbursts or small blowouts. They were major eruptions. We received some warning, but not enough to brace us for what arrived.

Beginning in Ashley's junior year, the anxiety attacks she'd experienced since middle school escalated to an unmanageable level. She hyperventilated, her heart raced, her palms grew sweaty, and her mouth dried up. Once again, Ashley felt like she was going to die. The only person who could calm her down was me. Often, I would rush to wherever she was and find her out of sorts, more than once sitting on a curb with her two girlfriends pacing around her. They felt helpless; Ashley's white face and worried eyes painted her struggle. On the occasions I couldn't get to Ashley, her dear friend Candice would call me and then hand the phone to Ashley. Without my presence, my voice became a necessary substitute.

In June 2005, I was overseeing a graduation event for my then-employer. The graduation took place in Ridgecrest, California, three hours from home. I received a call from Candice: Ashley was having an attack. There was no way I could get to her. My friend Joan was with me. Seeing my distress, she mentioned that her husband, John, had a cousin, Diane, who was a therapist—and a lesbian. Joan thought that Diane could serve two purposes: to help Ashley through her anxiety attacks and to serve as a sounding board for her sexual orientation struggles.

I returned from Ridgecrest and immediately made an appointment for Ashley to see Diane. Ashley instantly connected with Diane's calm, kind, and loving approach. She has been Ashley's therapist ever since. For a time, Diane became my only hope that Ashley would be safe. With her combined history of cutting and panic attacks, I saw Ashley falling back into deeper and deeper depression. Once again, I was baffled by this slippage. She now had friends with whom she related well and spent time. These friends accepted her sexual orientation, and Candice genuinely cared about her as a human being. I feared she would turn to drugs or alcohol; thankfully, that never occurred.

However, I could no longer avoid the glaring reality: her depression was leading her down a path of destruction. I prayed that she would hold on until she found answers that would make her stronger. I watched her every move as closely as I could while not letting on that I was concerned. I relied on Candice to watch over her when they were together, although I never attached any expectations. I trusted that Ashley's co-workers would also keep her safe and offer a place for her to belong. Then there was Diane, in whom I placed most of my trust. For a while Ashley met with Diane weekly. Candice and Diane were my hope, the women who made it possible for me to sleep at night.

I continued to live a seemingly happy, wonderful life. On the outside. At night, though, when I was alone with my thoughts in a quiet house, I languished. I wished that Ashley could find her true self and a life that would bring her joy. I didn't care who she was or what she wanted to be; I just wanted her to be happy. My nights were emotionally exhausting. The next morning, I would wake up, put on a happy smile, and pretend that things were okay. That's how I got through it all.

Now the finish line was in sight. Just six months remained until Ashley graduated. We successfully weathered the senior picture fiasco; Ashley was allowed to wear a tuxedo for her yearbook picture instead of the feminine looking drape. But when the holiday break ended, Ashley wouldn't return to school. The flu, she said. She didn't seem sick—she had no fever or other symptoms—but she refused to go back to school for a week. When she returned, she suffered a major panic attack and found herself in the nurse's office. The unsympathetic nurse sent her back to class assuming she was a slacker. Ashley came home and told me that she couldn't go back to high school—ever again.

Visions of my daughter becoming a dropout entered my mind. How ironic: I worked with a dropout recovery program as an educational director developing programs to help students clarify their dreams and goals, so they had a reason to finish school. I created experiences that changed the way these students saw themselves. Was this some strange, cruel joke? I built programs that helped dropouts graduate, but I couldn't help my own child get her diploma?

I called a meeting with the high school principal and vice principal. Although they didn't know about Ashley's struggles until the meeting, together, we formed a plan that allowed Ashley to work from home to obtain her credits and graduate. They stated she was so close to graduating that they would assist us in finding a way for her to obtain her high school diploma without transferring her to an alternative school. I will always be grateful for their compassion and their commitment to help her finish those final six months. Ashley held extra units as a result of her Health Academy involvement, a blessing, because she only needed a few more to graduate.

Ashley spent the next six months holed up in her room while her friends made plans for college and participated in senior activities like the prom, the graduation ceremony, and all night party festivities. It was a sad six months.

Many people, including her therapist, believed that the prospect of leaving home for college, after such a difficult four years in high school, triggered Ashley's agoraphobia, her fear of crowds, and being alone. Rather than face her increasingly unsafe world away from home, she chose to stay within the walls that protected and nurtured her. She felt safe in the high school administrative offices, and I encouraged her to go to school one period a day to keep her office assistant class. During that period she helped the administrators with whatever they needed, such as taking down and putting up bulletin boards. No bullying and harassment took place there and the staff enjoyed Ashley's helpful ways.

She also had a part-time job as a human resources clerk at the charter school where I worked. She enjoyed the job, her co-workers, but most importantly she was afforded a flexible schedule. If she didn't feel well, they allowed her to stay home or leave early. As long as she felt safe, in control, and not confined at the charter school, she would risk leaving home. Ashley only traveled to places where she felt secure and not imprisoned. If I asked her to run an errand for me—sometimes a ruse to coax her out of the house— she would only agree if she felt there would be no traffic. She declined to do anything that removed her from her comfortable environment. Friends came over to the house, but she rarely went out with them. Movies were taboo; even today, they are often too confining.

Since Ashley chose not to participate in her graduation, I hosted a party for her at the house. She was still pretty shaky, so she asked that I only invite a small number of people. Some of our dearest friends were not invited. When I gave her a special presentation with candles and a cake, she said only six people could be in the living room at one time. My brothers and their wives, along with Ashley's cousins and friends, patiently stood outside the room, waiting for their turn to enter. Thankfully, they were all very understanding. Once they came into the room, each presented his or her written wish to Ashley and lit a candle in her honor. In addition, every one posed for a picture to be placed in her special photo album, along with their graduation wish. Rod Stewart's "Wonderful World" played in the background. When the music started, Candice exclaimed, "Oh, no, not music!" Candice has such a sweet and sensitive heart that the music made her cry. But I loved how the music filled the room with love and hope, and infused those same feeling of love and hope into the hearts of all who participated in my candlelight graduation presentation.

I wanted Ashley to remember this moment more than all the horrible, miserable incidents of high school. I couldn't erase those hurtful experiences, but I tried to overshadow them with memories that filled her heart with love and acceptance. She deserved to believe that this could be a "wonderful world" for her, too.

Ashley graduated in June 2006, culminating an incredible seven-year roller coaster ride through the middle and high school years. Several years later, I asked her to sum up those difficult years. "My life seemed to always be an uphill battle . . . my adoption, my panic attacks, my sexual orientation, and gender identity issues. I had almost no friends and very few people to talk to. I felt trapped and then hit my limit. I am not sure whether my cutting was an attempt to end my life or a way to manifest my emotional pain through a physical act. I dreamed that if I just died, I could come back without all the problems I had."

Ashley's graduation from high school was a family milestone. I knew our difficult journey was not over yet, but I felt blessed that we had made it through the past seven years. I looked back with pride at many of the decisions and ways I supported my child. I looked back in sadness at all the things from which I could not shelter her. But I often told Ashley, "Everything will become clear in the future as to why we have had to travel this difficult road." I believed this with all my heart.

I just prayed that the answer would come soon.

CHAPTER FOUR

Finding Our Way

Following graduation, Ashley asked us if she could take a semester off rather than heading directly to college. Although she had been accepted to a number of good colleges and universities, her agoraphobia and panic attacks prevented her from traveling too far from home. Panic attacks hit Ashley with the fury of a heart attack. I knew quite a bit about these attacks, having experienced them following my hysterectomy in the early 1990s. I understood the truly tremulous, confined world that Ashley faced because of her agoraphobia and accompanying panic attacks. So Tad and I consented to her wish.

Our home represented safety and a place of comfort. Ashley still required time to gain strength emotionally to step into the college world. Tad and I agreed to allow her to set her own course, to feel more in control—exactly what people with agoraphobia need. We limited our input to showing possible directions and offering suggestions. This at-a-distance approach was easy for Tad whose laid back nature flowed well with standing back and watching things unfold. For me, an educator, whose job called for setting the vision and implementing that vision, I had to remind myself constantly to follow Ashley's lead, as she did not want any other pressure from her mother. What she needed was my acceptance and support—and to know that I loved her unconditionally.

I know what I *didn't* want: to see Ashley holed up in her room, hunched over the computer the majority of the day. I'd walked into that scenario many times during her senior year of high school and didn't like the degree of isolation and separation from the real world that life on a computer can easily create. I wanted her out in the world, not afraid of it. Ashley obliged by working almost full-time; consequently, she grew stronger by the month as she was surrounded by kind, understanding people. She still worked at the charter school where they understood her agoraphobia and she trusted them. And as I saw the cloud begin to lift from her, my own looming tunnel of darkness began to turn toward the direction of light. Without the pressure of starting college, through working with caring people and receiving a paycheck every couple of weeks, Ashley began to climb out of a hole that seemed to engulf her during her senior year in high school. As her life filled with more light, so did my heart. She lost her opportunity to go to four-year colleges, but a different path revealed itself to me. I hoped Ashley's willingness to work would translate into her feeling safe to enroll in a junior college classroom. She could live at home and take the next two years to gather strength and confidence to face the world, and then transfer to a four-year university. But this needed to be her decision, and so Tad and I sat back and watched, silently hoping for signs that our support would lead her down the right path for her journey.

But with every step forward, it seemed like adversity never seemed to release its hold on us. Ashley's diagnosis grew within her to become a dangerous hopelessness in her heart. This, I believe, led to her thoughts of suicide, which she confided in me years later. Although I sought medical and psychological help for her, I felt helpless when she withdrew. My entire approach with her always focused on open, flowing communication, where I would use whatever conversational topics I could find to connect with her inner world. I hoped I could always sense Ashley's mental and emotional state through communication.

"Hey, Ash, how was everything today at work?"

Ashley stopped and faced me. "It was good, but sometimes I wonder how come my life is like it is. Stefen seems to do so well. He is popular, doesn't have panic attacks, and seems happy. What is wrong with me, Momma? Why do I have to have so many problems: I'm adopted, I have agoraphobia, I have panic attacks, I don't have a lot of friends."

"But you do have a lot of friends," I said and began to name all those in her life.

"They are all in college now and I don't know if I am going to be able to even go to college."

"You will, Ash . . . you just need this semester to get stronger and then we will figure out the next step. Remember, we are following your heart and it will lead you in the right direction. And you know you can always talk to Diane or me if you need support, right?"

"Yeah, I know."

I believed if I stayed connected to how Ashley felt, I could get her the proper help or directly support her. We both faced the same nemesis: the thoughts that billowed in her head like angry thunderstorms, spoon-fed by the fear and panic that her agoraphobia dished out constantly.

When the spring semester arrived, Ashley decided to travel outside of her comfort zone to take one class on a junior college campus and one class online. *Progress!* I celebrated quietly. In my innermost thoughts, I feared that Ashley would never return to college when she took the fall semester off—a fear shared by many parents whose children's futures often detour during that first term following high school graduation, when their child wants to take a break after twelve or thirteen consecutive years of schooling. But she wanted to return to school, even if on an abbreviated schedule. Baby steps. How do you eat an elephant? One bite at a time. Maybe she would return to a full load the following year. Things were turning around. I felt cautiously hopeful.

As the spring semester progressed, Ashley seemed to be gaining confidence. She talked about her new friends and classes, especially sign language. Since this class took place in the late afternoon, most of Ashley's classmates were older. We laughed about how much slower older adults moved, talked, and even thought in comparison to the younger students. We didn't have far to find an example: when Ashley showed me how to sign my name, my head literally hurt from concentrating so hard. My face scrunched in concentration while focusing on directing my brain to tell my hands where to place my fingers. How is that for a linear approach to something a five-year-old could pick up in a second? Ashley could sign her whole name in the time it took me to sign the first two letters of mine. I could empathize and also admire these women who sat in class with Ashley, learning sign language after a full day's work. I could not imagine stretching my brain so hard to learn a new, specialized language after eight hours at my job.

Once again, life seemed to be returning to normal. But before the end of the semester, an event took place that sent her world spinning out of control.

One day, Ashley suddenly withdrew into a deep depression. What caused this about-face? She appeared to be growing stronger, then inexplicably she reverted to a guarded, isolated, and uncommunicative child again. When I pressed her for answers, she would shrug her shoulders or not respond, muttering something inaudible and walking away. Soon, she quit going to school and stopped doing the work for her online class. I only found this out later.

In a last-ditch effort to save her English grade for the semester, she paid someone with our credit card to help her with a final paper. Ashley often used our credit card for registration expenses, books, or supplies, but she always asked first, so we could anticipate seeing these charges. When Tad and I saw this expense on our statement, we could not recall talking with Ashley about this payment.

We decided to have a conversation with her. "Ashley, we need to talk about an unusual expense on our credit card," I said.

Her eyes flashed in surprise. She tried to conceal her response, but to no avail. She said nothing.

"It appears that you paid someone to help you with some type of paper," I said.

No response; her eyes were glued to the ground below. Something was amiss. "Do you know what this charge was for?"

Silence.

"*What is going on, Ashley?*"

Her gaze never left the ground. Any sound hid behind her lips. *To tell the truth or continue the lie?* I could feel her weighing these choices as Tad and I awaited her answer. The silence hung in the air for a long time, or so it seemed.

Then the truth came out. She told us everything; her words spilled out hesitantly and quietly. "I paid someone to help me with my English paper . . . I haven't been going to class because one of my friends died." Her eyes darted from the floor to our faces and then back down again as she spoke. "You didn't know this friend because I met him online . . . I knew that if I didn't turn in this paper I would fail the class. I didn't know what else to do..." The three of us stood frozen in place—Ashley too scared to move, and Tad and I shocked by her revelation.

I heard those voices inside my head again: *She hasn't been going to class? I don't understand. Her friend died? Why didn't we know this friend? Who was this friend?*

During all of her emotional turbulence in 2005 and 2006, Ashley connected online with a gay boy, who became her secret friend. Since I read plenty of sinister stories about online chat rooms, Ashley did not tell me about Anthony, fearful that I would respond with a lecture on sexual predators. Her perception was rock-solid. She knew me ever so well and wanted nothing to do with that conversation. She needed this friend.

Ashley's secret meetings with Anthony gave her a place to talk about her feelings with someone who truly understood what she was going through. She told us how she discussed telling her family that she was a lesbian, sharing her uncertainties about how to open this sensitive conversation, knowing that Anthony had successfully traveled this road already. Sitting around the kitchen table with Anthony and his mother, she practiced the words to "come out" to Tad, Stefen, and me. Anthony became one of her closest friends. His unconditional acceptance of her meant everything. She didn't have anyone else in whom to confide, as all her other friends were straight. Some could relate to her angst, but none could understand the anxiety and confusion permeating her daily thoughts.

Once Ashley took her relationship with Anthony into hiding, it became difficult for her to confess that she had been sneaking away to meet him and repeatedly lying to us along the way. She already experienced the consequences of being untruthful with us in high school during the prom incident and did not want to go through that again. Thus, when Anthony was involved in a major automobile accident in May 2007, Ashley couldn't share this heartbreaking news and gain the badly needed emotional support from her parents as her best friend's life hung in the balance.

Ashley visited Anthony in the hospital, hoping for his recovery while joining his family as they sat vigil at his bedside. A few days after the accident, he'd improved to the point where his prognosis pointed to a positive recovery. Wonderful news! Ashley and Anthony's family took a break from their bedside watch and prayers to rejoice over coffee at the hospital cafeteria. While they were soaking in the happiness of his turnaround, Anthony went into acute cardiac arrest. He never regained consciousness.

Ashley was devastated—but she said nothing to us. Confiding in us would be an admission of lying. This magnified the already profound sorrow of losing her friend because she had no one to soothe her troubled soul. Anthony's family could not comfort her. They could barely handle their own shock and grief. She didn't talk to many people, and he was definitely the only one with whom she shared her innermost feelings. To whom could she turn when her friend was gone and her family knew nothing? In her mind, nobody. She didn't know what to do. Privately, she grieved for her one true friend that understood and accepted her. Later I would learn that she attended his funeral alone. And I knew nothing about this—until she stood here, in the midst of this little credit card mess, finally telling Tad and me everything.

As she spoke, I felt shocked to the point of emotional numbness that she maintained and kept this relationship secret for not only months but years. Weren't we as close as any mother and daughter could be? Didn't she often share so much of her life that I thought, *Okay, I didn't need to know that!*

At that moment, I realized my culpability in creating this hidden friendship: the intensity of my feelings about online predators and my relentless motherly probing when I feared for Ashley's safety. She needed this friend; the thought of losing him motivated her to hide him from us. Suddenly, I understood her withdrawal. My shock turned to sadness that my daughter had to carry the terrible burden of losing her confidante and mentor. I wanted to run up to her, hug her tight, and tell her how sorry I was for her loss.

Instead, I stood back and calmly began to ask questions. I knew from past experiences that my emotions often overwhelmed her already emotional state, and my tears and feelings in turn would practically drown her. I retreated to a more rational and objective place. I wanted to support my daughter. I would deal with the fear, guilt and confusion of my own thoughts later.

"When did all this happen?" I spoke gently. Ashley gave me the details.

She talked about the simple funeral, the grieving mother, how his family had asked her to speak and Ashley's few words of gratitude for Anthony. I could sense that she missed him deeply. I thought about how close Anthony must have been to my daughter, and how close Ashley must have been to his family. In spite of the secrets she kept from us, I respected the person she was to them.

"How are the mother and father managing?"

"Not well."

"Can I call the family or send a card or flowers to offer my condolences for their loss?"

Suddenly, more than anything else, I wanted to visit Anthony's mother and offer my comfort while sharing my sincere gratitude for her affection towards Ashley. My heart reached out to the mother of this boy who had helped my daughter withstand years of uncertainty and isolation.

I saw grief fill Ashley's eyes as she replied, "I don't know how to reach them. They moved away." Unable to handle the death of her son, Anthony's mother fled from the happy memories of their home to places unknown.

About a year later, Ashley received a call from Anthony's father: Anthony's mother had died in a car accident. While attempting to escape her broken heart, she ironically died in the same manner as her son. Ashley and I both thought that perhaps unconsciously, she fulfilled a wish to join her son because she was incapable of living with the pain of his loss. Either way, she stopped the hurt that probably consumed her each day. I know the pain of feeling like you are losing your child. I do not know the pain of losing your child forever. Could I recover from the latter? I don't know. And I don't want to find out. I prayed that Anthony's mother could rest in peace with her son by her side, and his father and younger brother could find support and love to overcome not one, but two personal tragedies.

* * *

Ashley failed all her spring classes. With one year of college lost, what could I do to support her? No answers came. One thing for sure: I couldn't lose hope.

About two months later, a possible answer revealed itself. The Mt. San Antonio Junior College girls golf team sought players for the upcoming season. A friend told Ashley she should apply. Flattered by the friend's encouragement, she decided to check it out and called the coach. His upbeat, welcoming voice drew her in—a little. She liked how it felt when she talked with him. Still unsure about getting involved in golf again, she asked to meet with him. She liked Coach Mike immediately. She felt comfortable with how he worked to form a relaxed, heart-to-heart connection with her. He saw greatness in Ashley and focused on her many positive qualities, rather than the shortcomings that Ashley saw in herself. Mike shared with me that she possessed character traits like honesty, courage, and kindness that he wanted to nurture. He told me she was an amazing young person, first, and a talented golfer, second. Ashley told him about her sexual orientation. He didn't care and added if anyone gave her trouble, to notify him at once. He knew about her anxiety attacks but didn't focus in on it. Ashley trusted him implicitly.

Taking a huge leap of faith, she joined the team. Practice started in August, and competition began with the resumption of school in the fall. But there was one small detail: in order to play for Mt. SAC, as the school was known, she had to enroll. Suddenly, I was full of hope. This would place Ashley back on track academically and provide her a place to grow in a positive direction. As an athlete, she would receive free academic support. I could feel my heart cartwheel with pedal-to-the-metal happiness; no cautious half-measures of joy this time! Ashley would be back in school with a place to belong and a place to let her talents shine. Fall 2007 would be the start of a new life.

Ashley excelled. She received considerable publicity and recognition through Mt. SAC's college newspaper and local press. She not only found a place to showcase her golf but also became part of a team. Granted, it often appeared like an on-going soap opera, with others players often bickering and vying for position on the roster. But all that mattered to me was Ashley was back in school and traveling locally to compete, a major feat for an agoraphobic girl. At season's end, Ashley qualified to play at the California Junior College State Golf Championship. She set a goal to finish in the top fifteen out of forty competitors. I thought it was an aggressive goal, but she set it and I would be in her corner all the way. I didn't care whether she came in first or fortieth.

The state competition represented her return to a world of possibilities, not hopelessness. She qualified through sheer will and unwavering focus. She not only wrestled with her agoraphobia daily, but also a hand injury prevented her from practicing for weeks prior to the state tournament. While others built their entire practice schedules around this event, Ashley would have to walk into the tournament cold in order to rest her injured hand as much as possible. I saw signs that my determined and confident child had returned—eyes sparkling with anticipation, then steeled for intense competition, a certainty in her voice and posture communicated "I'm ready" and she walked with a relaxed stride filled with self-assurance.

At the tournament, I walked every hole with my daughter. Her skill and deep concentration, combined with the ease in which she approached the game amazed me. Was this the same kid who stayed locked in our home, only meekly stepping out in public? Unlike my daughter's calm composure, I held my breath more times than I could count, mouthed the words "come on Ashley" quietly at almost every swing, and shouted out "nice shot" not only to my daughter, but other players in her group. I walked to the final hole feeling as if I had played all eighteen holes myself. I was so exhausted and so proud of Ashley. I wished Tad could have been at this tournament, since this was his dream come true—to watch his baby girl play at this level with confidence. However, Ashley felt too much pressure when he stood on the sidelines. He would have dropped everything to be there, but he honored her wishes. I admire his unselfish ways every day.

As Ashley strutted up to the final hole, her injured hand throbbing, I saw her face light up when she noticed the leader board and realized she had exceeded her goal of being in the top fifteen in this state competition. She was tied for fourth. I double-checked the leader board, making sure I read it correctly. My heart soared ... then stalled in mid-flight, like a bird caught in a crosscurrent. *Tied for fourth? She'd have to return immediately for a sudden death playoff.* Her pained expression betrayed the deep trouble her hand gave her—how much more pain could she endure? Then I saw a familiar look return. She was operating "in the zone," that place where she blocked off any negative thoughts or feelings and focused her attention on just one goal. She would never concede fourth place. I knew without a doubt that Ashley would return to the first playoff hole without complaint.

After a short break, Ashley returned to the tee to start the playoff. This time, her face betrayed none of the pain that pulsated in her hand. An iPod earphone was stuck in one of her ears. I already knew what song was playing, Rascal Flatts' "Stand." And like the song expresses—in the midst of adversity if you "stand," you will discover an inner strength you may not have realized you possessed.

She faced off with her opponent; the winner of this playoff would take home fourth place. Both golfers made par on the first hole. I walked with the other spectators, wrestling with my thoughts running through my head. *Was she ruining her hand with all this added pressure? Was it worth it to fight for fourth place versus fifth place?* I knew Coach Mike would not be disappointed if she conceded due to her hand, but Ashley would have none of it. She would play on.

As she swung, Ashley's face now grimaced and she grunted every time she hit the ball. My face tightened with sympathy for her pain. On the second sudden death hole, the other player scored one less stroke than Ashley and took fourth place. Ashley was fifth. I breathed a sigh of relief that she didn't have to play on.

Ashley never used her injury as an excuse. She walked away proud of herself for all that she accomplished—and what an accomplishment! When she stepped up to receive her fifth place medal, only I and perhaps the coach knew what she'd faced and overcame to be one of the top five in the State.

After calling Tad and Stefen with the news of Ashley's great performance, I rushed home ahead of the college van to help my husband

and son put up signs and balloons around our front yard to greet her return. We were not only celebrating this day, but also rejoicing in all the other challenges that she had broken through. She was back in college, back at golf, but most importantly, back to having a meaningful life *in her own eyes*. What more could a parent really want? I experienced so many emotions that day: concern for her injury, happiness that she played eighteen fine holes under high pressure, and deep gratitude for a coach named Mike. The warmth spreading inside me did not emanate from the sun; instead, it came from fervent hope that life could be good for Ashley. It had been a long, long time since I felt that way. More than anything, though, I felt proud of my child who had weathered so much, but continued to "stand" and look to the future.

I felt like this was going to be the turning point. Instead of feeling like I was trying to run up a continual backwards slide month after month, I saw this as the end of many years of dark times. Her life was going to reverse itself from this moment on. I truly believed that ... but I had believed it before. And I had been wrong.

Coach Mike pulled Ashley out of her depression over Anthony's death and gave her something positive on which to focus. The coach had a successful year from the standpoint of the team doing well, but he constantly spent time smoothing ruffled feathers. Her golf talents caused jealousy and resentment from others, as she attracted the spotlight where once others garnered that place. In the end, Coach Mike came through for Ashley and she felt safe.

However, Ashley still felt discontent. When I asked her why, she told me, "I think Mike knew that I was still unhappy, because he would talk to me in his office and make sure things were okay. At the time, I didn't really think anything of it. I thought I was kind of happy. I had things that I liked. I liked playing golf. I liked competing. I didn't like how I felt, though, especially when I look back and I have all these medals and they're all for girls' golf. I mean, it's very much a part of my life, and I'm not someone who's going to burn it all or throw it away, but it's just hard when you look back and wonder how much different it could have been if I had played college golf as a guy."

As I listened to this, I heard an individual who wondered whether these accomplishments were real. Like any person who pretends to be someone he or she is not, there is a lie that stands between them and the events and relationships they form. If Ashley really felt like she was a guy, but she received accolades for being an accomplished female golfer, had she excelled under false pretenses? If she competed as a male golfer, but lived in the body of a female, would the pretenses have been just as false? It became more and more clear to me that she was caught between two worlds, each of which brought her unease and a feeling of being out of alignment.

Around the time of Anthony's death and prior to meeting Coach Mike, Ashley met another friend online. This friend became her new relationship. Although Julianna filled a great need for Ashley to have someone in which to confide, she did not share any motivation to attend college, nor did she nurture my daughter's broken side. To be honest, Julianna was often critical. This left Ashley feeling like she couldn't do anything right. "Even when I did something, that I thought was nice, it wasn't good enough—it wasn't the right thing, it wasn't the right one—so I was always in some kind of trouble. I was constantly being disciplined because I should have known."

From the beginning, the relationship was intense. Ashley fell in love, but her self-esteem seemed to fall. Julianna's mother was visibly shaken by the relationship and her daughter's announcement that she was lesbian. Ashley recalls, "The first time I ever went to Julianna's house, she introduced me first to her dad, and then she tried to introduce me to her mom. Her mom ran to her room bawling—really dramatic. If you don't like somebody you tolerate their existence, but she was in hysterics. She cried hysterically in her bedroom, I could hear it."

Despite the rocky beginning, Ashley grew so desperate to have someone permanently in her life that she bought Julianna a diamond ring—the type of ring you buy only for a long-term commitment. Or an engagement. When Julianna visited the house one day, I noticed the ring. I was not happy with this sudden move, but knew that fighting it would only alienate my daughter. Tad and I asked Ashley to wait until she finished school to consider getting married. If they waited, we would continue to pay for her education, car, car insurance, gas, and provide spending money. If they chose not to wait, they would be declaring their independence and would need to manage financially on their own.

I waited nervously to hear their thoughts. There were nights when I would lay in bed hoping that she would not make a rash decision. I didn't want Ashley to get married so young, bypass college, and create a life where she eked out a minimum-wage existence. However, I also knew I had no control over what she chose to do. If we attempted to control Ashley and Julianna's life, we would only cause them to bond more tightly together, united in a fight against us. Parents never win such battles, which almost always produce emotional reactions where everybody loses. In the case of Ashley and Julianna, they sat down and rationally decided what direction they wanted to take. The financial downside proved to be a bigger challenge than either of them was willing to assume. Even though both girls had jobs, they realized all their take-home pay would go towards living expenses, leaving very little for entertainment. They decided against a stark, monastic life and opted to defer marriage until Ashley finished school.

I contained my thankfulness, but inside, I was jumping in quiet celebration.

Soon, another challenge arose. They talked about moving to Oregon, where Julianna had lived for a short time with a cousin. Excited about this new idea, they planned the move and shared the "good news" with us. Tad and I were not happy, but we did not fight their dream. Ashley always knew where I stood, but as long as I didn't lecture and harass her, she tolerated my thinly veiled feelings. I'd learned to replace my historically long sermon-like lectures with bits and pieces of advice, dropped like sugar cubes into coffee or tea sparingly. My sermons were met with glassed-over, tuned-out stares. "Short and sweet" became my mantra.

Julianna planned to move to Oregon and find a place. Then, Ashley would follow. Our position remained the same. If Ashley continued her full-time schooling, we would pay her school, car, and basic living expenses. As Julianna's move date loomed closer and closer, I could see that their relationship was starting to unravel. I would notice Ashley at home and ask, "Where is Julianna?" With my heart so closely connected to Ashley's, I often experienced her feelings. Before she could answer, a cold, lonely, and scared sensation crept through me. It made me sad that she was so frightened, but privately I did not want her to move away. I couldn't see anything good coming from it. However, I sat back and watched the telling events unfold.

And unfold they did. Instead of spending every free moment with Ashley before moving ahead of her to Oregon, Julianna fulfilled a laundry list of people to visit and things to do—none of which included Ashley. That didn't feel congruent with someone leaving the one they loved for months.

A couple of months after Julianna's move to Oregon, the relationship ended. They had lasted a little over a year. Ashley pleaded to hang onto the relationship, until one night Julianna confessed all her infidelities both during their time together in California and after moving to Oregon. Upon hearing about the one bond she considered most sacred—trust—Ashley severed the relationship immediately. Meanwhile, I appreciated Julianna's honesty. Her truthful confessions allowed Ashley to move on, rather than hold on.

Ultimately, I saw their relationship as a positive learning experience. Julianna filled Ashley's lonely days, and she gave my daughter some insight into the kind of relationship she would need to feel successful and loved. At the end, Ashley held a huge credit card debt for an engagement ring, which took years to pay off, and held a transcript with very little to show for her college credits. Ashley understood on a deep level, without our parental lectures, that she had made some very poor choices. I see the results of that today in Aiden, whose focus is on making more responsible decisions, both financially and academically, understanding how and why they will affect his future. That year also presented valuable lessons in being more disciplined, listening to intuition, and recognizing a deeper awareness of the price you pay for what you do. I sat on the other side of this relationship, thankful for all the lessons Julianna not only brought to Ashley, but to me. We are both a lot wiser.

Later, Ashley reflected on why she stayed in the relationship so long. "It's not her fault, it's totally not, but we had such an unhealthy relationship. Between her problems and me ignoring my own problem, I feel now in retrospect this is why I clung so tightly to Julianna. I was desperately looking for companionship, someone to listen and be there for me. If Anthony would have passed away six months prior to meeting Julianna, I would have had some time to settle with his death before I started dating someone. It would have been different."

One of the most valuable things I learned from their relationship and from the many years of tough times with Ashley: I can advise and guide but cannot force my will on my child. If Tad and I told Ashley and Julianna they were too young to get married, they might have married each other to spite us. If we refused to let her move to Oregon, Ashley would have raced north on the I-5 highway to prove we were wrong. Instead, we told them only how we would be involved financially, hoping not to sound punitive, but objective. I trusted that our objectivity and respect for them would allow them to make decisions objectively and respectfully about their future. We wanted to be supportive, but if Ashley declared her independence from us, she needed to be responsible for that decision.

Still, I often wondered if Tad and I were making the right decision about our financial stand. I tried to put myself in her shoes. I wanted to be a responsible parent and support her financially, but I also wanted her to experience the realities of life. If she chose to move to Oregon and quit school, she would need to get a job. I believed making Ashley ultimately responsible for her choices made me a responsible parent, but nevertheless I held many a one-way conversation with myself:

Is this really the right approach?

Am I forcing my daughter to make bad choices because I won't provide more financial support?

Will I be driving Ashley away from the family and me because I am forcing her to be responsible?

Every time, a deep-seated anxiety rose to my consciousness, a small voice would whisper: *You can't save your daughter from life.* If we paid for everything after she got married or moved to Oregon, what would that say to her? We vowed to ourselves that we would make the best of the situation, even if their decisions were not those we'd ideally have made for her. Thankfully, Ashley's decisions aligned with our hopes—and what our accumulated life wisdom told us was a better course for her.

Regardless of the drama, the impetuous decisions, and the worry about Ashley moving to Oregon, Julianna gave Ashley one priceless gift: a reason to live. During her fragile years of torment and searching, Ashley experienced a relationship that brought a glimmer of hope into her life: the hope that she could find love. Because of what she gave to Ashley and all the growth she brought to our family, I am grateful to Julianna, even today.

* * *

Despite these seemingly challenging years for Ashley with Anthony's death and her breakup with Julianna, not to mention the constant effort to keep herself academically focused and her agoraphobia in check, we had some wonderful memories, too, such as her golf triumphs and our trip to Bali.

The idea for this trip began in April 2007, when a group of five women converged in the hills behind Escondido, near San Diego. My friend, Karen, dreamed of building a home in a place of solitude and peace, a place where she and her husband could get away from a week of work and tension. We were now guests at this dream home; I loved the spirit of love and tranquility that moved through her weekend home. We relaxed to a breathtaking view, listening to the wind swirling through the hills. I wandered from person to person connecting one-on-one or we joined up as a whole group.

That night, we all made "vision boards," pictures announcing our hopes and dreams for the year already in progress. As we shared our boards with each other, one of the women pointed to a picture of candles floating in the water in Bali. That became our group vision—and the perfect time to visit would be two months from now. One of Karen's friends who had traveled to Bali agreed to organize the trip. We decided that if our daughters wanted to come, we would bring them as well. The response was varied: Joan's three daughters agreed, Karen invited her only daughter-in-law, but Jennifer's daughter was too young. The fifth member of our retreat was Joan's daughter, Jamie, who was already included. I wanted Ashley to join me, but I couldn't conceive of her considering a trip this far from home, given her agoraphobia.

Ironically, my "vision board" contained a picture of the earth that I had placed there to represent my dream for Ashley. Underneath were these words: "A great mystery was unfolding, the more I devoted myself to it, the more it just kept opening up, as if the universe wanted to be recognized for its beauty and magnificence." Next to the picture I had cut out and placed the words "This is a safe place" and "Embrace the feelings."

Was this a sign that Ashley was ready to take a huge adventure? I approached her gingerly, not wanting her to feel forced or pressured. "Hey, Ash, a group of us is going to Bali, and I was wondering if you would like to go? I hear it is a very spiritual place. We are doing yoga every day. Karen's friend is planning the trip."

"Who's going?"

I gave her the names. She said nothing, but I could see the wheels turning in her head. I knew she wanted to go.

In order for her to travel to Bali, a huge obstacle would have to be overcome: her agoraphobia. She refused to take any medication, and still ventured only a few miles from our house. How would she travel almost twenty hours in a tightly-packed airplane when she could barely leave the safety of home and hated confined spaces? Her decision to join the Mt. SAC golf team was still four months into the future, so she was still staying very close to home. The obstacles seemed insurmountable. But if she and I were motivated, we would find a way. The questions were pretty simple, the same two questions we always faced when our respective desires intersected: How badly did she want to go? And could I keep my own wishes for her in check?

Days went by with no answer.

Finally, I approached her again. I had to: we needed to book tickets and accommodations.

"Have you decided what you want to do about Bali, honey?"

"Well, I think this is a trip of a lifetime," she replied thoughtfully. "I would be with an amazing group of women. I want to go, but I'm not sure."

I decided to push a little. "Would you be willing to take some medication to help you? I know that hasn't been your choice before, but Diane thinks it could help you. What do you think?"

"Let me talk to Diane and I'll let you know."

After speaking with her therapist, Ashley decided to go to Bali. Drawn into the trip by the spirituality that she felt and sought, and the camaraderie of the other women, she warmed to the option of taking medication.

Two months later, armed with a pocketful of prescribed medication, Ashley and I joined seven other women and one tour guide for a trip that even I saw as an adventure pushing me out of my comfort zone. We first landed in Hong Kong after thirteen hours and walked around the airport waiting for our plane to Bali. Then we faced another five-hour ride from Hong Kong to Bali. I watched Ashley carefully for signs of trouble; we sat together so I could keep close tabs on her. She slept a lot, listened to her music, and visited with our traveling companions. Finally, after more than twenty-four hours of airport check-ins, security, waiting to board, and seemingly endless hours confined to airplanes, we stared below at the small island that we had anticipated visiting for the past two months.

When the airplane wheels touched down in Denspar, I silently said a prayer that we had made it to our final destination. I wasn't only thankful for our safe travel, but for Ashley's ability to make it without incident. I turned to watch her as we landed and saw the relief flash momentarily across her face when she felt the plane rumble and shake as it hit the runway. Then I noticed an expression I rarely saw in the past few years, except on the golf course — a sense of pride. As she stared out of the window, our plane approaching the gate, she spoke without taking her gaze from the new country she would explore in the next eleven days. "Momma, I did it. I flew all the way to Bali."

Looking at her, I held back tears. "Yes, you did. And you did it all on your own." As Ashley predicted, it was the beginning of a trip that would change both of our lives.

I didn't realize how much Ashley would have to face in Bali. She slept in a building with two of Joan's daughters, and I slept in a neighboring building with Joan. In our home, she could get to my bedroom in less than ten steps. Would she be able to manage eleven days in a foreign place not in the same building as her momma? Once, she asked me to stay in her room. After a reflexology session, she felt nauseous. She wanted me close by. The next day, she said, "You can go back to your room tonight." At our next hotel, she slept in her own room across the hotel property. Getting to me quickly would not be easy. She had no problems.

We took many excursions to temples and other sites of interest. She often incurred panic attacks when she felt cramped into any situation from which she couldn't escape, such as long car rides or public thoroughfares where lots of people hustled and bustled. But in her back pocket, she possessed proof that she could be in close quarters and survive—her newly stamped passport. She also carried medication that became her safety net. Still, Ashley weighed the pros and cons of each jaunt to make sure she was up for the trip. Most of the time, she chose to hang out at the private villa where we stayed. I remained with her. I didn't want to leave her alone to feel like the odd person out. Besides, I could only melt away the stress of my work if I had a quiet, serene environment to recharge. We were perfect traveling buddies.

As the trip progressed, I relaxed and grew more at ease when I sensed Ashley felt braver and more adventurous. As her confidence grew, she ventured out more and more—with or without me. One day, Ashley went into town with the rest of the group to do some shopping while Joan and I spent the day at a spa. All of a sudden, as the organizer of the trip walked down the streets of Ubud, she saw Ashley on a motor scooter maneuvering through the traffic as deftly as a local. Kathy stared in disbelief, imagining my horror of Ashley taking on this dangerous activity. "Oh, shit! That's Ashley driving down the street!" she screamed.

Meanwhile, I lavished in a rose petal bath and lay in total bliss, getting a massage, not knowing how her confidence manifested itself. When Kathy finally told me the story, I laughed at the thought of seeing Ashley speeding through traffic, all the while thinking, *Thank goodness I wasn't there!* My reaction would have paralleled Kathy's, with perhaps less colorful language. Or perhaps more. The image of Ashley scootering down Ubud's bustling streets remains the picture I see of my daughter stepping into the world with more confidence and less fear. I love that image!

Ashley and I returned from Bali changed people. The love and spirituality of the Balinese people moved me in ways I will never forget. Their deep eye contact and warm, loving gestures left an impression on me that still remains. I have yearned for a more peaceful life ever since that trip. From that day, I began to plan how my life would be more serene. Also, the love and acceptance of the seven other women and beautiful organizer who traveled with us created a lifelong bond.

However, all of this only touches the surface when it comes to the feeling I had as a mother watching my butterfly emerge from her dark, ominous cocoon. Ashley predicted so accurately that this was a trip of a lifetime. Our Bali adventure became an important moment in Ashley's life. It developed within her the success and confidence that she drew on to step into unknown areas. For the first time, she saw risk in a more positive light. Hadn't she taken a huge risk going to Bali? The spirituality of the land and people also enabled Ashley to heal from a pair of deep losses: the loss of her senior year of high school and its accompanying memories to agoraphobia, and the loss of her dear friend, Anthony. Bali became her true graduation, not from high school to college, but from her present life to knowing the world could be hers. She no longer always viewed life as unsafe, but as a perpetual forum for discovery, learning, exploration, and growth. She also discovered that there were people who loved and cared about her beyond her family members. She began to trust. With that trust, she would return home willing to step into the unknown, perhaps cautiously at first, but nonetheless moving more for the positive. In spite of all the negative events of recent years, I instinctively knew that going to Bali would springboard Ashley into a new direction. Today, I see that even more clearly. Despite the fears each of us felt, we trusted our hearts and followed their voices. The heart never lies. And I have learned to listen to mine more closely, worked to keep it more open, and encouraged those I love to do the same.

CHAPTER FIVE

The Darkness Before the Light

I learned to be emotionally prepared for anything during Ashley's troubled years of adolescence—secretive relationships, confusion over her sexual orientation, periods of pitch-black moodiness, and the stifling effects of agoraphobia. Well, almost anything. Just when I thought we had encountered and overcome many of the challenges put before our feet, along came the one thing I feared the moment when I first heard the words "I am a lesbian"—physical violence.

Her first physical encounter happened at the local mall. As Ashley walked by herself, a group of kids walked towards her—three boys and two girls. As they passed Ashley, one boy began hurling derogatory comments at her. "Fag, fag, you fag," he said. She heard the same negative comments about her sexuality at school. She heard their shouts or whispered taunts while walking through the halls on campus. At school, she continued on her way, her stoic face masking the piercing effect of their words of harassment.

Once again, Ashley clenched her teeth, tensed her muscles, and opened her pouch of feelings to stuff in one more humiliating moment. Not this time. It would not fit. The pouch holding all her suppressed feelings bulged to overflowing. Not only was there no space left for further taunts and remarks, but all the emotions of the previous months started pouring out like an enormous, irate coiled snake forced into a jar too small for its size. Her frustrations exploded—and she swiftly turned around to face the guy who called her a fag. The guy spun around as well and shoved her. Ashley shoved back. More shoving and punches were exchanged. An employee from one of the stores ran out and asked, "Hey, what's going on?" "Nothing" was the answer, and the group quickly walked away to avoid any further interrogation.

I didn't hear about this incident until years later, which was really unfortunate because it opened a very difficult new chapter in Ashley's life that I wasn't initially aware of. Shortly thereafter, she was physically attacked again outside a liquor store. Due to her agoraphobia, Ashley always traveled with a soda or water to keep her mouth moistened; otherwise, she felt like she was going to gag from the dryness. On the way to work, Ashley walked inside the store to buy a drink. As she entered, she picked up an uncomfortable vibe from a couple of young guys on their way out. She dismissed the feeling, made her purchase, and went back to her car. Placing the drink on the top of her car, she searched for her keys. Before she was able to open her door, a fist slammed into the side of her head. As she reeled from the blow, the two guys drove away in their red truck.

This incident became another Ashley did not share with me immediately. One of my co-workers, Terri, happened to mention it to me, since her daughter and Ashley were friends at work. I was shocked. How many other attacks had Ashley hidden from me? And why?

When I confronted her, Ashley went on to describe the incident, avoiding my eyes as if she was ashamed.

"Why didn't you tell Momma about this, honey?"

"I don't know. I guess I didn't want to worry you."

I felt a deep rage begin to boil up inside me, rage beyond any I'd ever known. Not rage from my daughter confiding in others and not me, but a fury toward her unknown attackers who made her feel ashamed when she was blameless. This rage blinded me. It interrupted my thoughts throughout the day. And the minute I thought of this attack, I instantly went from being a loving and calm human being to a mother spewing hateful and violent thoughts. Every time I saw a red truck or passed the liquor store where she was attacked, the anger inside of me burst out. I imagined confronting these two cowards whose idea of dealing with their fear and prejudice was to blindside an innocent girl. All five feet of me wanted to track them down and scream in their faces, at the top of my lungs, "You are the lowest, most vile, and weakest of creatures!" I wanted to smash in the headlights of their truck and roar, "Do you feel like more of a man because you hit a girl? How small you must feel to be afraid of her?" I lived with this hatred for months.

Years prior, I remember reading that the sheer, dark power of violence could evoke the most irrational feelings in us all. This article's premise was that anyone was capable of murder. I didn't believe it. I couldn't grasp it. But through this brutal confrontation I knew: yes, I could retaliate with violence. And if I who lived a life wanting nothing but love and acceptance to emanate from my heart could be driven to violence and hatred out of fear for my child, was it that same fear that causes these acts of violence to spill over into racial and sexual prejudice? These thoughts have fueled my passion to educate people. I believe education increases awareness. And awareness can counteract the fear that causes violence.

After this incident, I searched for ways to protect my child. Tad and I talked about these frightful incidences and decided each of us would find a way to talk to Ashley. It wouldn't be a serious sit-down meeting, making her feel even more of a target than she already was. Tad would pull her aside and have a brief discussion. And I'd quietly process how I could make things better. Through my questions, I thought I'd find answers. *Why did they choose to attack Ashley? What did she do to cause this? Was it the way she looked? The way she walked? What could I do to stop the violence?*

I knew I couldn't handle this situation alone. I feared it would escalate. I called my police officer neighbor to get advice. My approach was that if you ask enough questions, you will find the answers. Sam explained that these types of "hate" crimes were hard to track down, but if Ashley filed a police report, at least there would be something on record.

She refused. On the one hand, I could understand her reluctance. What would she report? A white guy in a red truck hit her on the side of the head? She saw no license plate and didn't remember any identifying details. On top of the humiliation of being attacked, she might also have to face the embarrassment of making a report to police who saw this as a waste of time.

Still, I encouraged her to file the report, and bolstered my position by telling her I would accompany her to the police station. However, I decided not to force the issue.

No report was filed.

After receiving this serious blow to the head, which caused her vision to blur temporarily, Ashley saw our optometrist. He advised that another beating could cause permanent sight loss to that eye. I felt sick to my stomach, both from outrage over the situation and from one of the deepest types of fear any loving parent can experience—the fear of being unable to protect my child. How could I keep my daughter safe?

I didn't know what to do, so I worried constantly about Ashley's safety and whereabouts. When she ventured out alone and didn't return by the time I thought she should be back, I paced the house, staring out the window, waiting for her return. Often, chills would run through my body as profound as being frightened in the dark. My heart raced; the panic suffocated my sense of reason. Pictures would scroll through my mind of her being confronted by others and trying to fight back, but losing. I envisioned her lying on the ground with no one to help her. Then the voice in my head would begin this chant over and over again, *Please don't let anything happen to Ashley. Please keep Ashley safe.*

Unable to withstand another minute of this silent, private inner torment, I called her. Sometimes, she didn't answer. That heightened my sense of panic. I wanted to jump in my car and search for her—but where would I go? So, I called, called, and called some more. I didn't care if her phone showed fifteen missed calls. When she finally answered, I tried to speak calmly.

"Hi, Ash. Where are you?" My voice lilted too high in contrived cheerfulness.

"I'm running some errands at the mall."

"Oh, how come you didn't answer my calls?" I asked, trying to sound nonchalant.

"The mall has terrible reception in spots."

"That's right. I've had that problem, too. Okay, when do you think you will be home?"

"In a little while."

"In a hour?"

"Sure about that time."

"Okay, just checking. Love you, honey."

I know she heard the insincerity and perhaps panic in my voice. Nothing mattered at that point. I just needed to know that she was alright.

I used to believe that solving challenges and issues alone were qualities of a capable, highly skilled, and knowledgeable individual. My belief system evolved through the years; now I know that I don't have all the answers. When I fail to reach out to others, I end up worrying and spinning in circles trying to find the answers I don't possess. This circular spinning helps no one and invariably creates more emotional upset for all involved, especially me. But even with this understanding, it sometimes still remains difficult for me to ask others for help or support, unless my back is against the wall.

In 2005, I didn't immediately feel the need to reach out for support when Ashley announced she was a lesbian. Knowing that she was attracted to girls made me uncomfortable. *What would people think? How would they react?* These questions scrolled through my mind. But at that point I felt no long lasting fear. The threat of physical violence entered my mind, but eventually faded away. Who would hurt a girl? I confided in a few friends about Ashley's sexual orientation, but selectively chose my words. Books and my online research gave me information in a private setting. I was not ready to declare to the world in such a public way that I was a mother of a lesbian. My daughter had "come out," but her mother was not ready to do the same.

In 2006, when Ashley became agoraphobic, I grew more concerned and watchful. When physical violence entered our lives and began to escalate, my concern grew to fear. Feeling my back slammed against the wall and having no answers, I started searching for a support group that could help me deal with my fear.

I didn't realize at the time how important this group would be to my family and me.

I first ran across Parents, Families, and Friends of Lesbians and Gays (PFLAG) when I was in the south side of Chicago, setting up a school for at-risk youth. The hotel at which I was staying hosted a convention, and I saw the PFLAG sign. At first, I paid very little attention as I walked past it. A friend of mine, Cheryl, who had just disclosed to me on this trip that she had a lesbian daughter, walked by one of the convention tables and remarked, "Here is an organization supporting our kids."

Her words stopped me. I went back and inspected the literature and products on the table. I bought a T-shirt for Ashley and picked up some brochures for me. I thought the T-shirt would show Ashley I was supportive and she could wear it on top of some comfy shorts for bedtime.

Six months later, in 2007, I walked into my first PFLAG meeting. I went alone, as Ashley and my husband wanted nothing to do with attending a support group meeting and sharing some of their innermost feelings with total strangers. I decided that I would check it out first, and then convince the others to follow if that made sense. The meeting was held at the Neighborhood Church of Pasadena that proclaimed support for marriage equality. That was a welcoming start. As I walked into the room, I saw about twenty-five adults and a handful of teenagers milling around— and not one familiar face. People were talking with others they knew, so I slipped into an empty chair, tried to relax, and assured myself, *You only have to attend one meeting. If this isn't the support group for you, there are others.* I was uncomfortable but determined to give this a chance. Through my research, PFLAG appeared to be a well-established, nationally recognized support group for the LGBT community.

The leader asked everyone to sit down. He read a list of guidelines that we were all to follow, such as keeping everything confidential within the group, that no one was a professional, and various other parameters. We were all people sharing our experiences. He requested no one give advice, but only share their stories for others to gauge if that experience would be helpful to them. The rules created a feeling of safety and acceptance; I exhaled and settled back in my chair.

After the guideline reading, everyone was asked to say his or her name and anything else he or she wanted to share. People who only wanted to share their name were given that prerogative, but the leader encouraged everyone to share. As people began to introduce themselves and talk about some of the reasons they attended the meeting, I spotted the veterans—and the newcomers like me. As the introductions came closer to me, I felt my hands begin to sweat and my stomach fill with butterflies. Was I just going to state my name only? Or would I risk sharing more?

I decided I was here for support. I needed to be honest and vulnerable to get that support, so I swallowed my discomfort. When my turn came, I opened up my heart. First I gave them my name and told them I had a daughter who was a lesbian. My eyes welled up with tears, and words flowed freely as I revealed how afraid I was for her safety and future. I shared some of the violence that had already befallen her. I confessed that although I didn't care that Ashley was choosing to love another girl, sleepless nights were becoming more frequent as I worried about her growing up in a safe world and living a life that would be happy and fulfilling. I could sense people in the group reaching out to support and comfort me. Others knew my fear well; they lived through it themselves.

The turn to speak moved to the person sitting next to me and the introductions continued. About five introductions later, a nice-looking young man introduced himself and turned to me, "As much as you are afraid of what lies ahead for you and your daughter," he said, "just know that you have entered a community of people that will support, nurture, and love her and your family through wherever your journey will lead."

I felt a wave of hope as he spoke. I grabbed onto his words and wanted to believe they rang true for my family. Would this support group be the magical key that would unlock the door to a safe and accepting world for my child? I nodded my head up and down gently, thankful for the reassurance his words gave me. Then my thoughts rudely broke into the moment and questioned, *How could this be?*

Years later, I would tell this story when I introduced myself at PFLAG meetings, adding that his words were filled with more truth than I could have imagined at that time. PFLAG helped me get through some of my darkest days, not only because of the support from the group, but also because this organization gave my child a place to ask questions, be accepted, and blossom as a leader.

After my introduction to PFLAG, I went to the monthly support group sporadically. Since I traveled a lot to Chicago during this period, I missed many meetings, but the hope of entering this nurturing community never left me. One month, I took my husband to PFLAG, but he said this kind of meeting was not his "cup of tea." He agreed that he would go occasionally, but not regularly. I was happy that he would go at all. Tad proceeded to find his own ways to support Ashley that made both of them feel good. He generously donates to LGBT organizations and attends special events whenever possible. Stefen has attended a couple of events as well, but like his father, support group meetings and sharing feelings make him want to run for the hills.

When Ashley and Julianna started seeing each other, Julianna said that she would like to attend one of the PFLAG meetings with me. With Julianna's announcement that she was a lesbian and her mother's dramatic reaction, she hoped her mother would come to a meeting in the future. Ashley was not interested in going yet, so Julianna and I attended together. After hearing about the meeting from Julianna, Ashley decided that it sounded interesting, so she began to attend. Being in a place of acceptance enticed Ashley to come out of her shell, establishing herself as a person on whom others could depend. After the first couple of meetings we attended together, I intentionally stepped back to give Ashley space to share her issues without her mother infringing on her privacy. I would go to some events with my husband, but not the monthly meetings. For the most part, I wanted to play a more supportive role and allow my child to be the most visible Aizumi. I wanted people to know that I was the mother of Ashley, not that Ashley was the daughter of Marsha.

My absence from PFLAG allowed Ashley to find her place in the organization. I was happy that she was doing so well. Then one day she made a comment about me not attending PFLAG meetings and asked if I would return. Because she asked, I knew her presence had been established to a level where my return would not interfere with her place. She had even been elevated to a leadership position on the Executive Board of the local PFLAG. I was pleased for her.

I returned to the monthly meetings, contributing in whatever way possible to the organization. This time, I met people who would say, "Oh, you're Ashley's mother. We love Ashley." Hearing those words made my heart sing. My child had found a place where she could be herself and make a difference. I felt so grateful.

Although PFLAG supported our family in so many ways, a series of terrifying incidents occurred that pushed me over the edge and into greater action. The first incident occurred outside a Denny's restaurant in Arcadia, where Ashley stopped for a bite to eat with friends one night. Ashley walked outside alone to retrieve something she'd left in the car and wanted to share with her friends. A few Asian high school boys walked toward her; as they approached, they threw out the word "fag." One of the boys started fighting with Ashley. She fought back hard and defended herself well, slamming her fist into the side of her attacker's face, raising a huge bruise immediately. High school kids exiting the restaurant walked past at a distance. Nobody tried to stop the fight. Finally, the small group decided to leave before more trouble ensued. But Ashley had left her mark.

That wasn't the end of it. Ashley's car had identifying decals on it. On her back window, the words "No Fear" announced her feelings in bold white print. Originally an offshoot of the "Life's A Beach" surf clothing company, "No Fear" had morphed into popular sportswear among dirt bike motorcyclists, then again into one of the brands of choice for street fighters, hip-hop enthusiasts, and caged fighting. In other words, "No Fear" was synonymous with "Don't mess with me."

I saw the sticker another way. With her agoraphobia and panic attacks, it seemed like a strong, positive statement to motivate her to strike out and find her way in the world. However, if someone was to retaliate against her, this decal identified her easily, and also sent a challenging message.

A week after the Denny's incident, Ashley encountered the same group of boys at a local shopping center. This time, they were armed. The boy undoubtedly looked into his mirror, saw the bruises inflicted from his beating at the hands of a "gay guy" (imagine if he knew Ashley was a girl!), and decided to retaliate. I'm still not sure if it was a chance meeting or he intentionally hunted her down. Either way, the boy carried a bat—and he went after her.

Ashley ran for her life, but the boy caught up with her, swung and hit her in the back. She fell to the ground. Luckily, shoppers witnessed the daylight attack. Ashley said she believed they only meant to scare her and feel vindicated for what she had done to their friend. As she lay on the ground, they fled. Eventually, she pushed herself up and drove to a friend's house, where the friend's father, a medical professional, examined her. She was okay. She did not want to see a medical doctor.

Years later, as I write these words, terror and bitterness still course through my body. I must consciously release these negative feelings when they arise. Then the questions start scrolling through the screen of my thoughts: *What if it wasn't during the day with so many people around? What if they continued to hit Ashley while she lay helpless on the ground? She could have been hurt so badly.*

Again, Ashley refused to file a police report. But this time, I acted. I saw a very frightening pattern: the liquor store, the restaurant, and the parking lot incident happened within a few months of each other. This type of violence would only escalate, and I knew it. It crossed over racial lines, with some attacks from whites and others from Asians, each attack more violent than the previous. I needed to do something to stop it. However, I had to release my own anger in order to act most effectively. But how could I do that while I dreamed of sitting in front of the liquor store or strip mall parking lot, stalking the guys who hurt Ashley? Then I'd imagine tracking down the attackers, discovering where they lived, knocking on their doors, and confronting their parents. How brave would they be if I met with their parents and told them what their sons had done?

I also pictured myself standing face to face with these boys, my will to fight rising by the second. At that point, my rational mind would kick in and ask two simple questions: *What are you going to do when you find them? Yell at them, take a baseball bat, and chase them around the parking lot?* The image of me yelling or swinging a bat seemed ludicrous, but it was all I could think of doing because I was so scared for my child and angry with people who would want to hurt her. I couldn't believe that people would attack a girl so violently.

Ashley explained that these guys saw her not as female, but as a male. I was incredulous. "Can you grow out your hair," I asked, "so you look more like a girl, or change your choice of clothes to look more feminine?"

I wanted her to change anything that would stop people from beating her up. But my exasperated plea struck the deepest, most sensitive chords of her being. I now know that these requests probably hurt her as much as the beatings. She struggled with her gender, and I did not support the guy who screamed at her to come out. But all I could think about was her safety. Her gender identity appeared nowhere on my radar of importance.

I shared these incidences with a few people, but not the fury that consumed me. Red trucks seemed to trigger an instantaneous wrath within me, and my seething anger grew to a blinding state when I passed the liquor store or shopping center where she was assaulted. I began to detour away from these locations in order to avoid the rage that flew out of me. Then, sometimes for no reason, while doing the dishes or some other mundane task, images erupted suddenly like an awakened volcano blowing the top half of a mountain to pieces. Violent scenes filled my mind like a sped-up motion picture and sent shivers through my body.

This anger and fear held me hostage. By constantly replaying the vicious acts, I hurt myself and neutralized my ability to release these thoughts that occupied me. Those guys probably spent a few days bragging about being such tough guys, and then moved on to their next act of pseudo-masculinity. Meanwhile, I spent months reliving those incidences, sucked into the horrible whirlpool that threatens to take down any victim of repeated violence—or, in my case, the mother of a victim.

One of my friends, Jamie, made a suggesting comment that Ashley attracted this violence. Initially, I was appalled, but it made me stop and think. Eventually, I realized that her words rang true. The violence escalated as my fear rose—as the incidences ran through my head. The violence also grew as Ashley spent more time in our garage working out on her punching bag, glaring at quotes hanging on the garage wall like "If you're not training, someone else is training to kick your ass."

We were both attracting what we feared. The more we feared and fought, the more the violence seemed to enter our lives.

Thoroughly humbled and set straight by this realization, I decided to release those negative emotions and focus on the good in Ashley's life.

Ashley and I talked. I shared how angry I had been for months, wondering as I spoke, *Will you see that I, too, struggled with negativity? Will you release your anger and fear, too?* I pointed out the aggressive quotes on the garage walls, all of which conjured up imagery of her preparing for a fight rather than working out to be buff and proud of her body.

We tore the signs down. Ashley later told me, "I think I was looking for a fight. I was angry and stuck on fighting. There have been times now where I don't do anything, like when a drunken guy took a leak on my car. I was prepared in that moment to fight, not because I was looking for it, but because there was someone else with me."

Fortunately, that incident dissolved into nothing. The thought of a drunken man peeing on someone else's car seemed so childish. Like a dog marking territory, this guy had to proclaim his "manliness" by leaving his scent.

Determined to change our direction, we worked together to seek out a way around this violence. It began by emphasizing and focusing on all the positive aspects of our lives and what we could do to bring more awareness to others. We joined LGBT causes and supported them both financially and with our time. Ashley became more aware of her surroundings and the people within them. She learned to drop her energy intentionally, so as not to call attention to herself, a far cry from strutting and glaring challengingly at others. Previously, backing down from a possible confrontation was not an option for her, but now preventing confrontation became her goal.

We've come a long way since making that decision. We have attended candlelight vigils, spoken at events, and participated in peaceful protests. We strive to bring more humanity and love into this movement. As it turned out, all of the violence lifted us to another level of action and responsibility.

The encounters immediately dwindled, not only in numbers but intensity as well. Once, a guy kicked Ashley's books while she waited outside a college classroom for her teacher to arrive. She didn't react. People still walk by and mutter derogatory comments beneath their breath once in a while. However, those comments motivate both Ashley and I to do more to educate others, rather than wallowing in anger or feeling victim to the ignorance of individuals.

All of the deprecating comments spurred Ashley to go and speak to more high schools and colleges about LGBT issues, instead of physically fighting. My child shared her pain and struggle. She not only brought light to the feelings of LGBT individuals, but also her voice became a voice of understanding and acceptance. Could Ashley's words be the difference between LGBT youth choosing to live or feeling that life is not worth living? Could she open the minds of others so they'd choose to stop bullying or speak up when they witnessed others harassed? It was her hope.

My child no longer saw herself as a person who needed to fight, but one who needed to inform. She grew into a shining example of how to transform anger and rage into education and awareness. Fighting would not change things, but opening the hearts and minds of others could. Like Gandhi said, "Be the change you wish to see in the world."

Although Ashley began to spend much of her time working in the community, sadness and uneasiness still created a dark undertone in her life. Besides the violence, the most difficult thing for me was Ashley's withdrawal and depression. I was constantly unsure about her mental and emotional state. I often sensed that she was not doing well, but if I probed for answers in any way, she crept into a more solitary, silent place. She was eighteen and legally an adult, so I could not access private information, such as her therapy records. I had to trust that professionals were taking care of her. If she was truly in trouble, I had to believe she would come to me or I would notice something and find a way to help.

The only thing I could do was *love* her. After Ashley broke up with Julianna, she told me that she didn't believe in love any longer. When I would say, "I love you, honey," her reply was a flat "Okay." My heart sank every time. I tried not to take it personally, rationalizing that she would someday come around, but I couldn't convince myself. For a while, I started to tell her at the end of phone conversations or parting hugs, "I love you enough for both of us" when her response to "I love you, honey" was an "Okay" delivered in an unemotional tone. My feelings were hurt. I knew that Ashley loved me, but my feelings suffered from her inability to reciprocate with an occasional, "I love you too, Momma." I worried that if she couldn't tell me that she loved me, than she had truly given up on love. On the other hand, if she knew that I loved her, even if she would not reciprocate the statement, then I hoped she would never give up on life.

Little did I know that I was working with the truth – but not the whole truth.

Years later, she shared more startling news. "I didn't think I was going to live to see my eighteenth birthday. Then when I turned eighteen,

I didn't think I would live to be twenty-one." She added that she believed "there were only two options. Either I got beat up somewhere, or I did it myself."

During these darkest days, thoughts of ending her pain constantly filled her mind, which she shared with me in a conversation I will never forget. "I never planned suicide, but I did know that if I did it, it would be quick and painless and I would organize everything. At one point I remember cleaning out my room and I found my will. I had written it, not the night I was thinking of suicide, but I wrote it. I wanted all my movies to go to my cousin Stephie, because she likes movies so much. And all my music would go to my cousin, Lindsay because she likes the same music as I do. I don't even remember writing it now, but I found it and I thought, *Wow that's creepy*, so I threw it away."

During this period, our life seemed like a constant stream of challenges, compounded by Ashley's further social and emotional withdrawal. She was overcoming Anthony's death, Julianna's move to Oregon and their eventual break-up, her academic challenges, the agoraphobia, and the violent attacks. Still, the turmoil was broken up by some truly beautiful moments. We savored our trip to Bali and Ashley's golf success, using them to weather the difficult times. We handled each adversity as it came up, trying to eliminate any drama that could be interjected into the situation. Drama consumed too much energy. We needed to save our energy for resolving issues. One day, hope and joy radiated throughout our lives. The next, confusion and withdrawal reigned in all its suffocating darkness. Although our challenges did not seem dramatic to the outside world, the constant handling of daily occurrences wore on me. Because Tad and Stefen were more accepting and relaxed in their attitudes, their lives did not seem so deeply affected. However, I experienced things so emotionally. My biggest challenge was that I did not know what my child was thinking. I was often exhausted from the energy it took to suppress negative feelings, especially overcoming fear or halting the thoughts constantly streaming through my mind. Many weekends, I would wake up without the energy to leave the comfort of my bed. Every muscle in my body felt weak. When I would stand up, a torrent of weariness would sweep over my body, forcing me to crawl back to bed. I would blame my exhaustion on a challenging workweek or my business trips to Chicago, which occurred monthly or every other month. But in hindsight, the emotional issues concerning my daughter's safety and future happiness weighed heaviest on me and caused the most fatigue. I know that I got through these days because I had Tad and Stefen by my side, Joan at my back, and hopes of what the world could be for my child.

When I began this journey with Ashley, there were countless resources for support and guidance. But I needed to take the steps to reach out to them. Now that I've traveled this road, I can encourage everyone struggling with their child's sexual orientation, gender identity, or any issue to find resources that can support you. I have listed a few resources in the back of this book. If you don't live in the Los Angeles area, you might have to do some research to find resources closer to where you live. The Internet was a wealth of information, but I did not accept everything at face value. I talked to people, listened to their stories, and found organizations that supported my needs.

Each of us has struggled with some aspect of our child's coming out. Many parents who accept their child's coming out still face rejection from other family members, friends, or the church. Others may suffer from guilt or fear, as I did. In order to stay in a loving space to support our children, we sometimes need support ourselves. Go find that place where you feel comfortable to ask your questions and find your answers. If one place does not work for you, keep searching.

I could not support my child 100% until I was first able to find the support and answers I needed. I loved my daughter, but until I could work through my fears, my love felt like it had conditions. On the other hand, I did not want to blindly support my child without letting her know how I felt. Although Ashley's feelings might be different than mine, I asked her to listen respectfully to my thoughts. In the end we talked and shared, but my goal was always to respect her choices; as long as I understood how she felt, I tried to respect her path. If I felt uncomfortable with her choice, we talked until both of us were comfortable. This took time, reaching out to others to get answers, patience to listen, and worthiness to ask to be listened to. Ashley needed my unconditional love and support. Through the help I received from the LGBT community and through my own courage to work through my fear, I was able to get to that place.

Most of all, I could not embrace my child and her decisions until I forgave myself for the mistakes I had made out of ignorance and fear. I needed to love myself, to be kind to myself, release any guilt, and then I found that my heart was open and ready to take the next step in my journey with my child. Navigating uncharted territory takes courage—as well as people surrounding me with their love. I did not anticipate how my whole heart would need to be part of the journey. However, the love and support of others made me brave enough to step onto this unknown path. Others had made this journey with success. So would I.

To this day, when Aiden talks about that dark, suicidal period of his life, I cringe at what could have been. I am also filled with such gratitude for all the circumstances that came together to support his choice to live. Sometimes I wonder what kept him here with me. Was it how I listened to the voice that scrolled through my mind, which softly told me that it was time to find some professional help? Was it allowing him to finish high school from home, followed by our decision to let him take a semester off from college? Was it the presence of Anthony in his life, even for those brief years, and then being with Julianna? Or was it all the times that I told him I loved him, even when he stopped believing in love itself?

In my quiet, solitary place, a question rose from deep within: Does it matter what kept him here?

"No," a voice gently whispers. "It only matters that he is still here."

CHAPTER SIX

Gifts of the Season

Even in the best of times, the month of December is always stressful for me. There are eight or nine holiday events, gifts to wrap, Christmas cards to write, a house to decorate, and plenty of holiday cooking. The list goes on. Now with my daughter's big announcement that she wanted to transition to be my son, my list grew longer and my mind even more cluttered with thoughts.

On this particular Christmas season in 2008, I felt an entirely different kind of pressure, one I never would have imagined experiencing in my life. How was I going to get through this month with this life-changing news about my child transitioning to a man? How would my friends react? How would my family truly feel? As it was, I couldn't even get my arms around this new word: "transgender." What would it mean to my family and me? How could I explain it to others? Would we even be a family?

Not the type of questions you want to interject into the holiday hustle and bustle, I thought. I didn't know how much transitioning would cost or what the health implications would be. I wasn't clear on her course of action and even if I felt comfortable with Ashley's choices. There were surgeries to consider, as well as testosterone injections. Then, at some point,

I read that regular testosterone injections shortened your life, because men had a shortened life span and she would now become a man. How many years would we be cutting off her life between these injections and the cutting and sculpting of her outside body? Questions and thoughts continued to churn through my mind endlessly.

Questions moved through Ashley's mind, too. But she already dealt with the questions occupying my mind. Her mind reflected on what people would think about her. Who would be accepting of her desire to transition and who would outright reject her? And would Ashley's transition to male disrupt or sever her now warm and close relationships with family and friends, making future times together impossible? Even though she knew that Papa, Stefen, and I would stand by her side, those questions entered her mind about us as well. Could Papa accept her as his son? Would Momma, who dreamed of a daughter, love her new son as much? Would Stefen continue to admire and respect her as a big brother, as much as he did as his older sister?

For me, I just wanted the questions to stop swirling inside my head, but I could only stop this mental inquisition by addressing each uneasiness in a linear, objective way. I decided to take on every concern one by one. By proceeding in this manner, I kept my fears at bay and felt like I had a plan or reason to support Ashley's transition. For months, Ashley had been talking online with other transgender individuals. She had asked her "second mother," Betsy, a woman she'd met through PFLAG, about the experiences of her transgender female-to-male son, and searched the Internet for information to assist her in finding where she truly belonged. Ashley stood in front of the learning curve of transition, while I raced anxiously just to stay in sight of the curve. She was ready to charge forward while I needed to filter everything through my mother lens. I could only be completely supportive when I had enough information to feel like I was being a responsible mother, not just supporting my child blindly, but understanding what choices she was making and the risks and rewards of those choices. Again, time and patience became important factors.

Ashley and I talked about the cost of testosterone injections and having "top" surgery, which would remove her breasts. While not high on my priority list of concerns, the cost nevertheless loomed over our decisions.

Ashley decided it was best not to overwhelm us. She did that by revealing the procedures and costs in bits and pieces; the doctor bills, hospital bills, hormone therapy, court costs for name and gender changes, and incidental costs too numerous to list. Although her health and well-being remained my singular focus, the financial outlay often seemed endless and daunting. All of these costs added up to tens of thousands of dollars.

When I thought about the adverse effects of testosterone on her body, Ashley explained that a hysterectomy would offset the competition between estrogen and testosterone. Okay, I reasoned, that made sense. During the times I grew sad over the thought of her life being shortened by all the surgeries and hormones, I considered another angle: If she lived to seventy as a whole, happy, and fulfilled individual, rather than making it to eighty in a miserable and perpetually conflicted state, well, I could live with that trade off. As it stood, she often walked around in such a depressed state, that I thought I might lose her before she was twenty-five. Surgeries and hormones seemed less frightening compared to the thought of losing Ashley before she experienced all the joys of life—love, marriage, having her own family, and finding the uniqueness that only she could bring to the world.

My biggest concern still lay in her making a mistake with all the surgeries. Since Ashley decided on just surgery for her breasts and eventually a hysterectomy, the question that plagued me was, "Were all of these irreversible acts?" On one hand, I thought, "yes," but then I realized that she could have implants if she wanted her breasts back. I also realized that, like me, she could adopt children after her uterus and ovaries were removed. Although the finality of losing her reproductive organs unsettled me, if having a hysterectomy would result in her body not fighting the testosterone, I felt relieved. With each concern that I tackled, I grew more and more at ease with Ashley's transition. I slowly felt reassured because I could see a plan unfolding and I was comfortable with the plan. But most influential, during this December, I could also see my child returning back to me day by day—a Christmas gift I joyously welcomed. I felt her climbing out of a dark abyss, and I sensed a ray of hope return into a spirit where hopelessness had dwelt for years. When Ashley returned to college and began to play college golf, she had climbed out of this hole before, but this time things felt different. Previously she climbed out of depression for someone, like Julianna, or for an event, like a golf tournament. This time she rose out of darkness, not for something on the outside, but for something deep inside of her. She was transitioning not for others, but for herself. Despite the daunting nature of this transition and my initial, overwhelming feelings of conflict, we were moving in the right direction. I could see it in her eyes, feel it in her spirit, and sense it in her new zest for life.

As comfortable as I was as we moved towards Ashley's physical transitioning, thoughts would occasionally enter my mind about losing my daughter. At those moments, I felt so sad. When Ashley came out as a butch lesbian, a gay man explained that I would grieve for the loss of my daughter and all I dreamed her future would be—wearing a flowing white wedding gown and veil, carrying a child, watching that child grow within her, and shopping together for cute baby clothes. I had visions of finding that perfect wedding dress together, also mother, daughter, and granddaughter teas, and sharing special girl time at a spa. When those dreams vanished, I mourned their loss, but I still had a daughter. I would need to put away all memories of my girl—take down pictures that hung around the house, no longer say "she" and "her," and soon begin to call her a different name, a boy's name. For the past few years, I had let go of my daughter bit by bit, but now I would need to let her go completely. But then I would turn my attention to the child that stood before me, who was more hopeful than ever, and my sadness lessened. Yes, I was losing my daughter, but I was giving birth, so to speak, to a son who would finally feel whole and as a result my thoughts turned to the possibilities that lay ahead of us.

Suddenly, the packed month of December became a time of optimism for me. Little did I know this would be the most memorable holiday season of my life. On December 6, 2008, the day Ashley asked for my support and my love as she began to transition into the person she was meant to be, I made a choice to travel every step with her on this journey and love her through whatever transpired. I didn't realize how my life would transform with hers, but I would soon find out.

Ashley boldly decided to announce her wish to transition at the first holiday party we attended together. She felt that this Bali group could be a safe place to come out. We headed to my friend Jennifer's house for the party that was a combination of a holiday celebration and Bali reunion. My best friend, Joan, and her three daughters attended; so did Jennifer's young daughter, Abby, and my friend Karen.

Before dinner, I pulled Jennifer aside and said, "Ashley is planning to hand out letters announcing her wish to transition to male. How should we handle this 'coming out' in front of your little girl? I want to be sensitive and respectful to you and to her." I knew Jennifer as a colleague would be okay with this announcement, but I wasn't certain how she would react as a mother. My protective instinct as a mother sprung up out of nowhere in many different situations, so I wanted to be sure this wouldn't ruffle Jennifer's feathers—or her daughter's.

Jennifer looked at me reassuringly. "I want Abby to learn to accept all people. Don't worry about her. She will be fine."

I will love Jennifer forever because of those words.

The evening continued with dinner, and then everyone retired to the family room to exchange gifts. Each of us brought a gift that expressed our New Year's wish for a member of the group. Since we weren't sure of the recipient, the gift had to fit all. Rather than draw numbers to determine the order in which we would select our gifts, we included Abby allowing her to pick a gift and present it to the recipient. Before the recipient unwrapped her gift, the giver shared her wish, either through a verbal explanation or a written note. Sometimes, these types of gift exchanges result in subsequent participants "stealing" an already opened gift. We decided that whatever wish you received could not be taken away.

I received my gift early. My wish came from Joan's youngest daughter, Jodi. Her wish for me was to experience "grand adventures, happy memories, and enjoy life." I unwrapped a journal that had the words "Enjoy Life" at the top with a garden of flowers appliquéd on the cover. This gift was light, airy, and felt full of creativity. Ironically, Jodi didn't know the adventure on which I would be embarking in 2009 and the memories that would be created along the way. As the cover of my journal pointed out, I could "enjoy life" or suffer and begrudge my plight. An easy choice for me.

Ashley received her gift early on as well, in a recycled gift box from another of Joan's daughters, Jenn. The box contained this wish: "I wish you recycle and reuse. Enjoy being GREEN and taking care of the environment."

Five other gifts and wishes peeked out of the recycled gift box:

A bath ball that would dissolve into a bubbly bath – "I wish you take the time to pamper yourself."

A journal titled "I Love" – "I wish you are grateful for the blessings and challenges in your life."

A paper binocular – "Find new perspectives and enjoy the search."

A box of crayons – "I wish you live your own life and color outside the lines. Be child-like!"

A beautiful orchid plant – "I wish you show your beauty to the world. Re-invent yourself. Re-bloom...and nourish yourself."

For a person who was embarking on a new chapter of life with a new name and gender, could you imagine gifts more tailor-made? I couldn't.

After the gift exchange, Ashley passed out her transition letter to the group. It was the same one she had given to Tad and Stefen. Joan knew this reveal would take place tonight, as well as Jennifer, who I had spoken to earlier, but most of the others probably wondered why Ashley was passing out a letter. Walking around the room, she silently handed each person her announcement, disguised innocently in a plain white piece of paper that was tri-folded. Her eyes made contact with some, with others she looked shyly away as she walked from person to person, handing them her letter. At times, she looked up briefly, hoping to get a glimpse of their reaction as they read. Joan and her daughter, Jamie were Ashley's bosses at work. They would set the tone for the future of her job – a concern to Ash. Would she be accepted fully? Or would there be women, starting with these two, who would not be comfortable with her decision? I believed that all these women would embrace Ashley without question. They were friends who I trusted and felt close to, but this was Ashley's first encounter with others outside our immediate family. I sensed she anticipated the worst, but wished for the best.

As individuals began to read her letter, stillness filled the room. All tried to grasp what she was saying. I held my breath, praying that my intuition about my friends would not betray me. Joan, with whom I had already shared the news, would accept Ashley's decision. Would the others? Joan cried quietly, sniffling gently as she read the words. Finishing the letter, she walked up to Ashley, tears trickling down her face, and hugged her longer than she had ever hugged my daughter before. As others finished reading Ashley's letter, they walked up lovingly to show their acceptance with a hug or a kind word.

Although no tears stained Ashley's face, she radiated softness, coupled with a relaxed smile. "I felt good inside," she remembers warmly, "relieved, happy, and accepted." All had opened their hearts to her words. It was a good place to start.

The next "announcement" opportunity for Ashley came at a holiday party with some girlfriends of mine from a church youth fellowship group. Except for one individual, who I'd met while in college, the remaining four of us had known each other since our teens—over fifty years. And we had been getting together during the holidays for four decades. We witnessed each other's weddings, sometimes as guests, some of the times as bridesmaids. We'd watched our children grow up and get married themselves, celebrated the birth of grandchildren, and supported my maid of honor when she lost her husband unexpectedly to a heart condition.

Every year, we selected a special place to have dinner, reminisce and catch up on a year's worth of "current events" about our respective families. During the middle of dinner, while eating and exchanging updates, my cell phone rang.

It was Ashley. "Momma, can I come by and visit all my 'aunties'?"

"Sure, honey. What time will you be by?"

"I finished work and thought I would come now."

"Are you bringing your letters?"

"Yes, I am." My heart fluttered and my stomach did a quick flip. She never indicated she wanted to do this tonight. Once again, I thought I knew these women and they would accept my daughter's transition, but would they? I couldn't bear to see my child hurt if I misjudged the situation, so I felt nervous for her. And I felt nervous for me. I didn't want to lose these longtime friends, but I also knew that if I must choose, my choice would always be Ashley.

About thirty minutes later, Ashley walked in and greeted her aunties. She declined to have dinner. We were almost done anyway. Her agenda was clear, at least to me. Up until now, her announcements had gone well and I felt less tension with each "coming out" that ended up positive, but a twinge of doubt always hung over our heads. Before Ashley would hand out her letter, we decided to move to another restaurant for our dessert. I read the relief on Ashley's face, a brief reprieve.

Though her decision was made to tell her aunties, she seemed uncertain about informing my oldest friends. Ashley was waiting for the proverbial "shoe" to drop. She heard so many stories that did not end well. I had not heard those stories or perhaps with my tendency for optimism chose not to acknowledge them, so any concern seemed to vanish more quickly for me. I am the kind of person who hears a person honking loudly and thanks him for looking out for me. Or if someone gives me the middle finger, I choose to think that person had a really bad day and I happen to be the one receiving all his or her frustration. Sometimes Ashley would stare at me sideways shaking her head, like what planet did you come from? But it always made me feel better to see these acts as helpful gestures, or at least not a personal attack on me, rather than be pulled into the anger, impatience, and frustrations of others. After all, I would surmise, life is a choice and I choose to think the best of others so I can feel the best about myself. Call it naïve, but it has worked for me.

At the second restaurant, we ordered and passed around an array of desserts. Ashley sampled the different dishes, trying to appear calm and composed. Then a moment of silence lay in the air. Why was Ashley here? She had never come to one of our dinners before, so it felt as if people were questioning her presence. Ashley seemed at a loss on how to proceed, so I prompted her by asking if she had something she wanted to share with everyone. Ashley handed out the letters and waited while everyone read her words. Auntie Judy was the first on her feet, her arms opened wide to give Ashley a big hug. Ashley later recalled, "Auntie Judy was teary. Auntie Janice, maybe not crying, but I think teary. Auntie Jeanne was crying. And then Momma, you were crying, because everyone was crying. You mostly cry because everyone is so loving. I think Auntie Susie was crying, too, but she's kind of funny. I like her."

The tension that filled the air a few minutes ago evaporated with tears and hugs. I felt happy for Ashley and pleased that my oldest friendships would stay intact after seeing the reactions of my childhood friends.

After that, Auntie Susie led a lively discussion about what would be a good name for her new nephew. Throwing out names, Ashley chimed in with her own opinions . . . some thumbs-up, a few thumbs-down. We all laughed at some of the suggestions that people made. We started with names beginning with "A."

"Alexander or Alex?" No, that didn't fit Ashley.

"Anthony or Tony!!" Noooooooooooooooooooo! Everyone laughed

"Ashland!" Auntie Janice volunteered. No takers.

"Ashton!" Ashley nixed that name.

"Christopher?" Ashley's cousin's middle name, so that was eliminated.

"What about names like your father?"

"Takashi?" Possible

"Takeshi?" Maybe

"Takumi? Your Grandpa Tak's name?"

"Not really" was Ashley's response.

Discussing all names suggested, both English and Japanese, the conversation slowly drifted into other areas.

I breathed in the moment to remember every detail of the evening, especially the ease in which Ashley joined the discussions. She seemed comfortable and content as she effortlessly took part in the conversation. I sat back and watched her soak in the positive attention and acceptance. As we left the restaurant, Ashley turned to me with a huge smile. "You have really good friends, Momma." I had to agree.

I drove home feeling lighter than ever, filled with more gratitude and love than I ever thought possible. My high school friends had just given me the greatest gift any friend could give—the unconditional love and acceptance for my child who was searching to find her true self. No other gift in the future will ever surpass what they gave me that night. Although these girlfriends and I have had forty-plus years of get-togethers, this will always be the moment that defines our friendship and their love for my family and me.

Ashley's next step was to reveal her wish to transition to her co-workers. Unlike the more festive, light-hearted parties with my friends, this involved a multiple-step process that occurred throughout the month of December. Ashley began leaving letters on the desks of co-workers to whom she felt closest. Gauging the supportive reactions of those she considered close friends gave her the courage to approach others whose reaction she couldn't be as sure of. For four years, Ashley had been working part-time as a Human Resources assistant. During that time, her co-workers had watched her change after she had revealed her sexual orientation as a lesbian. She'd cut her hair shorter and shorter, and also dressed more masculine to the point that her general attire consisted of pants and a collared shirt. By now, announcing her wish to transition could not have been a total surprise, even to those who did not know her well.

Since the corporate office takes a two-week holiday break every year, Ashley planned to let everyone know of her transition before the break, then give them the ensuing two weeks to get used to the idea. She would leave work before Christmas as Ashley and return in the New Year with a new male name. Ashley's supervisor, Vrej, reacted in both a compassionate and methodical way. He set out a plan to announce to the regional supervisors, by email, that Ashley would now go by the name Aiden when they returned from holiday break in January. The email would request that the regional supervisors notify their lead teachers, so most of the top leaders would be aware of the name change. Being a man's name, it clearly indicated that she was no longer female. One regional supervisor, I remember Ashley talking about. When Jenner Jose came into the office shortly after the email was sent, he gave Ashley a huge smile and a warm comment, showing his support. As luck would have it, Jenner would eventually become the supervisor overseeing a program that Opportunities for Learning (OFL) opened up at the Los Angeles Gay & Lesbian Center.

The only person Ashley was too scared to inform was the superintendent, whom, she felt, would not be comfortable with the announcement. Although the superintendent, Gordon, was a kind, deeply sensitive individual, he was much older. Having been lured out of retirement, Gordon carried the dignity and the respect of an "elder statesman." The thought of telling him about her wish to transition sent chills up Ashley's spine, so she chose to stay quiet. Perhaps a strategy or plan would emerge.

But no strategy appeared, so Ashley decided that she needed to tell

Gordon because he would feel bad if he didn't know. "It was kind of a weird period, where everyone was adjusting. At the same time, no one knew what to do because they didn't know what to call me when Gordon was around. So it was very confusing for everybody because they would call me Aiden in front of me and other people, but they would go back to Ash or Ashley and use female pronouns when in front of Gordon". Ashley enlisted Joan's help. As one of the founders of the company, Joan had the authority and respect to assist directly in bringing Ashley and Gordon together. This gave Ashley the impetus needed to move forward. "I was still so scared because he is older and I thought, *Good Lord, he's not going to be okay with this, like, how is that possible?*"

"It was Tuesday, because it was a day that Joan was going to be in the office. Joan said to Gordon, 'Do you have a minute to meet with me?' He actually thought he was in trouble because he thought maybe he offended me in some way. So we were sitting in Joan's office, Gordon and I both on her couch. I'm sure it looked like we were in big trouble, or at least he was or maybe me. But he was sitting there and I handed him the letter, the same letter I was giving to everyone. He started to read it. It felt like it took him forever; when he was done reading it, he was kind of tearing up, and I was a little freaked out by that."

"Then he told me this story: he had all these different jobs all over the world. He met a guy while he was working in a different country and they became really close, like family friends. They hadn't talked recently so Gordon decided to write his friend. And Gordon received back something he said 'was like a book' explaining that his name had changed, that he was transitioning to female, and would prefer to be called by his new name. Gordon said that they're still very close. He even invited this friend to his daughter's wedding, and she attended as a woman. It was very unexpected. He gave me a hug and told me if I ever needed anything I could ask him. He said I was a good kid."

Ashley had scaled a huge hurdle; she would be accepted in the workplace as a man.

One more big reveal to go—the biggest. It was a family Christmas dinner at my brother's house. I had no doubt that my brothers, Marty and Paul, and their wives, Leslie and Arlene, would be supportive, but Ashley reminded me that sometimes the people you least expect to react are those who react the strongest. And then her cousins, Stephanie, Lindsay, Matthew, and Jonathan, would need to be told as well. She paced around our home, pensive and fidgety before we had to leave. She played music in her room. She loved her uncles, aunties and cousins so much, but would they betray her love? Would they no longer be close? I could sense she anticipated trouble.

It never materialized.

My husband's side of the family held a Christmas luncheon at a restaurant. More letters—more silence, more acceptance. When Uncle Drew wiped away tears, I started dabbing my own eyes. Once the silence was broken, the questions began to flow. By now I'd bolstered my knowledge of transgender individuals, the LGBT community, and countless issues that surround this monumental decision, so I could provide some answers. Ashley was still uncertain about her new name. Aiden seemed to be a frontrunner, but she had not yet made her final decision, since that announcement would be made in January. Tad and I thought Ashton could be a good name, enabling us to continue to use her nickname, Ash. That would make the transition a little easier for us, but Ashley had other ideas. She wanted to make a clean break by choosing a name that spelled out differently and sounded totally different.

As December progressed, I watched with increasing relief, gratitude, and admiration as Ashley's friends joined her immediate and extended family in rallying around her and embracing her decision. Ashley's godfather, Uncle Bob, was very supportive, though we found out later that he was caught off-guard by the news. You would have never guessed by his reaction. He has loved her from the first moment he carried her in his arms, so Ashley's Uncle Bob and Auntie Bonnie addressed her with nothing but acceptance and love. With each letter passed out, my confidence grew that Ashley would not be shunned by those we loved. Still, although many people had joined us in supporting Ashley, I knew some would not understand the decisions she and we were making—decisions that would lead to changes none of them had ever conceived.

Every one of us experienced awkward moments during this final month of Ashley's life as a female. Many of them centered around her name change. In her letter, Ashley asked that we begin using male pronouns and see her as a guy. In a small boutique, one nice saleswoman referred to Ashley as my daughter. I hesitated for a moment, thought for a few seconds about how to correct her, and then blurted out, "Oh, this is my son." The saleswoman blushed with embarrassment and apologized profusely. When we left, she commented that she had thrown a few extra goodies into our bag of purchases.

Another mother, seeing how kind Ashley was to me at the market, made a comment about my sweet daughter. When I corrected her, she hurriedly pushed her cart away from me, a look of horror screaming across her face. I stood in place, frozen. I couldn't figure it out: Was she horrified because I was allowing my child to be a boy who looked like a tomboy? Or because she had mistakenly called him a girl? If I'd have known more at that time, I would have been able to explain things better to her, and perhaps the scene could have been different. But I was still uncomfortable myself to some degree, so my reactions were often slow. I tried to hide my discomfort from Ashley, but in honesty I still felt like I lived between two worlds myself—a mother with a daughter and a mother with a son. I wasn't sure what to say to others and my child in these months of transition. I wobbled on a tightrope, not wanting others to feel uncomfortable and also trying hard not to offend my child. I made countless mistakes.

However, I grew from each slip of the tongue by others. My courage to correct them increased—and so did my comfort level over the reality of being the mother of two sons. "You don't stumble around so much now, Momma, when people make a mistake about who I am," my son remarked with pride in his voice.

I was proud of myself. I was getting more comfortable, and it was beginning to show with the ease and compassion with which I corrected others.

Since Ashley still had not decided on a new name, we called her by her old name. When she requested that we use the male pronoun, my husband and I tried to remember to say "he," "his," "him"—but with the same female name, our minds were conditioned to using female pronouns. We were correcting ourselves all the time; Ashley rolled her eyes, or should I say *his* eyes, when we made mistakes. I explained, "We are not trying to be disrespectful, Ash, but you have had this name for twenty years. We can't change what is programmed in our brain so deeply." He pointed out that others could do it. I began to feel old and feeble, unable to get through a day without a gender mistake. Patience was the operative word for all of us. Sometimes the patience came from allowing Ashley to be frustrated with us and to not feel guilty. We were doing the best we could. At other times we had to be tolerant of our own mistakes. Tad and I possessed no roadmap with which to navigate our way. I realized this was how I felt when I first became a mother, but I had had more books, resources, and parents to turn to for guidance back then. There was no Dr. Spock for parents of transgender children.

After Christmas break, Ashley would decide to adopt her new name—Aiden. She had made a list of names she liked, surveyed some friends through Facebook and email, thought about what would sound good with a middle name of Takeo, and then decided to go with Aiden. I had suggested Takeo as a middle name after hearing a books-on-tape recording of a samurai who was both courageous and compassionate, a wise leader and loving father. In Japanese, Takeo meant "strong as bamboo," and also depending on the Japanese characters written could mean "fierce or brave warrior." I thought how appropriate that Takeo represented who Aiden was at this moment and who he aspired to be.

Returning to work in January, people struggled to remember to use his new name. Finally, Aiden grabbed a nametag that stated "Hello, My Name Is," and filled it in to remind his co-workers that he had a new name. If anyone called him Ashley, he would just point to the nametag. Meanwhile, at our house, my husband would say "Where is Ashley tonight?" and Stefen would say, "Who's Ashley?"

"What do you mean, 'Who's Ashley?'" Then slowly, Papa's face began to show comprehension and we all laughed.

In the midst of this mixture of the good, awkward, silly, humorous, unsettling, and stressful, one day in particular threatened to erase all the goodwill that had accumulated throughout the month. It actually started off wonderfully—perhaps an omen, similar to the day of the parade.

As comfortable as I was becoming in referring to Ashley as male, I still had not fully processed all the steps needed to complete her transition.

In fact, I often felt overwhelmed by all the information thrown my way through my research and my child wanting to do everything yesterday. I needed time to absorb all that was being thrust in my direction.

I had just finished meeting a friend for a holiday tea and returned home to pick up Ashley. She was housesitting for a family and needed to stop by to pick up some things. I decided to ride with her to the house, so I could tell her about my afternoon with Betsy and keep her company. As she drove us over to the house, we started to discuss some of the aspects of transitioning, especially the hormone treatment and surgery. Somewhere between our house and our destination, our voices started to escalate as Ashley began to talk about how important surgery was to her. I felt like she was pushing me too far, too soon, and I pushed back.

"Ashley, I can't make a decision about surgery and testosterone without more information. I need to know the total cost, what is involved, what are the risks, and a lot of other answers."

"But surgery is a priority on my list. It's not like I have to have it now, but it is more important to me than my hormones. Do you know that fifty percent of trans people who don't get the physical stuff like surgery or hormones commit suicide?" Ashley countered.

"Commit suicide! Do you mean if you don't get these things right away you might kill yourself? Don't put that on me, Ashley!" I was screaming at her now. "I can't make a decision about this immediately." I had grown cold inside hearing the words "commit suicide." It was the type of chill that grabs hold of you, creates a tunnel vision of fear, then spirals in your head, leaving objectivity somewhere in the distance. Then without warning the icy terror exploded into boiling anger, forcing out words so full of rage I couldn't believe it was me speaking.

"That's not what I mean! I'm just trying to tell you how hard it is for me to wait."

"If you don't have surgery tomorrow or the next week or the next month, you mean you might kill yourself? That's not fair to put that pressure on me!!"

"You're taking this all wrong, Momma! It is just so hard, that's all I am saying."

"I can't believe that after all we have been through that you would try to kill yourself!"

Ashley didn't utter another word while she drove angrily to our destination. But she was thinking, *Wooah, what is going on? Momma is not even rational or making sense. No matter what, I am not saying another word.*

The conversation had shot up to a point where I thought Ashley was going to kill herself if she didn't get the surgery right away. According to Ashley, "I was more explaining that if I had to wait another year I didn't know what was going to happen because it was already hard enough," she expressed to me afterward.

I couldn't say where my anger was coming from. Nor could I stop it. I had never felt such fury, not even when Ashley was physically assaulted. This rage erupted from a place deep within me. As much as I wanted to stop screaming, it continued to pour out. I would pause and try to figure out how to repair the damage I had done, but instead of moving to a gentler place, I would begin screaming again.

Later, Ashley told me, "It was very scary, you've never yelled like that before. You were screaming at me and yelling in the car. And I was foot to the pedal, cause I was, like, 'Oh, man, this lady's yelling at me and I was pissed.' I think it was lots of miscommunication, but it was very frightening. We never had a fight ever and this was horrible. We went from zero to fifty. And then I just remember I kept driving fast because I was so mad."

Ashley shut down. A voice inside me said, *This isn't good,* but I felt out of control and after the fury, only silence remained between the two of us.

When we arrived to where Ashley was housesitting, she went inside and stormed into her room. I drove away, still seething. About a mile down the road, I realized that I couldn't go home without apologizing and trying to make things better. I felt so remorseful; why had I screamed so much? What was the point? Why had I alienated her when we were doing so well?

I turned the car around. The family that owned the house had returned that week to celebrate Christmas. I knocked and they let me in. I went to Ashley's bedroom and she opened the door, thinking it was a member of the family for which she was housesitting. When she saw me, her face steeled with anger. She tried to slam the door to prevent me from entering the room. I wedged my body against the door so it couldn't close.

When she realized I was not going anywhere, she just turned her back on me and flopped heavily on her bed. She lay with a computer on her lap, like a wall separating us, not talking, looking at me, or answering anything I asked. I apologized profusely, but to no avail. She had every right to rebuff me—I had closed her spirit.

I sat at the edge of the bed for an hour and a half, trying to get her to talk with me. Finally, I decided to leave. I was exhausted, Ashley was still furious, and it seemed like staying would only further fuel that anger. I said everything I could think of saying. There was nothing else to say.

On the drive home, I felt sick. Someone else drove the car while I was sitting in the driver's seat. So it seemed. My stomach filled with dread and my mind searched to find an answer that would fix all I had done. When I got home, I told Tad about the argument and its devastating extent, then crawled into bed. I searched for solutions, but there was nothing I could do. I fell asleep.

Meanwhile, Ashley called her friends to pick her up and take her to our house, ten miles away. She had no car, so she was stranded. She waited all night for the friends to come, but they didn't, so she eventually slept.

Christmas Eve day dawned the next morning. I woke up feeling as sick as the night before. Usually a fairly early riser, especially during the holidays, I couldn't get out of bed. My body felt lifeless and bleak, drained of all its blood. I had no energy or desire to do anything. Why had I erupted like that? It was so out of character for me. I felt sad and hopeless, afraid I had ruined my relationship with my daughter - soon to be my son. Why should I get out of bed when my child wouldn't even speak to me?

My husband gently encouraged me. "Call Ashley."

"She won't talk with me." I curled into a fetal position, pulling the covers tightly around me. The empty ache and emotional chill of hopelessness consumed my body with a pain that I'd never experienced before. It felt like I had actually lost my child, that she had died. For the first time I truly understood how people could contemplate suicide. When you are in that much emotional pain, you just want it to stop. It helped me to realize later what Ashley was referring to when she told me she couldn't wait another year. With my pain, I didn't know how long I could last. A week? A month? Certainly not a year.

My husband didn't like this situation at all. He felt determined to fix this problem. It was Christmas Eve, and the next day was Christmas. He was not about to allow a disagreement to cost his family the spirit and love of the most sacred of holidays. He made a call.

"I woke up 'cause Daddy called me kind of early," Ashley recalls. "He left me a voicemail that said I better call him back. So I called him, scared out of my wits. He said, 'You better call your mother and apologize or don't expect support from me.'"

Not knowing that Tad had called Ashley, I picked up the phone and dialed her number. I was not hopeful that she would pick up after her reaction last night, but I had to try. She answered right away and her voice was soft, like a small child's: "Daddy said that if I didn't talk to you, he wouldn't support me."

Although I felt bad that he resorted to such a threat, I knew he only wanted us to begin communicating again. My heart filled with love for my husband, who made it possible for us to reconnect. All I could say to Ashley was how sorry I was... how afraid and miserable I was not being able to talk with her. I must have apologized five or six times. I could feel my sadness, so desperate and hopeless less than an hour before, float away as Ashley responded with forgiveness. Hope returned to my heart. Everything was going to be all right. Another present had been placed at my feet; suddenly, Christmas looked wonderful again.

I asked Ashley if she wanted me to pick her up. She said, "Yes, I called my friends last night, but nobody picked me up. One friend was supposed to come and get me, but then he decided last minute to go to Vegas with his friends. And then another friend was going to come get me, but she was out with her friends, so she didn't come either."

I picked up Ashley. We said all the words each needed to hear and vowed that we would never fight like that again. In spite of everything we have faced since then, we have kept that promise.

A week later, I talked to Joan. "It was like you were coming from a very primal place of fear," she said softly, her eyes compassionate and pensive.

Suddenly, I knew why I had reacted so violently. It was primal, one of the most primal fears a mother can experience. This fear transformed me from a loving, nurturing being into a protective guardian instantaneously—

the thought of losing my child. The notion that Ashley even considered taking her own life before giving herself the opportunity to live as the person she was meant to be scared me so intensely that all I could do was scream and make her stop thinking of that act. As a mother, I knew that I would never recover from something so devastating. I would never be the same; I would crawl in a hole and want to die, or maybe I would follow Ashley to the same end. It was a horrific thought, so I responded with rage.

Even though I understood the reason I screamed at my child, today I still feel pangs of guilt for doing so. I wish I had found a better way to communicate my fear. I pray that in the future nothing pushes me over the edge again to react in such an extreme way. But I also realize that no matter what I do, no matter how insensitive my communication, and no matter what terrible mistake I may make, my unwavering belief in love and acceptance must always rise above it all. Without that belief, my life would be without hope. And hope is everything to me.

One final lesson came out of Ashley's "coming out" to our friends. We gave Ashley's letter to dear family friends, a married couple with two children. Unlike the others thus far, I could feel a wall beginning to form between us, because they didn't know how to handle the news with their children, especially their youngest. In her desire to remain close with us, the mother called me and asked to meet one night to discuss the situation. We sat in my living room and she was visibly anxious. Nancy shared this was one of the hardest things she ever had to do. I respected her enormously for being so vulnerable with me and caring enough to have this conversation.

"I want to talk to you about Ashley's decision to change to a guy. I am very uncomfortable, because I told my children that Ashley is a girl and now I don't know what to say."

"Well," I replied, "can you just let them know that Ashley talked to us about a different name and we said that if the judge said okay, then it was okay with us?"

"Actually, I don't know if that would be good. My oldest child will understand, but you know how Kevin is. He might ask a lot of questions and if he asked why Ashley has a boy's name now, I don't know how I would respond." I could see her concern as a mother, but then I was Ashley's mother, so I wanted to find a solution for my child, too.

"Are you afraid that if Kevin sees Ashley transitioning that maybe Kevin might want to be a girl? Ashley showed signs of being masculine at a very young age. Kevin doesn't have any signs, so I don't think he will even have that thought."

"I don't know . . . he is so young." Nancy suggested, "What if you said that Ashley moved away for college?"

The suggestion assumed that if she weren't home, the subject of transitioning would not be a topic for discussion. I felt we would only be postponing that discussion, and what would that say about how I felt in regards to Ashley's transition?

"But that wouldn't be the truth." I replied softly. Lying seemed to equate to being ashamed of my child, and I couldn't do that. After going back and forth and neither of us finding acceptable solutions, we ended the evening without resolution. Nancy and I both decided to take some time to think about it, then talk again.

I came up with additional solutions about a week later and we talked by phone. Nancy wasn't comfortable with any of my added ideas. Eventually our busy lives took our focus away from this issue.

We didn't hear from our family friends for months. One day, Aiden came to me and said he had seen Nancy and her husband, Dexter, at the mall and they ignored him. He felt that they were embarrassed to acknowledge him now that he was a boy; he felt shunned and wounded.

I wasn't going to let that happen to my son. I swung into action. I called up Nancy and asked if both Dexter and she would meet my husband and me for breakfast. I explained what Aiden had told me. I also told her that I knew she and her husband would never do anything to intentionally hurt Aiden, but because we had not come to any resolution, he felt rejected by them. They agreed to meet us for breakfast.

The meeting began awkwardly. Tad and I ordered breakfast, but Dexter and Nancy said they had already eaten.

"Thanks for meeting us," I began. "Because we haven't resolved the situation with Aiden, he is feeling rejected by your family." I explained how he had seen them at the mall and he thought they ignored him. " I know how much you care about him, so I hoped to sit down and discuss how we can honor your concerns, but also address Aiden's feelings."

"First of all," Dexter began, "we love Aiden and nothing has changed about that. We just don't know how to handle the questions our kids may have, especially Kevin. Kevin is very young and we don't know how he will take it."

And so, this is how our conversation began, as Tad and I acknowledged their challenge and we shared that we were also struggling with what this change meant to our family. Laying out our feelings, we came up with some solutions that worked for both of us. We decided that when they came over, either Dexter or Nancy would always be with Kevin, so they would know what was being asked and what was being answered. They still did not know how to respond to the gender questions, but they felt comfortable leaving that open as long as they knew what conversations were taking place between their children, Aiden, and our family. They wanted to let their children continue to use the name Ashley or Ash. I had already addressed the name issue with Aiden and he was comfortable with Kevin using Ash, but not Ashley.

What we didn't address was how the adults would address Aiden when their kids were around. Each of us naturally gravitated to the name that seemed most comfortable for us, so Dexter and Nancy didn't use a name often, and when they did, it was usually Ash. Tad and I, who were having trouble with the name change as it was, used Aiden most often with an occasional Ash if we could remember to do so.

Since then, we've thoroughly enjoyed our time with this family. Dexter and Nancy's fears seemed to have lessened. They attended two of Aiden's twenty-first birthday parties, one I threw for family and one for his co-workers and friends. In the beginning, they seemed to hang around Kevin when we got together. Today, that is no longer an issue. These days when Kevin sees Aiden, his gender is still a little confusing to him. We say "he" and sometimes Kevin shouts out, "No, 'she.'" Aiden says no need to correct him. Children adapt. He will automatically shift when he's ready. Kevin says, "Hey, Aiden, Ash, whatever!" as they play in our front yard and we all laugh. That seems to say it all. It doesn't matter what name he is called, it only matters that there is love, respect, and acceptance between us all. Our acceptance and respect for each other's family has allowed all of our children to be accepting and respectful of each other. I will always appreciate Nancy's courage to reach out to us and Dexter's expression of love for Aiden. They are part of our journey and we feel so blessed to have them along with us.

We bade farewell to 2008 by also saying goodbye to our wonderful daughter, Ashley Akemi Aizumi. Tad and I loved her with all our heart. Though we were sad to let her go, we knew that she belonged in our past. We began 2009 welcoming our new son, Aiden Takeo Aizumi. He belongs to our present and future. With a new name and a new sense of self, Aiden was going to find his way. We were all finding our way. The new year would be a year filled with transitioning for all of us. We stood ready to take in every amazing moment.

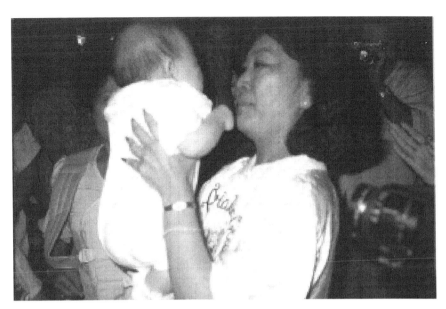

Holding Ashley for the first time.

Our tomboy starts to appear.

Zorro for Halloween.

A Power Ranger fan.

Golfing with Stefen.

Ashley, 2002.

Ashley in Bali, 2007.

Aiden lived to see his 21st birthday.

Aiden soaring after transition.

Aiden receiving the Youth Leadership Award.
Photo credit: Beck Starr

Celebrating Christmas with cousins, 2010.

Christmas 2011.

The Aizumi family excited about Creating Change.

PART II

Aiden

"Nothing happens unless first a dream."

—Carl Sandburg

CHAPTER SEVEN

Beginning Transition

Shortly after Aiden revealed his wish to transition from female to male, I could feel his urgency to begin taking action as soon as possible. Aiden spent hours doing research on transitioning and what that meant for him. "I watched a 20/20 TV special about transgender children and hearing what they had to say spoke to me. I felt a connection to it." After studying hormone therapy, name change, legal gender change, the emotional and social aspects of coming out and surgery, Aiden felt prepared to move forward now.

On the other hand, I was still settling into being a mother of a lesbian, so news of Aiden's desire to transition to male took me back to square one. At Aiden's suggestion in December 2008, I watched a YouTube five-part video called "My Secret Self," which was a 20/20 special hosted by Barbara Walters. I couldn't tear myself away from the computer screen until I watched every segment at least twice. I sat my husband down to watch it for a third time. These children and parents weathered so much. I kept thinking, "They could be telling our story."

I identified with the families of younger transgender children wanting to protect their child, support their child to have a good and full life, while mourning the loss of the child that no longer existed. I loved Aiden with all my heart, but I missed the daughter I had dreamed about and loved for twenty years. I recognized the same jealousy over sibling toys and clothes, the panic attacks, the moodiness, unhappiness, depression, the bullying, the internal struggle, the pain, and sadness that led to cutting—we shared those identical experiences. But what struck me so deeply was the courage it took for these families and these transgender kids to stand up and say this is who I am.

I bonded with these families, who took a risk and shared their stories on national television. I felt the tears of the parents. I felt the hurt and humiliation of the children. But in the end, the love spoke out the loudest to my heart. *Could I be that courageous and unselfish? Could I love so openly and deeply?* Even though I had no thoughts of writing my story to share with others at that time, in some ways I believe their bravery inspired me to write this book. I wanted to change the world, as these families had changed my world through their vulnerability and openness. My son deserved to live in a more loving and accepting world.

It needed to start with me.

My education began by sitting in front of the computer for hours during the month after learning of Aiden's wish to transition. The books I ordered to supplement my online learning over the next two to three months helped me gather information about Aiden's options for transitioning and issues he must face: the hormone injections, the top surgery, and other options I never even considered, such as a hysterectomy. Then, issues such as bathroom safety, choosing a new name, coming out to family and friends, and obtaining documents with correct gender designation started to broaden my awareness of what we would face in the future. I truly did not grasp the extent of all we would encounter, but I got a sense that there would be many checkpoints along this journey and many hurdles to overcome.

In my research, I noticed how each individual's transition was so personal. Not every transgender person followed the same route, but the experience of searching, and the pain involved, was haunting and true for all. I studied *True Selves: Understanding Transsexualism for Families, Friends, Coworkers and Helping Professionals* by Mildred L. Brown and Chloe Ann Rounsley. It provided me with some basic information about the transitioning process, while describing the many issues and feelings that transgender individuals experience. I sat for hours propped up in bed, highlighting everything that applied to my son: the anger, the fear, the guilt, the self-mutilation, the shame, the despair, and thoughts of suicide. Once again, our story rose out of the pages of this book. As I read the words, my heart ached for how much my child had suffered alone. A sick feeling in my stomach emerged as I thought, *Was I so unaware of the depth of his pain? I am his mother.* At times, I wanted to put the book down as the sadness and feelings of guilt overwhelmed me, but I knew I needed to press on.

At the end of the book, I had a greater knowledge of what our family would have to confront and a deeper understanding of what my child had endured all these years. Not wanting to focus on the past, which I could not change, I chose to move into our future. I now knew some of the decisions that would have to be made. Aiden was very clear on what he wanted to do and what he was willing to forego. He wanted hormone replacement therapy (HRT), top surgery, and eventually a hysterectomy. Armed with facts from my many hours of research, and given time to process the information I was beginning to accumulate, I now felt comfortable moving forward slowly. It was time to find people who could quell my fear about all the future changes. I needed to talk to individuals and ask the questions that made me most afraid.

It started with one of the families featured in the *20/20* special with Barbara Walters. Betsy and her son were part of our local PFLAG group. I did not know them well, but Aiden seemed very close to Betsy. She was the mother I mentioned in an earlier chapter. And she was the one I met with before Aiden and I had the huge fight. I decided to reach out to her to see if she had time for lunch. I emailed her. She responded quickly, and we connected immediately, as two mothers—one sharing her journey after transition and one just stepping on this road with her son to begin transition.

We met at an intimate little tearoom, sharing stories over tiny tea sandwiches and freshly baked scones with lemon curd, Devonshire cream, and raspberry jam. I chose a calm and cozy place because I wanted to know everything there was to know about this journey in a place that felt like we were two friends talking in my home. I took lots of notes. Betsy provided me a wealth of information. I began to catalogue every fact, shared story, and recommendation for future reference. This added knowledge comforted me as much as the warmth of my drink. As a businessperson and educator, I felt I was doing my due diligence. As a mother, I felt I was more prepared to ask the right questions of the professionals who would help us through this transition. I wanted to support Aiden's decisions, but also wanted to feel like my support was based on understanding the consequences of each choice. I was determined to operate in "true choice."

My Asian background often puts pressure on me to choose roads that my ancestors and family members might approve of, not roads that reflected my hopes and dreams. The concept of "true choice," which I first heard at the "dream" seminar I attended, really resonated with me as a way to honor both. As I saw it, true choice meant that I looked to myself and decided what the right decision was for me. Of course, I considered the feelings of others, but the final decision rested with me. I knew I was in "true choice" when my heart felt right after making the decision. The opposite of this was "false choice," which put the feelings of others before my own. In most cases, decisions I made out of false choice had left my heart feeling sick or sad. I knew I had compromised my feelings for the approval of others.

With Aiden's transition, I recognized what my true choice was: helping my son live a life of integrity, while knowing deep within that I had asked the questions that needed to be asked and communicated my concerns in a compassionate and honest manner. Unlike my past, where I had avoided facing issues out of fear, only to live with the resulting guilt, I promised myself to share truthfully my apprehension, question those things that made my heart uneasy, and listen with an open and understanding mind. Oh, if I could only do that, I would feel like such a good mother to my son!

I looked for opportunities to support my son in finding his way while confronting concerns that still lay unanswered. One of the first opportunities to practice my new approach came when I visited the doctor whom Aiden had chosen to perform his top surgery, Dr. Michael Brownstein, whose office is located in San Francisco.

When Aiden and Julianna split up in 2008, Aiden had already booked a plane ticket to visit her in Oregon. Though sad about the breakup, he thought he would now re-book his ticket to visit friends in San Francisco over the President's holiday weekend in February 2009. This gave him something to look forward to, instead of brooding over lost love. One night as we talked about his plans to visit San Francisco, Aiden turned to me and said, "Hey, Mom, would you like to go to San Francisco with me?" He didn't need to ask twice. We both loved San Francisco. Plus, any chance to spend one-on-one time with either of my sons was a mother's dream.

Aiden appointed himself Momma's San Francisco tour guide, showing me the Castro District (a predominantly gay and lesbian area where activist Harvey Milk lived until he was assassinated in 1978) and other interesting sites that he and Julianna had discovered. I had never heard of The Castro. This visit opened up a whole new area of exploration. We strolled down the main street of The Castro as many LGBT and straight couples enjoyed the day. Aiden wanted me to see Harvey Milk's camera shop, which now housed a gift store. Then he took me to a Castro bakery that displayed interestingly shaped cookies—shapes of male and female anatomical parts stared out at me from behind the bakery display case. As much as I tried to seem unaffected by them, the straight-laced upbringing inside my brain screamed, "Oh my gosh, those are woman's breasts staring back at me!"

Aiden also wanted me to meet some friends he met though the Internet. I had come a long way from thinking that all online friends were sexual predators. His willingness to invite me to meet these friends confirmed this thought. Between the Castro, the bakery, and meeting online friends, my paradigms were shifting rapidly.

Aiden also had another scheduled stop while we were in San Francisco. Prior to flying up to the Bay Area, he had asked, "Momma, can we make an appointment to see Dr. Brownstein, who specializes in top surgery? I have heard he is the best on the West Coast. I have seen his work, and I want him to do my surgery." Aiden knew a couple of people who had used Dr. Brownstein, so this surgeon came highly recommended. Betsy's son had also used this doctor, so I felt assured that this wasn't a back alley quack that preyed on fragile transgender individuals. I agreed to the appointment, sensing the excitement of my son and picking up on the excited feeling myself. But I also felt uneasy. I saw this as a fact-finding visit, but I could sense that Aiden wanted to set a date for surgery as soon as possible. I wasn't quite ready for someone to cut out parts of my child's body, but Aiden was on the move.

Dr. Brownstein is a surgeon who speaks honestly and directly. His methodical and organized ways comforted me. I felt like my son would be in safe hands. Dr. Brownstein also sat in a huge, whimsical high-backed chair like something out of *Alice in Wonderland*. This initially threw me off balance, but after talking with him for a while, I realized his throne chair fit him so well. Performing top surgeries for FTM individuals, let's admit, takes a special type of surgeon. He, like his big chair, made a statement to the world and I liked what his statement said.

Dr. Brownstein met with Aiden, but allowed me to sit in because Aiden gave his permission. The doctor could sense my discomfort during the visit, but he made it clear that this decision belonged to Aiden, who was over eighteen years of age. In reality, though, it was a joint decision. Aiden simply did not have the eight thousand to ten thousand dollars to cover the medical costs, transportation, and the ten-day stay in San Francisco.

Prior to travelling to San Francisco, Aiden's first choice was to have surgery during his spring break in two months. I thought that the timing was too soon. If he needed to be in San Francisco for ten days, he would miss too many college classes. However, I said nothing. I found that stating my opinion before getting information made it appear that I was blocking his progress. So I sat back, smiled, and listened.

Tad and I had discussed previously how much this procedure would cost and agreed that surgery during the summer would be the best for Aiden's school schedule. Tad is a generous man and wonderful financial provider. And I like to put money aside for a "rainy day," so we had the finances to pay for this surgery. I received no objections from him about spending the money.

After some discussion of Aiden's health history and a few other preliminary questions, Dr. Brownstein asked, "So, when were you thinking of having your surgery?"

"I want to have surgery as soon as possible. I am in college, so I have a spring break in two months. Do you have anything available in April?"

April! That's too soon—I need more time, I thought in a panic, even though I knew he would request this date.

"Well, Aiden, I am booked during that week."

Thank goodness, I thought to myself as I exhaled quietly.

"Well, my next college break would be summer vacation. Do you have openings after mid-June?"

"Yes, I could do the surgery on June twenty-third. Does that date work for you?"

"Yes, June twenty-third would work great!"

"Okay."

June 23: Four months to get comfortable.

Dr. Brownstein continued by giving us information about pre-op visits, post-op visits, payment structure, and other details that flew over my head. Aiden also needed a letter from his therapist indicating that she believed that he needed to make this transition. Since he had been presenting himself masculine for years, and had continued regular visits with Diane, she was comfortable writing this letter after a conversation with me. As I listened to every detail of what would take place in June, all I could think was, *You have four months to get comfortable with this surgery. Would that be enough time?*

Although disappointed that surgery would not be in two months, Aiden stood up from his consultation with Dr. Brownstein knowing that a June 23 surgical schedule showed Aiden T. Aizumi written in. I stood and noticed a big, radiant smile on my son's face. He could not hide his happiness. How could I not be happy for him? I had not let my fear stop me from supporting my son's dream. And my son could now see himself moving closer and closer to being the man he always dreamed he could be. We both walked out of the doctor's office feeling good.

When Aiden returned home, he turned his attention to things that would move him closer to transitioning during the ensuing months. One of the first things to do: get his name officially changed. He'd already filed paperwork at our local court for this name change, paid the fee, and obtained a court date before our San Francisco trip. Upon returning from San Francisco, he hoped to stand before a judge and legally be granted his male name.

When I found out that I had scheduled an out-of-town business trip on the same day as Aiden's court date, I felt terrible. Changing my flight would cost one hundred and fifty dollars and required a lot of re-shuffling of meetings. I decided to talk to Aiden.

"I am going to be in Chicago when you have your name change. I can change the date, if you want me there."

"Don't worry, Momma. I don't think it takes more than a couple of minutes."

"But this is a big deal, honey. I'll try to change my trip, or Papa can come."

"It's okay if Papa comes. No need to change your trip."

Tad agreed to support this important part of Aiden's transition. My husband and I were such a good team. I was so lucky to have married this man.

On February 26, 2009, Ashley Akemi Aizumi legally became Aiden Takeo Aizumi. This proceeding took about five minutes. "The judge asked me why I wanted to change my name. I remember telling him, 'Because I'm going to transition from female to male and I want my name to match my gender.'" After the judge pounded his gavel, signaling Aiden's request was granted, Papa patted his son on the back and said "Congratulations!" Then, without any fanfare, Tad left for work and Aiden was off to change whatever documents he could with his new name. I called Aiden from Chicago, asked for every detail of the five minutes, lavished my *ooohs* and *aaahs* on him and probably overdid my congratulations. I am sure that Aiden was glad that his Papa accompanied him to court. I try to restrain myself, but I am a natural gusher. My children know it all too well!

Besides providing the moral support for this court date, another important role that Tad and I played in these proceedings was to pay all the fees. Between the court filing fee and the required newspaper posting of the name change, both handled before the court date and purchasing copies of the official name change document, this simple five-minute court proceeding cost between four hundred and five hundred dollars. Looking into the eyes of your child who now has a name that matches how he feels on the inside, however, cannot be measured in dollars. Yes, MasterCard—some things *are* priceless.

With court documents in hand, Aiden drove to the Department of Motor Vehicles for an updated driver's license, and then to the Social Security Administration for a social security card with his new name. With these two legal documents in hand, all of his bank accounts and other records, such as school documents, could be updated as well. The only sensitive issue remaining was his gender. Still considered a female, his driver's license showed an "F" under gender where an "M" needed to appear. Aiden would not be able to change his gender officially until after top surgery.

Nonetheless, the legal name change was a big step for him. Showing his driver's license often proved to be a mortifying public experience. Aiden's old driver's license and its picture of him with longer hair, a female name and gender brought him much distress, especially after he began looking more and more masculine. Standing in line to charge a purchase or use his debit card, Aiden often squirmed uncomfortably, knowing that he'd need to show his license. People did not believe the license belonged to Aiden.

"Is this your license?" he would be asked.

"Yes," he'd reply.

"It doesn't look like you at all. I need to call the manager."

His humiliation only grew as customers in line observed this interrogation. So even though he was still considered female on his license, his new picture and name deflected attention from his birth gender.

I remember clearly the day his license arrived in the mail. He waved it in front of my face, his eyes joyful and giddy with delight. Then when his papa came home, Aiden once again shared this milestone. In just a few months, my sullen and emotionally unstable child became hopeful and more positive in attitude. We were definitely moving in the right direction.

With surgery still months in the future, Aiden hoped to take another step toward transitioning: hormone replacement therapy. I read that HRT was irreversible. When I read or hear the word "irreversible," I also hear "be careful on this decision!" I wanted to tread cautiously and carefully in this area. In a paper Aiden wrote for his college psychology class entitled "Second Chances: A Research and Reflection on being Transgender," he described the HRT:

The Harry Benjamin's Standards of Care stated that a person had to have a letter from a psychologist saying that they have a gender identity disorder before they could receive hormone therapy as their medication. It also states that the person should live in their chosen gender for a year before being allowed on hormones. These are outdated now, although doctors still use them. They aren't required by law. My doctor didn't require them and just did a blood test and also asked me if I knew the health risks of being on testosterone. I said I did. I had done tons of research about it.

The risks of being on testosterone include high blood pressure, high cholesterol, increased red blood cell count, increase chance of stroke, and heart attack. Alongside of that there is an increase of body hair, shift in hairline, shift in body fat distribution, and the cessation of the menstrual cycle. You have the option of receiving testosterone a few different ways. One is through Intramuscular (IM) injection in the thigh or buttocks. There are three different types of injectable testers: testosterone enanthate, testosterone cypionate, and sustanon. Another is through a patch, gel, or cream. Examples of gels and creams are AndroGel, AndroDerm, and Testim. The most effective way to receive HRT is through intramuscular injection. Most of the changes brought on by testosterone are irreversible. If I were to stop testosterone my voice would remain the same, my body hair would most likely stay the same, and any hairline change would remain permanent. The things that would change back would be my body fat distribution, my period would return, if I haven't had a hysterectomy, and body shape would change back to a more feminine look.

I knew I had to quickly move up my timeline to get comfortable with all the aspects of transitioning, especially the irreversible HRT and the surgery. Even though surgery was several months away, we would have to put up deposits to guarantee the surgical date with both Dr. Brownstein and the hospital. I asked Aiden if he would be willing to spend some time with me answering questions I had about transitioning. "I do not want to block anything that you want to do," I said to him. "I only want to feel like a good mother that is participating in your transition to the fullest. Maybe we can go to a movie, then go to lunch and talk. What do you think?"

Aiden had other ideas. "Going to a movie is anti-social, Mom. How can we talk during the movie? Why don't we just stay home and clean my room?"

Clean his room? Wanting to clean his room with me—now that was a first!

We selected a Saturday to start our little "spring cleaning." I thought if I needed more time, we could go into Sunday. I didn't anticipate a marathon cleaning session, although Aiden's room could conceivably take that much time. He loved to collect things.

From the day I first heard we would be cleaning Aiden's room, I began to make mental notes about the questions for which I wanted answers. I thought that if I obtained all my answers, then at the end of the day I would feel comfortable with Aiden's transition decisions. I wanted to walk away from our cleaning day together, knowing without a shadow of a doubt that I could offer 100% support to all the areas of transition that Aiden chose. I didn't know how I would know. I didn't know what I needed to hear, but I knew at the end there would be no hesitancy in my heart, questions about surgery, nor fear about HRT. I hoped to feel confident we were making right decisions.

We began our cleaning day fairly comfortably. I felt determined and convinced that I would be able to ask and receive all the information I needed. With my stated goal in mind, I committed myself to delve into all my areas of fear and not back down. This was not a day to be tentative. I would exhibit boldness with respect and compassion.

As we sat on the floor, sorting what items Aiden would keep, what would be tossed, and what would be donated, I began to ask him questions. I wanted to start slow and easy.

"How are you feeling about what we have done so far?"

"Good."

"Are Papa and I supporting you okay?"

"Yes." "Is there anything we can do better, so you feel more supported?"

"Nothing I can think of. Everything seems good."

"Tell me about all the things you want to do to transition and why."

Aiden talked about the HRT, top surgery, and a little bit about the hysterectomy.

My next question: "Tell me about all the things you won't be doing to transition and why?" Aiden talked about genital reconstruction, also known as "bottom" surgery, which he felt was not perfected and would not be an option at this time.

Hours passed. We filled more and more trash bags with his stuff. We cleaned and organized more shelves, drawers, and closet space. Still, I felt no certainty in my heart. I began to feel I set too lofty of a goal to be without any doubt. We kept talking, laughing, cleaning, and arranging things. We were having fun. I rationalized to myself, *At least, Aiden's room will look good and I will have spent time with my son!*

About four to five hours into our time together, I felt more and more doubtful about finding all the answers I needed to feel comfortable. Finally I asked Aiden, "How do you know for sure that this is the right thing for you to do? What happens if you have top surgery, go on HRT, and then decide you should have stayed a girl? How do you know that you should be a guy?"

He stopped what he was doing, thought for a moment and then said, "You know, Momma, I have spent a lot of time thinking about this. And I know that this is something that I have to do to be happy. You know how much I am afraid of being alone in the world and never finding love."

"Yes, I know, Aiden. But I have no doubt you will find someone to love. You will not go through life alone."

"Well, I have thought about this a lot. And it comes down to this: I know I may never find someone who will love me as a guy. And I know I may end up alone in this world if I transition. But knowing this fact, I would do it anyway — as long as I could be the man that I feel inside. I would give up love to be who I am."

Instantly, I began to cry: he spoke the truth from the core of his being. He would even give up loving another and having someone love him for the rest of his life to live in alignment with the man who lived within. I didn't need to hear another word, another reason, another answer. In that moment, I knew without a shadow of a doubt that my child needed to transition.

I don't remember asking any more questions. I don't even remember how long we continued cleaning. I had my answer, and I knew that nothing would stop me from helping my son be his true self.

On April 3, 2009, Aiden received his first injection of testosterone: another milestone and another moment to celebrate. For the first ten months, Aiden received shots in the buttocks every two weeks by a nurse.

Since then, he has been doing his own injections every week in his thigh.

One day I asked Aiden if I could watch him give himself the injection. It was a more complicated procedure than I thought. First, he iced his leg with a package of my frozen vegetables (don't worry, dinner guests, I have not served you those vegetables!), and then he wiped off the vial of testosterone with alcohol and pulled the syringe back before he inserted a needle into the vial. Once he inserted the needle into the vial, he pushed the air out, and filled it with testosterone. He then removed the old needle, now dulled from the process of drawing from the vial, and threaded on a new needle. He removed the bag of frozen vegetables, wiped his thigh with alcohol, and found the quadrant of the thigh safest to inject.

Up to this point I observed without expression, but as he started to go for his thigh with the needle, I noticed how large the diameter of the needle was. Aiden said it needed to be large because of the density of the testosterone. My hands got clammy. I squeezed my eyes shut halfway and grimaced, anticipating the prick of the needle in his leg as he pinched his thigh. He explained that he would need to pull back on the syringe to make sure he had not hit a vein. If he drew blood, then he had to push a little further or pull the needle back a little, so he did not inject in the vein. I was feeling a little queasy at this point, listening to the explanations and thinking maybe this wasn't such a good idea to watch. Aiden looked over at my face and said, "Don't look like that, Momma. It makes me nervous."

Finally, he withdrew the needle and began to massage his leg, signaling the end of this ordeal. I wanted to be part of every aspect of his transition. Some parts are harder for a mother to watch than others.

Going on testosterone was such a high point for Aiden. Every new hair on his belly or leg was a sign that he was becoming more of a man. In the beginning, I observed only small changes, but gradually more and more hair began to appear. He often lifted up his shirt, thrust out his chin, or pulled up his pant leg to show me how much hair was growing. He would be so pleased with all the new hair sprouting up that I couldn't help but be excited for him. I would rub his shin or his face and exclaim, "Wow, honey, you are getting really hairy." He would smile back at me, proud as he could be, and my heart would fill up with so much happiness that I thought I would float to the ceiling. Those were some of the moments that we shared, mother and son. They may seem small and unimportant to others, but for a mother who lived through some bleak and depressing days and a son who thought there was no hope for his future, these moments began to replace those memories.

When I first heard that Aiden planned to go through hormone replacement therapy and he told me his body would begin to transform to be more angular and muscular as a result of the testosterone, I felt a bit disheartened. But since the change occurred gradually, I seemed to have time to adjust to how his body was molding into a more masculine frame. In addition, any brief moments of losing my daughter vanished instantly when I looked into the eyes of my son whose joy filled the room. His happiness swept away any feelings of loss. And soon, I could only remember Aiden being my son and not my daughter.

Aiden's voice also changed. In the beginning, like all young men who go through puberty, his voice would crack. Aiden would say, "I was ordering dinner tonight at a restaurant, and my voice cracked like a teenager. It was embarrassing!" Sometimes when I called his work, it shocked me how deep his voice sounded. To Aiden, however, the change seemed unnoticeable. "I hear myself talk all the time. Sounds the same to me." But when he listens to recordings of his pre-HRT days and early days on testosterone, he can hear the difference.

As Aiden began to take steps to transition to male, I noticed huge positive changes in him. Less moody and angry, he returned to that happy, communicative, and open person I knew before the middle school years. Now more confident of his future, his self-esteem soared. Like a child at Christmas, Aiden saw the wonder and possibilities at his feet. Like anyone who is full of joy and living life with hope, opportunities rushed towards him like a magnet. He was asked to speak at high school and college campuses. He received a PFLAG scholarship and was selected to be part of the Youth Advisory Council, a group that serves as a liaison between youth nationwide and The Trevor Project, as it relates to young people and the issues surrounding suicide, sexuality, and gender identity. (The Trevor Project is best known for its twenty-four hour suicide hotline for LGBT youth in crisis.) Aiden began to feel empowered and inspired rather than beaten down and insignificant. He marched in Washington D.C., in 2009, sponsored by a San Francisco-based group called One Struggle, One Fight which fights peacefully for socioeconomic justice and full equality under the law. The year 2010 brought him even more memorable moments as he continued to evolve as a man. Socially, his calendar began filling up. Academically, my child returned to being a student with good grades. At college, if people gave him a disapproving stare or made a snide comment, Aiden had the LGBT community and his own confidence to balance out the negativity.

As an example, Aiden hoped to be a fireman. He approached his college professor, a local fire captain, and discussed the possibilities of pursuing this career field as a transgender FTM firefighter. Encouraged by the captain, but also cautioned to stay away from rural areas where acceptance could be more difficult, Aiden still loved his fire class. Every time he saw a fire engine, it was a positive trigger device for the job of his dreams. However, being in a class with potential fire candidates gave him a glimpse of what his working world could be like. Many of the guys were "macho" men who wanted to boast and talk about their sexual conquests, saw women as only a means to an end, and stared at Aiden with suspicion. During this period, my son received a Facebook posting riddled with disdain and ridicule. The post shouted with contempt, "I knew there was something off with you." Perhaps it came from one of the fire course students, perhaps a student from another class. Clearly it showed that someone felt threatened by who Aiden was.

I have a relative who is a firefighter. I even found communities of gay firefighters and gay paramedics on Facebook. Many firefighters and paramedics are compassionate, respectful human beings who are not threatened by Aiden's transgender identity. However, like the fire captain indicated, there are some aspiring and current firefighters who hold the same kind of homophobic viewpoints that, in a station call, would make it difficult for Aiden to feel they would have his back and for them to feel he would have theirs. You can't have that kind of uncertainty in a field where trust can and does often mean the difference between life and death. A firefighting career was definitely not my dream for him.

As much as Aiden loved the thought of being a fireman, he finally decided that this career field would not be the best choice for him. I was relieved. I imagine him working with co-workers who valued him as a loving, talented human being, not scrutinizing him with mistrust and condemnation. He is still searching for his perfect career path, now considering psychology, LGBT Studies, and education. I always thought he would be a wonderful therapist. He has a kind heart, is a good listener, and loves to help others. Recently, he began to think about pursuing his teaching credential and being a safe space for kids in middle school or high school. And he also talks about running his own non-profit organization. He wants to serve the LGBT community and believes his experiences will contribute to the community as well. I do, too.

During those agonizing months of waiting for surgery, Aiden made steady progress on his road to officially becoming a man: a new name, a new driver's license, a deeper voice, and hair beginning to grow on his face and legs. Every month, we celebrated quietly the successes that became part of our lives. Aiden carried a full course load at the local community college, held down a twenty-four-hour-a-week job and actively participated in the LGBT community in between it all.

Life was good. Could it get any better?

CHAPTER EIGHT

Transformation

When Aiden announced his desire to transition to male in December 2008, the most unsettling part of his transition for me were the types of surgeries he planned to undergo. Women agonize over mastectomies when they are diagnosed with breast cancer. They struggle to come to terms with their feelings of being less than a woman when this part of their body is removed. As a mother, I went through the same agony as a woman having a mastectomy. *What if we made a mistake? What if he changes his mind? What if I didn't look into all the ramifications, and we regret this decision?*

All valid questions – but they came from the mind and heart of a woman and a mother. I needed to step into the shoes of my son, a man. Breasts reminded Aiden that he lived in the wrong body. He viewed his breasts as unwanted masses of fatty tissue for which he had no use. As far as he was concerned, he couldn't get rid of this part of his body fast enough. It was no surprise that he wanted to have the surgery immediately, but I needed time to make sure he wouldn't have second thoughts. Fortunately, I had the whole spring to prepare mentally and emotionally. Aiden would have the whole summer to heal.

We both got what we needed.

On Sunday, June 21, 2009, we began our momentous drive to San Francisco to begin his transition. For our lodging, I chose a hotel chain that provided a suite, because I wanted to be near Aiden all the time while having a place to work and relax as he recovered and slept. We would need to stay in the San Francisco area for ten days. I needed to be available to my staff for questions, and I needed to take care of my son after surgery. As an educational director for a charter school, I oversaw programs in California and Colorado. In addition, I traveled often to Chicago to oversee a contract school. I had people handling much of the day-to-day activities, but when it came to critical issues I needed to be involved.

On Monday, June 22, my phone rang early with disturbing news. My principal in Chicago had accepted another position; his last day would be at the end of the week. He only gave me four days' notice. The timing couldn't have been worse. All I wanted to do was focus on Aiden and his transition. Now I faced a major problem with my school in Chicago. Fortunately, I work with supportive and highly capable people. The Director of Human Resources, Mike, and my program specialist, Patrick, assured me that they would handle everything, keeping me in the loop, so, in their loving words, "please just take care of Aiden." I decided to follow their advice and trust that after a number of phone conversations, the situation would be managed. Only a phone call away, I felt confident that if anything critical arose, I would be contacted. I allowed the stress of this situation to fall away, and returned my attention to Aiden. My big question: what did he want to do the day before his surgery and over a week of recovery?

Our day started with a pre-surgical visit with Dr. Brownstein. He needed to examine Aiden to establish the type of surgery he would be performing. Dr. Brownstein would determine this by the size of Aiden's breasts. He also gave us final pre-surgery instructions. In the college research paper Aiden wrote earlier in the year, he described the options for top surgery and the requirements to have the surgery performed:

There are different procedures for top surgery. One is to have a double incision bilateral mastectomy with nipple grafts. Another is to have a keyhole/peri-areolar incision, which is only recommended for small-breasted people. Because of my chest size, I had to go with the double incision, which leaves a noticeable scar across my chest but is totally worth it. I call it now, my battle scar. There are hoops to jump through to get top surgery, just like there are the ones for hormones. These are a little bit more set in stone, because surgery is so irreversible. You have to have a letter stating that you indeed have gender identity disorder. They recommend that you are already on hormones, because of the way your body changes shape.

Armed with all the information and papers we needed for the hospital, we ventured over to Fisherman's Wharf for lunch at Bubba Gump's. It was one of Aiden's favorite places from a previous trip to San Francisco, and he wanted to share it with me. We walked around after lunch, shopped a bit, drove back to our hotel to relax, watched a movie, and got ready for the "big day."

Aiden remembers, "I was nervous. I never had surgery before. I thought, *What if it came out badly?* Then, I would be excited thinking, *What if it comes out good!* In the end, I was more excited than nervous, because I hoped the surgery would come out good."

June 23. Surgery Day. Aiden and I arose early. "Mom, can you not eat in front of me?" he asked before I could get breakfast; he was not permitted to eat prior to surgery. I grabbed a quick bite in the hotel coffee shop, out of his sight. Neither one of us was very hungry. He was even more nervous and excited today. I was just nervous.

We arrived at the hospital to check-in and were escorted to a private room. I watched while he was prepped for surgery, his vitals taken, and IV inserted. Then we waited. Attendants came in and out of the room explaining what would be happening and what roles they performed. I listened carefully, trying to ignore my churning, anxious stomach. Then we waited some more.

Suddenly an orderly walked in with a gurney. Scheduled to go into surgery at 10:50 A.M., the orderly wheeled Aiden out of his room at 9:30. Dr. Brownstein's first surgery had finished ahead of schedule. How often does that happen in a hospital? Part of me felt happy that we didn't have to wait another hour and twenty minutes, especially on this day when time seemed to tick by agonizingly slow. The other part of me was caught off guard—I thought I had eighty more minutes to prepare!

My reaction to Aiden going into surgery early had nothing to do with me losing my daughter. The moment he wished for was finally coming true. I knew how much it meant to him. I just didn't want him to leave my side so suddenly. Those eighty minutes would have given me time to let go slowly. Instead it felt like they were pulling him out of my arms before I prepared myself to hand him over to their care.

Riding down the elevator to the operating room, I held tightly to the rail of the gurney, my heart beating rapidly, the voice in my head anxiously repeating, "It's too soon... I'm not ready!" But Aiden was ready. This was the day he'd dreamed of for years, long before the meal after the parade where I first heard of my daughter's desire to become a man, long before the letters to friends, family members, and employer, long before our last trip to San Francisco to schedule the surgery.

Then he was gone.

Before the attendant took Aiden into surgery, he pointed in the direction of the waiting rooms. Rather than go back to Aiden's hospital room, I walked to the waiting room. I observed a woman sitting nervously, a concerned look on her face, at the first room I encountered. She seemed like she wanted to be alone, so I decided to check on another waiting room. Before I even entered the second room, I sensed that it did not match how I felt. People were talking to each other, sometimes noisily; not the place to feel solemn. I desired reflection time and isolation, so I returned to the first waiting room, walked in, took a seat, and quietly read a magazine. The nervous woman faced the door, obviously in anticipation. I imagined doctors operating on her husband, and every thought imaginable running through her worried mind. I prayed silently that everything would work out for her.

Unexpectedly, Dr. Brownstein walked into the waiting room. I sat up, thinking he was here to brief me. Instead, he walked directly to the other woman. Dr. Brownstein explained that the surgery went fine, her son was doing well, and being monitored in recovery. Her body relaxed; a big smile replaced her worried look.

Suddenly, I understood. My eyes welled up with tears. Her wait was over. My wait had just begun. Dr. Brownstein then noticed me. "Oh, hi, Mrs. Aizumi; your son is next." He explained a few things about the timing of the surgery and then walked out.

I turned to the other mother, whose name was Rosie, and we exchanged introductions. Rosie's body relaxed even more when she realized why I was waiting. I leaned toward her, now knowing that I would not invade her privacy and shared my story. Rosie shared her journey as well. We had so much in common—our hopes and our fears as mothers who loved their sons. Our dreams that the world would accept them and see all the good within them. Just knowing we both had FTM sons, I skipped all the superficial talk, threw open the doors of my heart, speaking about some of the most private parts of my journey. She did the same. We did not hesitate disclosing some of our most tormenting experiences, such as the cutting, the thoughts of suicide, and worry about our sons being harmed. We spoke about our days of concern, our nights of tears, and our fears that often appeared out of nowhere to haunt us. We talked freely and openly, understanding the heartache and courage that it had taken each of us, mother and son, to arrive at this day. Besides the pain, we talked about the hope we saw in the futures of Aiden and her son, Trent. We spoke the whole forty-five minutes that Trent remained in recovery—it felt like we were suspended in time—and no one entered our waiting room or my consciousness. It was just Rosie and me; two mothers coming together and finding each other for the first time.

Rosie provided me with comfort and a welcome distraction. Without her, the time would have inched slowly by and I would have fought off negative thoughts while Aiden lay on the operating table. In those few minutes, we bonded more closely than most long-time friends. In a sense, it was like two mothers giving birth on the same day. We supported each other as our boys, who had been crying to be born, finally came into the world in their correct body. Today was Aiden and Trent's real birthday.

After talking with me, Rosie walked to Trent's room to see if he had returned from the recovery room. As it turned out, Aiden and Trent had adjacent private rooms. Rosie and I exchanged cell phone numbers. We decided that we wanted our sons to meet.

When Rosie left, my waiting began.

Aiden was away for three and a half long hours. The time crawled by. I tried to read, but couldn't concentrate. I caught myself studying the same paragraph again and again, comprehending nothing. I put my magazine down, picked it up, flipped through the pages, and then put it down again. I paced a little in the tiny waiting room. I could only take six steps before turning around. I stepped outside the room and paced the hall a few more steps, but didn't want to walk far, fearing Dr. Brownstein would come in and I wouldn't be there. I worried about Aiden coming through surgery okay. I knew there were always risks involved with surgeries. And Tad's brother had died going through a surgery that everyone believed was just routine. I never worried about losing a daughter and gaining a son on this day. Those thoughts I had already come to terms with during my discussions with Aiden, cleaning his room. I just wanted Aiden to come out of the surgery healthy and happy.

Rosie came back once and suggested that if the boys were up to it, perhaps we could all go to San Francisco Pride together. I liked that plan, but told her I would defer to Aiden about attending. Finally, Dr. Brownstein walked into the waiting room and announced that Aiden had come through surgery without incident. Like Trent, Aiden would be monitored for forty-five minutes and then taken back to his room. Before he turned to leave, Dr. Brownstein said, "You can stop shaking now, Mrs. Aizumi." I realized that my legs had been shaking the whole time Dr. Brownstein updated me on Aiden—a sure sign of my nervousness.

With the news that Aiden was fine, I realized that I was starving. I headed to the hospital cafeteria and grabbed a Lean Cuisine, which I microwaved and ate in the hospital room while waiting for my son to return. It wasn't a day for gourmet meals. I just wanted to keep my energy up.

Without warning, I heard voices talking outside the room. Knowing that Aiden was just coming out of recovery, I dismissed them. Then I looked up, startled to see my son being wheeled back into the room. He and the orderly were talking and laughing. His alertness stunned and confused me. *Didn't he just get out of surgery?* I pictured him returning to the room asleep or at least groggy, but apparently pain roused him from the anesthetic. He asked for some pain medication, and then dozed in and out of sleep. In between, he called friends and co-workers while plenty of texts flew about. He was so happy that not even the pain could dampen his mood.

He had recently begun a relationship with a girl he had met at PFLAG named Mary. Many of his conversations and texts seemed to be with her. She was completing a master's degree program in school psychology, which did not allow her to accompany or visit Aiden on this trip. I know this made Mary sad. She wanted to be by his side, showing her support. But I believe things always happen for a reason. I needed these ten days to take care of my new son alone, and to see his newfound happiness compliments of his surgery. I will always treasure these days, for they gave me a chance to watch the transformation of my child privately and time to acknowledge my worthiness as a mother. I had listened to my son. I had asked questions as a responsible parent. But most importantly I had balanced both his needs and my feelings as his mother.

Now on the other side of surgery, I relaxed and donned my Florence Nightingale "cap" to prepare for the next few difficult days ahead. I knew from my own surgical experiences that the following days would be uncomfortable. I prepared for his mood to shift as he fully felt the discomfort of his incisions and drain tubes. Drain tubes measured the amount of liquid seeping out of the left and right side of Aiden's surgical area. In order for the drain tubes to be removed, the drainage amount had to decrease to an acceptable level.

Nurses came in to monitor Aiden's vital signs. I decided to go next door and meet Rosie's son, Trent. Sensitive to the anesthesia, Trent was drifting in and out of sleep, but his sleep was deeper. He couldn't seem to stay awake. Aiden showed signs of recovering much faster, as his waking moments were filled with much conversation and activity. At 5:30 P.M. Aiden was discharged and we prepared to go back to the hotel. Next door, Rosie decided to keep Trent overnight, since he could barely function during his waking moments. As we said goodbye to Trent and Rosie, I saw in her eyes that she wished she were taking her son home as well.

While driving back to the hotel, Aiden felt nauseous. I stopped to get him some ginger ale and he grew very impatient with me. Even the slightest bump and unexpected jolt to his body warranted a glare my way. I attempted to drive slowly and carefully, but the harder I tried, the more bumps I encountered and the more lights I hit. Aiden stared angrily at me, like I was intentionally driving erratically to make him uncomfortable.

Back at the hotel, Aiden walked carefully the fifty steps to his room. Thank goodness, we got a room close to the exit door and on the first floor. Initially, I hoped for a room with a better view, but I felt the closeness to the exit could be important when we returned from surgery. It was a good call. Once comfortably tucked into bed, Aiden apologized for his sour mood. Having undergone a number of surgeries myself, I knew that you could only be a little nicer than you feel. I gave him space to be grumpy, but also appreciated his apology.

Finally, my exhaustion from the day took over, and I slept heavily through the night. On the other hand, Aiden went to the bathroom, fed himself Wheat Thins in the middle of the night, and took another Vicodin for his pain. I woke up the next morning, refreshed, but feeling guilty that I didn't hear a sound. I admonished Aiden lightly for not getting me up to help him and vowed to be more vigilant that evening.

The days following surgery still seem like an uneventful blur. I fed my son, emptied his drains, helped him to the bathroom, washed his hair over the bathtub, gave him sponge baths, and tried to cater to his needs. I also read, checked my email, watched TV, or slipped a disk into the portable DVD player that I brought with me while my son slept. Aiden was a good patient, except that he dreaded the drainage tube ritual. Who wouldn't?

Wanting to be the best nurse ever, I followed the hospital directions to a "T" on how to measure the draining liquid from tubes on each side of Aiden's chest. With Aiden propped up in bed and me sitting by his side, I would squeeze the liquid from each of the two tubes coming out of his chest into the plastic drainage bulb attached to the tube. I would then remove the drainage bulb, determine the amount of liquid that had drained, record the amount of liquid in the two drainage bulbs on a piece of paper, throw out the liquid and re-insert the tube in the now empty bulb. Aiden loathed this procedure, especially the tube squeezing, since I would sometimes inadvertently tug on the tube as I attempted to squeeze out any blood into the bulb. Aiden feared that I might accidentally pull out the drainage tube and sometimes clearing the tube hurt.

Later on, I heard from Rosie that she just measured the blood and liquid in the plastic bulb, and decided to forego squeezing the tubes. She feared she would hurt Trent. I wish I would have done the same, but I diligently followed the hospital instructions a couple times a day to Aiden's dismay. Amazingly he never complained, although he told me afterwards he hated this part of his recovery. The measurement was needed to verify that

Aiden's drainage was decreasing in order for the tubes to be removed on our first post-surgical visit, which was our goal. According to my records, things appeared promising.

When Aiden woke up the day after surgery, he asked about Trent. I called Rosie. We celebrated Trent's release from the hospital. Trent anxiously wanted to return to their hotel, and Rosie looked forward to taking a nice shower and putting on clean clothes. She had slept all night in a chair next to her son, wanting to make sure he would be okay. A mother's love knows no boundaries.

After I talked with Rosie, I gave Aiden a report on Trent. "I can't believe he hasn't taken any pain medication," I said. "His strong reaction to the anesthesia probably helped deaden the pain for him."

"No pain medication at all!" Aiden's face showed disbelief. "I can't believe he hasn't taken anything!"

Although Aiden's male competitive spirit emerged upon hearing the news, it disappeared quickly when his pain signaled time to take another pill.

Trent and Aiden would form their own special bond on the computer as they each lay in bed recovering from surgery. Both had proficiency for computers, so typical for their generation. But besides having technology, a surgery date and being female to male transgender individuals in common, they appeared polar opposites in other areas. Trent was reserved and contemplative in nature, while Aiden more spontaneous and talkative. Trent was Caucasian, tall and lanky, presenting himself as a man, not a transgender man, due to living in a state not as accepting as California, and sporadically involved in the LGBT community. Whereas Aiden was Asian, medium height, broad shouldered, totally out in the LGBT community as an FTM person living in a city where he did not have to hide who he was. But none of those differences mattered. They had a connection that was personal, private, and everlasting. I understood that bond and so did Rosie. We shared that same bond ourselves.

The most remarkable thing that occurred the day after surgery was the re-emergence of Aiden's self-confidence. I remember watching him get out of bed, pass a mirror, and pause a moment to glance at his reflection. What I saw in his eyes, carriage, and spirit was a sense of being at ease with who he was. It felt like he had finally come home to the place that he belonged.

Even for me, I saw him differently. His profile was more masculine. Although I never really noticed how much his breasts, even with the binding, made him seem more self-conscious and more feminine, he just *appeared* different. Even a day out of surgery, he stood taller, no longer pulling in his shoulders to hide his chest. His broad shoulders spread out more proudly, as if to showcase all his workouts at the gym. "I didn't realize how much your chest made you look less masculine," I told him. "It is so noticeable. I can't believe how different you look!!"

"Really, Momma? I seem that different?" He gazed from the mirror to me and then back.

"Yes, and now I know why trying on that suit at Macy's made you so uncomfortable. It could never fit you properly before surgery. Now we'll be able to get you a suit that really fits you. You look great, honey!"

I felt a special bond form as we talked about his new body. We were now bonding as a mother and son. It would mean changes in the way we thought and interacted. On this trip I reserved a room with only one king size bed. I actually should have reserved a room with two doubles so we would each have our own private space as mother and son. In the future that is what I would do. We were figuring our new roles out and we would make mistakes, but I believed the most difficult part of our journey lay behind us. I knew we were going to make it now.

The conversation drifted off, but not the feeling. From that moment on, my son began to radiate a light from deep within that expanded further out than I had ever seen. When people talk about auras that glow around certain people, I now understand that image. It's as if he possessed a joy that could not be contained, one that spilled out from every pore of his being. That joy touches you and draws you in. Sometimes, I think that all the darkness that he walked through allowed him to unleash this unrestrained joy. I believe we all have this joy inside of us. Because of all the years of hiding who he was, Aiden was able to release his joy in its fullest splendor. He felt so good about himself and it showed.

Aiden doesn't exude joy every moment of every day. There are times he feels upset, angry, or sad. But the negative feelings take hold less and the joy arises more. Friends and family who have experienced the withdrawn Aiden still comment on how much he has changed since his transition. It's as if he lived one lifetime, miserable, withdrawn, and unaligned. And now he lives a second life, happy, engaged, and knowing who he is. Of course this makes sense. As a female, his life provided so much pain, loneliness, and inability to tell the world who he really was. Today as a male, his life consists of authenticity and openness: he is free to be himself. How can bliss not spring from someone who now feels so alive and liberated?

The day after surgery also provided Aiden some distraction as a few friends stopped by for a short visit. Then he returned to bed. My son always healed very quickly. It was never more evident than after this surgery.

Two days later, we returned for Aiden's post-surgical visit. Rosie and Trent didn't have a car, so we picked them up. The timing worked perfectly as the boys' appointments were a half hour apart.

Another cause for celebration: the drains come out for both boys! According to Aiden, pulling the tubes out from his chest was painful, but the aftermath worth the few seconds of pain. Initially Aiden only wanted to see Dr. Brownstein, and then return home, but removing the drains changed everything. He was up for a little sightseeing and lunch with our new friends. We drove over the Golden Gate Bridge, stopped at the visitor's center on the Marin County side, and took a few pictures of the San Francisco skyline. Rosie and Trent had traveled from another state, so their eyes lit up as they absorbed the beauty of San Francisco and this often photographed symbol of the city.

For lunch, we stopped at Mel's Diner. Aiden and I had eaten there our first night in San Francisco, meeting my niece Stephie and her boyfriend, Dan, for dinner. Aiden liked the casual old-time feel of this restaurant, the milkshakes, and easy parking, so his suggestion to eat there again was met with unanimous approval. We conversed lightly and laughed easily, all four of us comfortable with the slow-paced conversation, moments of quiet in between the slurping of milkshakes, and smiles all around. Since Trent and Aiden only communicated by computer after surgery and hadn't met until today, the two mothers, already tightly bonded, did most of the talking, encouraging their sons to join in. Aiden, the more social one, chimed in often. Trent's softer spirit contributed more quietly and gently.

At the end of the meal, Rosie and I fought for the bill. I won. What a gift she had been to me the past few days. Without her support, I would have been so alone. With her, I had a mother who understood everything I felt—the worry, the relief, the hope I had for my son. I spoke of my gratitude for her. Tears formed in Rosie's eyes and she brushed them away. We had a special connection, and no one could take that away.

The short outing exhausted Aiden. After our return to the hotel, he climbed back into bed and I flopped on the living room sofa for an afternoon siesta. Later on, revived after our mid-day rest, Aiden wanted to go out for dinner. His choice was Thai food with mango and sticky rice for dessert. The perfect ending to a wonderful day!

On our seventh day in San Francisco, it was San Francisco Pride Festival and Parade day. Exhausted from a San Francisco bus tour the previous day, Trent opted to stay in and bypass the parade. Aiden feared being jostled and bumped in the chest by rambunctious parade goers, so we stayed in as well...for awhile. In the afternoon, he emerged from his room and announced that he wanted to go to the Pride Festival. There was no entrance fee, so we agreed that if Aiden only wanted to stay five minutes, we'd lose nothing. I was kind of excited. San Francisco Pride, I had heard, was the flagship event, the biggest and the best. I was off to another adventure, courtesy of my newly transitioned son.

We arrived and saw a fairly open event. When crowds appeared, we moved to less crowded areas. For the most part, Aiden was comforted by the large open areas into which he could maneuver himself. We bought some T-shirts and leather bracelets. Aiden bought a bracelet for Trent, since we were not sure he and Rosie would show up.

Even though I was a relatively seasoned Pride event attendee, Aiden forgot that his mom is also still a conservative Asian lady in some respects. As we walked around the event, I noticed quite a few men wearing *nothing* below their waist. No briefs, no boxers, just their birthday suit with some adornments such as things around their neck or waist. At first, I couldn't believe what I was seeing. I turned to take another look. *Oh my gosh, it is true*; nude men were strolling around the festival area uninhibited. I stared in disbelief and couldn't take my eyes off of them. Aiden noticed me and whispered, "Mom, quit staring." I tried, but I couldn't help it—another naked man walked past me. Then another. But after a while, I quit gawking, the shock wore off, and eventually, I didn't notice them anymore. Perhaps they all hid from my intruding eyes, or much more likely, I no longer saw this as so shocking. Nudity isn't evil; it's just unusual in our society.

Aiden and I wandered around for a while and then decided to head back to the hotel. After two hours, he landed back in bed, so his body could continue to heal. He didn't realize what a toll surgery takes on a body. Why would he? He was only twenty-one. But it had been a momentous day—my new son with his new body out in the world, feeling proud of who he is.

Finally, ten days after our arrival, Aiden was released to return to Los Angeles. Trent was released as well. To celebrate, we returned to Mel's Diner for one last meal complete with those famous milkshakes. This time, it was Rosie and Trent's treat. We gave hugs and farewells to our new friends. I felt sad because they snuggled their way deep into my heart. Now they would be returning to their home in a distant state. We continue to stay in contact over the phone, and Aiden and I are friends with Trent on Facebook. I feel certain that whether or not we ever see Rosie and Trent again, we will always be friends. Those ten days that we shared began a new road of hope and happiness for two mothers and two sons. That kind of connection stays with you for a long, long time.

This experience of transformation with my son was the beginning of new life for us. With renewed confidence compliments of a body that finally felt in alignment with the man living inside of him, Aiden talked about the things he looked forward to. He couldn't wait to go swimming without a shirt. He couldn't wait to buy that new suit. He couldn't wait to get his new driver's license with the letter "M" under "gender." The world held a whole new set of possibilities. His spirit anticipated the next exciting step forward in life. What a change!

I began to change as well. My words of hope and possibilities for Aiden felt honest and sincere. I saw the world opening up for my son. And I knew, as only a mother knows, that he would somehow find his way now and contribute in a way neither of us believed possible during those long, painful years that preceded this moment. I looked forward to seeing his life unfold.

CHAPTER NINE

Marching Again

Aiden continued to heal during the summer. In the beginning, he would show me his scars, which were thick and bright red. I would think, *Those scars look so bad. I hope they get better over time.* Even Aiden confessed that he had moments when he thought, *What did I do?* But as the months flew by and the scars began to fade in color and thickness, those thoughts became less frequent and eventually stopped altogether.

With his new body and new attitude, Aiden threw himself into the LGBT community, volunteering whenever he could. As an openly transgender individual, his name was passed around if a speaker was needed for a panel discussion or event. In high school, my son could not attend regular classes due to his agoraphobia. Now he was speaking in front of large groups of people, sharing his story!

In the months after his surgery, I also began to volunteer. On one of my volunteer visits to the Los Angeles Gay & Lesbian Center, Michael Ferrera, Director of LifeWorks, happened to mention that he was going to recommend Aiden to a Northern California group that was sponsoring individuals for an Equality March in the fall. This group had talked to Michael and asked if he knew a transgender individual. Michael couldn't think of a better representative than Aiden. I was so proud that Aiden's reputation had grown into one of such responsibility and maturity that Michael would want to recommend him to others.

A short time later, Aiden announced that a community organization from San Francisco called One Struggle, One Fight would pay for him to go to Washington D.C., to be part of the Equality March. They wanted Aiden to represent the transgender population. It excited and honored him to no end. Even though I asked him if he wanted me to join him, I sensed he wanted this to be his time of independence, without me hovering. He politely told me that on this trip he would fly solo. That was fine with me, as I had a business trip to New Orleans the week before, so taking two trips in a short period of time would have been exhausting.

As the trip neared and Aiden received more details, I also could sense some concern on his part. Having been agoraphobic and occasionally still experiencing panic attacks, his internal dialogue started up between going on his own, and wanting me to be there to support him should his anxiety surface without warning. Furthermore, to save on costs, most sponsored participants—up to 300 people—would be staying at a church and sleeping on the floor.

Hearing about the 300 participant church "hotel," Aiden made his decision; he would see what my plans were. A few weeks before the scheduled trip, he approached me casually. "Mom, I was thinking about something. You seemed like you wanted to go with me to Washington, D.C., and I want you to know that if you want to be part of the march I am okay with you coming along. I don't want to tell you not to go if it is something you want to do."

With a combination of Aiden's concerns about his agoraphobia, sleeping with 300 strangers, and his desire to include me in LGBT events, my son encouraged me to march with him. Aiden enjoys introducing me to these new experiences, and I believe, somewhere deep within, he prides himself on being my guide on this journey we are taking together.

"Are you sure, honey? I don't want to cramp your style," I told him.

"Well, I really don't want to tell you not to go, because this could be a once in a lifetime experience."

"Where would you be staying?" I asked.

"On a church floor. With a bunch of other participants. If you went Momma, where would you stay?"

"Not on the church floor, Aiden! You know Momma; I'll probably get a hotel room at one of the Westins and if you want me to go, you can stay with me."

"Well, I was thinking that staying in a place with three hundred other people and my anxiety might be a little overwhelming, so if you want to go, could I stay with you?"

That was all I needed to hear. I picked up my phone and began to make airline and hotel reservations. Still, there were a few details to iron out. My husband would also be out of town traveling with his sister to Chicago on a brother-sister getaway week. My son, Stefen, who is old enough to take care of himself during normal daytime hours, would be at home alone. Not comfortable with my younger son staying alone, I asked our neighbors, Sam and Lisa, to watch out for him and maybe let him stay one night with them. "No problem" they said without hesitation. With everything set, I relaxed and began to think about this new experience.

The week before the march was our monthly PFLAG meeting. I was tired from a business trip the previous week, but decided to attend, as I was really trying to get the word out to people about a high school diploma program opening at the L.A. Gay & Lesbian Center. These monthly meetings offered a chance to network with other people who might know a family in need of a program like this, or an organization with which I could meet to provide more information.

The meeting turned out to be very eventful. After opening introductions, the large group broke down into two smaller groups. A lot of transgender families attended, so the groups broke down into a transgender family cluster and all others formed the second cluster. Aiden and I, of course, joined the transgender group circle. During our group discussion, Aiden began to relate the big fight we had ten months before.

"My mother and I never fight, but one time we had a huge one. She was yelling and screaming at me when I tried to tell her that I needed to transition, because it was getting so hard for me."

Caught off guard, I felt unprepared to share this painfully private and vulnerable moment in such a public way, so I responded hesitantly,

"Well, honey, you were talking about committing suicide, so I just got scared."

"But I wasn't going to go out and kill myself the next day and you kept yelling at me."

"I realize that now, but at the time it felt different."

"You couldn't stop screaming at me."

Feeling my face begin to flush with embarrassment and averting my eyes to the group, I calmly answered, "I think we just had a misunderstanding, Aiden."

The moderator of the group stepped in as things escalated to an uncomfortable level. Not feeling like I had a chance to explain my primal response, so I didn't seem like an irrational, out of control, awful mother, I sat quietly as the group continued on with other families discussing their issues. After about thirty minutes, the two groups were brought back together for closing comments.

As I pulled my chair over to rejoin the larger group, I felt sick inside. I hadn't been able to explain fully the reason for my reaction to Aiden's wish for surgery, and Aiden's account made me relive an extremely horrible experience. Further, the discussion left me appearing like the most terrible mother on earth, a woman who screamed at her child at his most vulnerable of times. I wanted to quietly slink out of the meeting, claiming I needed to leave early, but hung in there even though I felt ashamed and mortified.

As the meeting closed, Aiden raised his hand to share some news. He told the group about his sponsorship to march in Washington D.C. Everybody was excited for him, but I still felt sick to my stomach. He wasn't done yet. "And I want to tell you how awesome my mother is, she is going with me and will be marching by my side."

People turned to me and smiled. First, I was shocked by his announcement, so public and so filled with pride. Second, it dazed me. Wasn't it just a moment ago that he described me as his screaming mother? He sat forward in his chair, beaming.

On the drive home that night, I had a chance to process the unexpected events of the evening. I came to understand a few things that continue to define a part of our lives. Everything about this journey Aiden and I are taking is new and uncharted for us. I am not always going to say the right things or perhaps make the right decision on the spot. I must forgive myself for that. I am truly doing the best that I can, and as long as I have not abandoned my son physically, emotionally, or spiritually, our relationship will endure these moments and our bond will grow stronger. The horrendous fight we had had arose from our mutual fear. Today, I do not believe I would have reacted so horribly. I am less fearful and more knowledgeable. So is Aiden. But at the time, I responded the only way I knew how.

The juxtaposition of talking about our fight and Aiden's announcement about me marching beside him took two very private moments and made them public. Everyone who attended the small group meeting was aware we were not a "perfect" family without flaws and missteps. We were trying to find our way, just as they were. But these two events illustrated to the group our commitment to love, understand, and forgive each other. That is the image I hold in my heart and mind whenever I am faced with adversity. Our family, arms linked together, marching side by side, determined, demonstrating our commitment to each other, and expressing our love whenever possible.

One final thought that crossed my mind during the drive home was how glad I was that I didn't leave the meeting early. I would have missed the moment that Aiden proclaimed how proud he was of me. Sometimes when I feel sick and scared, I want to hide. But that night, I realized that hiding would rob me of those moments that can never be replaced. If I want to be there for the joyful moments, I must also release the times that I felt less than the mother I want to be. Today, when I want to run away, feel defeated, and consider quitting, I remember that night in all its warmth and unexpected affirmation and it spurs me through whatever adversity I must face.

Even when I feel darkness all around me, I seek out the light. It is always there.

Our trip to Washington D.C., was a huge adventure for both of us. Shortly before the boarding time, I checked the departure board and my heart sank. Our flight was delayed, which meant we would miss our connecting flight. Luckily we were able to find another flight and scurried off to catch our re-booked flight, which was non-stop. Lucky us! The only downside, Aiden and I would be sitting rows apart.

Usually a very private person when I travel, I was somehow drawn to my seat partner. Karen was traveling with her daughter, Kim. We began some superficial conversation and then I opened up about Aiden, our journey, and the reason that we were traveling to D.C. I could feel her begin to soften and open up. She proceeded to tell me that her daughter was sent to a six-week camp in lieu of incarceration. They were returning home on this flight. "If she went to jail, I knew she would not survive. She would be changed forever in a negative way, and I could not and would not allow that to happen," Karen said. A musician, she struggled to raise money for the costly program, but received welcomed help from fellow musicians. She continued to relate how the camp shaped her defiant daughter into a happier and more loving child.

Later, Kim walked up the narrow aisle to talk to her mom. She was an edgy-looking but beautiful girl of eighteen or nineteen. What I noticed most, however, was how much she loved her mother. Her eyes peered straight into her mother's eyes, and her affection was open. I sensed the prevalence of both peace and joy when she talked. I saw both sides of this child: the defiant and the peaceful. I hoped that the peaceful continued to win out as she returned to her everyday life.

Karen and I talked a lot during the cross-country trip. We shared stories of adversity and triumph with both of our children. But mostly we shared tears of relief that our children seemed to be finding their way after many years of searching and struggle. Once the plane arrived, we went our separate ways. But even today, I think about Karen and Kim and wish them well. As one mother to another, those five hours together connected us on a very deep level. I may never see Karen again, but I will always be inspired by her love for Kim and how much a mother would do for her child.

We arrived in D.C. As expected, no luggage. We checked with the baggage office and were told our suitcases would arrive later and be delivered to our hotel. I didn't see how it was possible, since our bags were probably stuck in St. Louis, but I decided not to stress about it—yet. I thanked them and obtained contact information in case our bags failed to arrive later.

On the Super Shuttle to the hotel, I sat near a man who I thought could be in D.C. for the same reason Aiden and I were here. We struck up a conversation. "What are you doing in D.C.?" I asked.

"I'm here to protest at the Capitol. And what about you?"

"Oh, I am here for an Equality March."

He looked at me rather strangely. I could feel Aiden's eyes rolling around in his head. I realized at that very moment we were here for the same event. Suddenly it dawned on me: I was here as a protestor. *Oh my God, even in the days that I was growing up with hippies, I had never protested anything. My parents and all my ancestors are going to sit up in their grave. I hope that my face is not going to be plastered all over the media.*

Then I relaxed. What my conservative ancestors may have thought, I needed to cast aside. I was here to march with my son. This was part of the adventure.

The following day, I took a "spiritual renewal" day in bed while Aiden explored the city. He came back filled with excitement of all that he had seen: the Natural History Museum, the Smithsonian Castle, the Washington Monument, and the Spy Museum. His eyes grew wide from all the history he had taken in.

However, we still didn't have our luggage. We smoothed our rumpled clothes, which doubled as pajamas the previous night, and headed out for dinner. On our way to dinner, we met two guys headed off to protest at the Human Rights dinner where President Obama was scheduled to speak. They were here for the march as well. I nodded my head in acknowledgement. I'm sure Aiden was holding his breath, hoping I didn't say something naïve, like, "Oh, yes, I met someone yesterday who is protesting—I am, however, here to march for equality." Aiden was practically turning blue, thinking, "Good Lord, I can't take you anywhere, Momma!" but his fears were unwarranted, as I managed not to embarrass myself again.

After dinner, we returned to the hotel room, hoping our luggage had arrived, especially since we had an early day because of the march tomorrow. No luggage. We decide to watch a movie and relax. A few hours later, around midnight, a knock on the door: our luggage!

We woke up early, anticipating an exciting and awe-inspiring day. We were not disappointed. Aiden was supposed to meet his sponsoring group at the local park, and then we would all walk over to the parade line-up area. We took a taxi to the park and waited for others to arrive. Slowly people began to congregate. I met Aiden's sponsor, David, who headed One Struggle, One Fight. Aiden and I also met some of the other people marching in the group. They brought along a banner with their organization name, and some people came with their own protest signs. We were empty-handed, as we didn't attend any of the pre-workshops where they made signs. I began to feel out of place with all these young, energetic, and verbally extroverted individuals, so I located a vendor selling rainbow flags. I bought one for Aiden and one for me. Now we had something to carry in the parade.

Aiden instantly connected with Jake, a UC Berkeley student who was a transgender FTM individual. He was intelligent, spirited, and very welcoming. Not wanting to steal any of Aiden's thunder, I attempted to drop my energy really low and become invisible. This was his arena, his community, and his honor to be sponsored. I wanted his star to shine brightest. Since I am one of those parents who openly and proudly supports her LGBT kid, I often receive a lot of attention and accolades. Kids admire the fact that Aiden's mother would come out to be part of his experiences. On this day, I wanted everything to be directed at Aiden. I became very quiet and unobtrusive, often sitting off to the side.

We moved from the park to the parade site and met up with more people. I noticed a number of families and couples, but grew more and more uncomfortable as I realized that I was part of one of the loudest and most demonstrative groups. We had bullhorns, signs, and rehearsed chants that were louder than most of the other groups around us. Withering inside from being pushed way past my comfort zone, I waited for the march to begin, my head swimming in thought as I tried to figure out how I was going to show up and what statement I was making.

We began to march. People on the sidewalks chanted along with the group, cheering and applauding. I meekly chanted, "LGBT, we demand equality," while the other side of my brain was protesting, *I don't like to demand anything. I like to talk with people and build bridges. This is not my style.*

Eventually, I found somewhat of a comfort zone. Any new experience that pushed me past thinking of myself to thinking about others, seemed to melt my discomfort. When I thought of myself, I would often feel embarrassed and self-conscious. When I thought about others, especially my son, my voice grew louder and I waved my rainbow flag more vigorously.

A few opposition protestors yelled derogatory statements from the sidewalk, but their numbers paled in comparison to the numbers in favor of LGBT rights. Jake took off his T-shirt and proudly marched with his scars from top surgery, indicating what his gender used to be. Then the chant changed to "Trans rights now!" All of a sudden, my voice rose to a yell, my rainbow flag flew higher, and my fist pumped in the air for everyone to see. I became a voice for my son. I experienced the moment for what it was: a time of ultimate empowerment; a moment when a mother spoke out for her son, who deserved to be recognized, loved and respected like any other individual given rights by the Constitution of this country.

I realized how far this reserved, polite, and proper mother had come. Being the kind of person who never wanted to rock the boat and made sure everyone had a comfortable seat on that boat, I had found my voice without compromising those things that were important to me. I could still be respectful. I could still be compassionate. But I could also speak my truth in a way that I felt good about myself as a mother and as a human being. I wanted to model for my children how to effect change while remaining kind, honest, and loving.

We marched by the White House and continued to Capitol Hill. At the end of the parade, people sat on the lawn of the Capitol building, basking in proud feelings and observing who came out to march for equality. It was estimated that more than 100,000 people marched. I was overwhelmed by all the faces of hope. After twenty minutes of listening to singers and speakers, and watching the lawn continue to fill with people, we were told that the protest parade was still seven to eight blocks long.

While I sat with our group, relaxing, and listening to others talk about their experiences, I received a call from my husband. In Chicago, he and his sister accidentally encountered an equality rally in the downtown area. They stood, watched, and supported the event. Unable to march with his son in Washington, D.C., Tad found a way to show his support for Aiden even if in another state. When I shared this news with Aiden, he smiled deeply, knowing both of his parents joined him on this adventure. What a comfort for him to know that he would not have to face his travels alone.

My seeds of activism began to grow at this march. They grew not only from seeing my son in this community lending his voice, but also from seeing all the other families and individuals who just wanted to be accepted for the person that lived inside of them. I met and talked with a retired judge from Rhode Island who came alone to march for his lesbian daughter. I also observed a middle-aged Hispanic lesbian couple with their teenage daughters. The daughters carried large poster boards announcing their moms had been together sixteen years and asked that their mom's love for each other be recognized. I thought about all the heterosexual couples who don't stay together for that long, who take marriage for granted, and then walk away from their relationship. Yet these two women chose to stay together, despite facing the typical adversity associated with marriage plus all the social pressure associated with being lesbians. I wondered if the adversity made them more committed to each other and their children, or perhaps the adversity made them more determined to prove to the world that their love transcended time and rights.

The love of these two groups of people—the father and lesbian daughter, the lesbian couple and their girls—touched me in a special way.

But the two images that left an indelible imprint on me happened while we waited for the march to begin. In line for the march, two fathers waited behind me with their two children. The children were adopted, as they were Hispanic and the fathers were not. The little girl was being carried on one of her fathers' shoulders. She was a tiny thing, perhaps three or four years old. She carried a sign written in small child's letters on poster board that said, "I love my two daddies." The other father was with their other child, a son who appeared to be about five. As he talked to his son, I heard his gentle, loving voice. When he turned to his partner to speak, the look that he gave his son and then his partner was filled with more love than I had ever seen come out of the eyes of another human being. It struck me how deeply this man loved his family. And it moved me beyond words to see the love he had for his partner. The love that I saw in this man's eyes was so vulnerable, open, and filled with truth that I had to turn away, fearing I had unintentionally witnessed a moment intended for only their eyes, voices, and hearts.

As we began the march, I turned back to look at this family one last time. The moment was gone, but I will never forget the feeling that came over me when I saw them gaze into each other's eyes with such love. I hope that is the love that my husband and children see on my face when I speak to them. And I hope that is the love they feel deeply within their hearts when I tell them, "I love you."

A few minutes later, my eyes were drawn to two young women walking in front of me. One had her arm gently wrapped around the neck of the other. As they walked, I could see her whispering into the other's ear. I did not overhear the conversation nor did I actually see their faces. What I did feel was their love. As the taller woman spoke softly, the smaller woman sank into the arm of her partner and listened. I could imagine her telling her partner that one day the world would not only know how much she loved her partner, but would also know that the law and society acknowledged their love. I brushed tears from my face as I felt and understood how much this march meant to them. In front of God and thousands of people, they were marching quietly and humbly for the world to see their love. Because of those young women, because of those two fathers, and because of my son and transgender individuals like him, I am determined to further the rights of LGBT individuals. Those moments etched images in my mind that I will never forget.

By the late afternoon, we were both starving and trying to locate a place to eat. We ate with a group of marchers from North Carolina and a girl that Aiden had met online from California. Upon our return to the room, we crashed. An even earlier day awaited us the following morning, as we were to be picked up by Super Shuttle at 5:15 A.M. Aiden watched a movie, but I could barely keep my eyes open.

As I drifted off to sleep, I realized how memorable this day was, and how many exciting new adventures I would be experiencing in the future. Like in the Robert Frost poem, "The Road Not Taken": "Two roads diverged in a wood, and I, I took the one less traveled by, and that has made all the difference."

CHAPTER TEN

Inspired to Activism

As I became more visible in the LGBT community, people began calling me an activist. An activist? Me? Oh no! You've got to be mistaken. I would never participate in protests, carry signs, chant catchy sayings, or yell into a bullhorn. I am just a mother who loves her son and wants the world to be safer for both of her children. An activist—no, that is too visible for my Asian comfort zone.

As I reflect back, I see that I had been travelling down the activism path in my own quiet, Japanese way.

Before I marched in Washington, D.C., I had been working on a project. With Aiden's transition behind us and my son finally moving toward success and happiness, I thought about how I wanted to use my time as I looked forward to retirement. I felt so grateful to the LGBT community that had helped me weather many precarious years. I wanted to give back to this community that had supported our family each step of the way—but how?

As I asked the questions, the answers slowly came into view. With the harassment and bullying Aiden experienced, his struggles academically due to depression, anxiety attacks, and agoraphobia, I wondered if his high school years could have been different. If he hadn't been bullied, would agoraphobia have ever entered his life? If he had attended a school that understood his struggles, made his safety a priority, and accepted him unconditionally, would his high school years have been filled with more hope and less sadness?

I played the "what if" game many times. *What if I tried to communicate more with Aiden when he withdrew? What if I had forced our family back into therapy? What if I didn't work and stayed home with my children? What if... What if... What if...* However, dwelling on "what ifs" only kept me in the past. I also knew from my son's words that everything positive and negative, even the bullying, isolation, depression, and physical violence had shaped his character—and he would not have changed a thing. His compassion, his courageous and authentic voice, and the motivation to share his experiences with other young people came from all he had gone through, both the affirming, but primarily, the disheartening. In the dark, lonely moments, he needed to stand taller and move into the discomfort, not away from it. In the beginning, when Aiden was struggling with who he was, my son couldn't find the worthiness to do so. But as he grew more confident with whom he was, as he began to speak with authenticity and pride, his belief in himself created a stronger and more resilient individual.

Thankful for this knowledge that lifted some of the guilt from my shoulders, those "what ifs" developed into a foundation for how I wanted to change the future. My dream emerged of finding a place for LGBT youth to have a safe and nurturing environment to graduate from high school.

Where would I start? Or go for support? I began with the charter school for which I had worked, and now served as a consultant. Aiden transitioned while he worked for this same public charter school, Opportunities for Learning (OFL), so I knew how much they valued mutual respect, integrity, and compassion. These are the school's core values, along with mutual trust. I also knew that the founders, John and Joan Hall, had open hearts for all at-risk youth, and LGBT youth were a part of that demographic. Of all the people in my life, outside my family, the Halls have been the greatest supporters of my dreams and goals. I love them dearly and respect them even more. John and Joan gave their blessings for me to meet with Deputy Superintendent Bill Toomey and discuss the possibilities.

Bill, a Chicago-born educator, gathered loyal people around him, because of his genuine passion for helping at-risk youth and the trust he created with his honest and direct communication. I liked Bill and hoped he would be on board with this idea. I knew from working with the Halls and Bill that although this project fit into their mission of serving underserved kids, it would have to be financially viable in order for them to support it.

I called Bill and said I would like to discuss with him a new idea. "I want to see if we can provide some type of diploma program for the lesbian, gay, bisexual, and transgender students who are dropping out or at risk of dropping out of high school." Bill knew some of Aiden's story, so he understood why this could be something close to my heart. "John and Joan are on board with this idea. What do you think?"

"Sure," Bill replied. "What are you thinking about?"

"Well, I was hoping to do something at the centers where we can create a cohort of LGBT youth, give them support, and have discussion groups and speakers. Is that possible?"

"Hmmm, we could coordinate something with the centers currently having night school and see how that goes."

"That would be great!"

With Bill's approval, the next steps would be to find a way to reach those LGBT youth who were either dropping out of school or at risk of doing so, and then come up with a plan that Bill would be comfortable supporting. During this time, a name kept popping up as someone who could help me reach out to the LGBT community and get support.

I loved Stephen Jimenez from the first time I heard his voice. Stephen works for Los Angeles Unified School District as the Project 10 Specialist. Project 10 is a program out of LAUSD that offers schools technical and educational support for LGBT students. The mission of Project 10, in accordance with the District's Nondiscrimination Policy and the California Student Safety and Violence Prevention Act of 2000, is to "ensure safe, supportive, and welcoming campuses free from discrimination and harassment for sexual minority students." In Stephen's spare time, he is involved in various other projects. I hoped this would be a project that piqued his interest.

His voice was kind, helpful, and warm. I could sense that he connected with my dream and wanted to assist me in any way possible. Stephen sent me a list of people who I could contact about the high school program. I began to call each name. When I introduced myself as someone who was referred by Stephen Jimenez, the doors opened up for me. People seemed to trust me easily because I knew him. One by one, I checked off names of people who said that this would be a great asset to the community and they would be interested in hearing more. Things progressed and I felt pleased.

Bill and I agreed on utilizing three centers for the LGBT cohorts. Stephen thought Huntington Park, Studio City, and Pasadena could be good centers. Studio City would be near the Los Angeles Gay & Lesbian Center, drawing from organizations near the Center. Pasadena could serve the San Gabriel Valley, and Huntington Park would be good for the greater Los Angeles area.

I began to plan orientation meetings, send out flyers to the community, and invite students and organizations to come to an informational open house. We enjoyed a good turnout for most of the open houses, and people involved in the LGBT community attended to hear about this new program. At our Studio City orientation, attendees included Michael Ferrera, Director of LifeWorks, an LGBT youth mentoring program; Steve Krantz, Regional and National Director of PFLAG; Stephen Jimenez; and Dr. Johanna Olson, an adolescent medicine physician specializing in gender identity disorder, who dropped by to provide some resource material. People thought it was a wonderful idea, because GED programs existed in the community, but not a high school diploma program from a Western Association of Schools and Colleges (WASC) accredited school. People said that I drew the attention of many influential individuals in the community. I felt enormously hopeful.

I encouraged Aiden to get involved. This project was my passion, not his, but he supported me by coming to the informational meetings and speaking about his experience. I watched in awe as he got up and spoke about his harrowing years in high school with only a hint of discomfort to a group of people he didn't know. Was this the same child who, in sixth grade, would break down in tears over the thought of doing a presentation in front of a class? Or suffering an anxiety attack every time the situation became stressful in high school? Tad and Stefen also came to one meeting for support. I felt so lucky to have my family around me as I pursued this dream.

One of the areas that Aiden and I work on is finding a place where our advocacy meets and where our connection to each other needs to be separate. I always believed we should follow our own passions, wherever that may lead. In some areas of our work, our passions seem to intersect and in others they seem to diverge. I loved the idea of working with Aiden on things that I passionately pursued, but felt disappointed when my passion for something relating to our journey did not spark a passion within him. I have learned that I can be strong with or without him. Previously, I needed his support to feel confident to do things as an advocate. Today, I ask if he wants to be involved and if he doesn't, I decide whether I want to continue on without him. Aiden confided in me recently that he hesitated to say "no" when I proposed ideas because he wants me to feel his support. But when he has no passion for what I do, I can sense it in his reluctance and his slow response to my requests. In our discussions, we have given each other permission to act out of "true choice" not out of obligation. I like this way we work together—it is honest, open, and respectful of each of our individual journeys.

As much as I promoted my program and talked to people, we were not getting any enrollments in the school sites. I called the three centers regularly and asked if there were any enrollments. The answer was always, "No. I'm sorry, Marsha."

"Don't give up hope," Stephen consoled me. "I'll send a few more announcements out and see what happens." His words reassured me.

Stephen and I talked regularly. He called me his new friend, and I felt so fortunate to have him as a mentor and adviser. One day as we were discussing the cohorts, he asked, "What do you think about me talking with Michael Ferrera at LifeWorks and see if they are interested in sponsoring this high school diploma program? They are moving to the L.A. Gay & Lesbian Center, and I think Michael has always wanted to do something educationally for the youth."

"I think that is a great idea," I responded.

The diversity cohorts never gained traction and the program didn't open in the three centers. Sometimes, though, the seeds don't germinate where you first plant them. The idea of a satellite school at the L.A. Gay & Lesbian Center seemed to be gaining momentum. My dream still burned strong. Stephen got back to me saying that Michael was on board with a collaboration. I set up a meeting with Michael and Bill Toomey. Stephen and I attended as well. In less than an hour, details of the program were hammered out. Michael would provide the space at no charge to house the school and Bill would provide the teacher, curriculum, and supplies at no charge to the L.A. Gay & Lesbian Center. This seemed like a great partnership with LifeWorks incurring no additional costs and Opportunities for Learning not having to pay any rent. A memorandum of understanding signed by both entities sealed the deal to open the program in late 2009.

Once again, response was tepid. Since the L.A. Gay & Lesbian Center housed the program, I thought students would flock to the school, especially those who were harassed and bullied. I was certain organizations would flood the school with referrals, but that wasn't the case. After a couple of months, we only had two students enrolled. This low number would not sustain the program financially, so I grew increasingly nervous about its future. The regional supervisor of the area, Jenner Jose, suggested an open house. That became our next step in getting the word out to the community about this program called our Hollywood site.

A couple of days before the open house, Stevie St. John, the Communications Manager at the L.A. Gay & Lesbian Center, submitted a press release to the news media. In response, the *Los Angeles Times* sent a reporter. The day before the open house, the *Times* ran an article called "A Harassment Free School." Little did we envision what happened next: two major news channels sent their crews to the open house, one Spanish news channel sent a news van, and a number of small local newspapers interviewed individuals involved in the program. I was ecstatic. Now we would get the publicity that would reach the kids in need of this program. I envisioned the phones ringing off the hook.

We did get calls, but only a handful of enrollments.

I knew the program was in jeopardy. After such great publicity, we were stuck at seven or eight students. Then, in September 2010, a rash of tragic suicides hit our LGBT community. Campaigns such as "It Gets

Better" hit YouTube and took off virally. Along with many others, I received an email blast from the CEO of the L.A. Gay & Lesbian Center, Lorri Jean, about one of the boys who took his life. I asked her if she could help us promote the program. A meeting was set up to discuss strategies. A follow-up meeting with Stevie St. John kick-started more publicity to the community. As a result, our numbers in 2011 are between fifteen to twenty students, so we doubled in six months. Our goal is to have forty students enrolled in this LifeWorks/Opportunities for Learning program so a full-time teacher can be devoted to these students.

I knew in my heart that this program worked. Opportunities for Learning had a proven model that has been graduating students for over twenty-five years. Our first Hollywood enrolled student said she planned to graduate from the school. Our second enrolled student was a straight ally who attended our program while taking care of her new baby. She also plans to graduate with us. Both of these students are still enrolled in the program as of Spring 2012. One of our students has already graduated. Students who could not travel to our Hollywood site were encouraged to go to enroll in one of the seventy-two charter school centers in Southern and Northern California. Students who went to centers other than our Hollywood location also found places to graduate. I know one student who enrolled in Fall 2009 in one of our centers. She recently emailed me and announced that she has turned in her final unit, so she will have graduated in June 2012. I attended her graduation.

Also on track to graduate in June 2012, is a student who came to our school after he was bullied, harassed and beaten at his previous school. Taking himself to the emergency room, because he had no family to take care of him, he later found his way to the LifeWorks/Opportunities for Learning diploma program. Our numbers may be small at the present time, but I believe our impact on students who have or will be graduating are enormous.

Since this Opportunities for Learning model has a low student to teacher ratio (5:1), teachers can invest their time and energy into getting to know their students. This creates a strong bond of trust. In addition, teachers respond quickly when students are struggling academically or emotionally. They seek out tutors, mentors, or whatever support the student needs. Partnering with LifeWorks has brought another wonderful source of support and resources for LGBT youth that a traditional school cannot always provide. These include discussion groups on LGBT issues, a weekly dinner program where LGBT and ally youth can be a part of a socially inclusive environment, special after school programs, and weekend activities such as martial arts, photography, ice skating, and other field trips. Michael Ferrera's vision and support of the high school diploma program has brought a much-needed educational component to the Los Angeles area and to LGBT youth in this city. I am personally so very grateful for Michael's tireless work and unwavering dedication, since Aiden used many LifeWorks' services, including being part of their mentoring program. Aiden also received a LifeWorks' scholarship to help him with college.

The two individuals responsible for opening the Hollywood high school diploma program, working with Michael and his staff, are Opportunities for Learning regional supervisor Jenner Jose and lead teacher, Molly Sircher. Jenner says of this satellite program, "I'm concerned with human rights. And the LGBT population is experiencing something that I could never understand and something that I think nobody should ever have to go through. If I can have a part or a hand in trying to alleviate this prejudice and discrimination then I want to be a part of it. I just hope that those of us who can make a difference are doing what we can."

When I sat down and discussed the school with Molly, she shared her thoughts. "I believe in education—the most important gift we can give ourselves. I think they (students) should be able to pursue their education and not have to worry about being judged or being taunted. I would never want anybody to have that dread coming to our school." Molly goes on to say, "I wish there wasn't a need for a separate school that was LGBT-friendly, but until society evolves to accept everyone, my students shouldn't have to suffer now. Our school is their hope and I am proud to be a part of it."

Educators like Jenner and Molly bring a special devotion into the work they do. I feel so privileged to be working with people who care so much about moving students towards graduation, especially those students who were previously bullied and taunted for their sexual orientation and gender identity, as Aiden was.

The Washington, D.C. March took place in October 2009. After returning to Los Angeles, I was even more determined that I would help students get their diplomas in an environment that allowed them to be themselves and see the greatness of who they were.

The LifeWorks/Opportunities for Learning program officially opened in February 2010 with our open house. Throughout 2010, I worked to keep the high school diploma program supported and growing. Stephen Jimenez was right by my side, encouraging, sending out announcements, and doing trainings for tutors and enrichment programs.

I also began to search for other areas that could open programs. I talked with Long Beach, Orange County, San Diego, and San Francisco about piloting similar programs. Nothing materialized. I also met with Chicago, but Chicago Public Schools, immersed in their own financial problems, could not provide additional seats for us to run a small program at The Center on Halsted. I am still hopeful about Chicago and have a few influential members of the LGBT community who have expressed interest in helping me start something in the future. Perhaps Chicago will be my next location to help students get their high school diploma. Or maybe there is another city out there, one that is ready to help these young people.

My activism was quiet and very much behind the scenes. I attended some candlelight vigils, Models of Pride (an annual LGBT and ally youth conference in Southern California), supported fundraising events, and a scholarship program. Aiden's godfather and uncle even gave out LGBT scholarships. Since I was still working and had begun writing *Two Spirits, One Heart,* I chose my participation carefully. With Stephen proving to be such a wonderful resource to me, I usually chose events in which he involved himself. I wanted him to know that his support didn't go unnoticed.

With the high school diploma program feeling more stable, I tried to find ways to support our teacher Molly, who was giving so much of her time and energy. Some students who I met at a candlelight vigil in Santa Barbara wanted to come and speak to our students. These Santa Barbara Junior College LGBT students had received a small amount of money to do outreach, and they chose to spend that money on gas for the drive to Los Angeles. I was touched. I contacted local organizations, like The Trevor Project, and arranged for them to visit the program. If I knew an advocate for LGBT programs planned to visit Los Angeles, I asked them to come and observe our program. The more outreach I did, the more confident I felt we would find the students who were out on the streets looking for an alternative.

In late 2010 and early 2011, I committed myself to completing *Two Spirits, One Heart* and building a social platform. I set up a Facebook page, website and blog. Through all my social platform building, opportunities began to arise for me within both regional and national communities. I contacted people about speaking on radio shows, being interviewed for newspapers, submitting freelance writing pieces, and contributing thoughts to articles written by others. I also responded to controversy that arose, something I still can't believe I put myself out there for. But my need to speak my truth welled up and demanded expression. I felt a deep yearning that pushed me to not be silent any longer with things that would hurt my son and those in the LGBT community. As far as I saw it, my silence equated to approval. I couldn't be silent and look at myself in the mirror each morning and still feel good about who I was.

There was, however, a limit on what I could do. Once again, I chose wisely, knowing that I would be investing my precious time in whatever involved me next. Soon, one such moment arose and caught my attention. I noticed posts from a number of individuals regarding the Monrovia School District canceling the production of the play *Rent*. From the postings and news articles, it appeared that the cancellation was in response to families who did not want their children to see such a "dark" play, even though the drama teacher advised the school board that they would be presenting a toned-down version. My initial reaction? I felt this school district, and in particular the superintendent, Dr. Linda Wagner, had backed down due to homophobic fears in the district. My blood boiled: this district bordered the city in which I lived! Was homophobia creeping into my backyard?

I wrote to the superintendent. In hindsight, my tone could have been nicer. Surprisingly, I received a prompt response filled with warmth, assuring me that this decision was not homophobic. Furthermore, the superintendent wanted to meet with Aiden and me. I responded that I didn't live in her district. She didn't care. She wanted to hear from a son and his mother about their experiences in school. She wanted to gather information. And so Aiden and I went to Monrovia to talk with Dr. Wagner over a cup of coffee.

Our meeting lasted about one hour. In the end, she didn't change her position on the cancellation of *Rent*. What originally upset me, I now understood. She took the time to communicate with my son and me, and has carved out a different way to address my concerns. She has asked for our help and we are more than happy to do what we can.

Having coffee with Dr. Wagner has given me more hope that leaders in education will do something to stop the behaviors that are causing youth around the country to believe their lives have no meaning. She has vision, she has courage, and she truly cares.

Dr. Wagner and I are friends on Facebook now. She has met with the Monrovia High School Gay Straight Alliance (GSA) and Aiden has been to the district to speak to their GSA. Her school district ordered Safe Space Kits from the Gay, Lesbian, and Straight Education Network (GLSEN). They also initiated a Day of Silence. And she has visited a training that Stephen Jimenez conducts for staff about LGBT issues.

I believe I made a difference in Monrovia, because of my email and meeting with Dr. Wagner. If nobody said a word to her, but complained only when *Rent* was cancelled, all of which occurred in that district to support the LGBT youth may have developed more slowly. It really does take only one voice to create change. I applaud the courage of those who step forward daily. I also silently patted myself on the back, knowing I had been courageous and had done something meaningful and positive, small as it was.

Whenever I follow my instincts about anything, I am generally led in a direction I may not have recognized previously. Meeting with Dr. Wagner made me realize that I could bring resources and support to districts, but in 2011 Aiden and I met with only three districts. This was not the way, I thought. So in 2012, now on the Board of Directors for PFLAG National, I began to reach out to PFLAG chapters in our Southern California/Hawaii regions to see if interest existed to work together on a PFLAG Safe Schools Initiative. I hoped through collaboration with other chapters that we could reach more superintendents and bring more resources and trainings that will eliminate the bullying and harassment in schools. In the beginning stages of development, about seven chapters are now working together. I anticipate that this group effort will bring about greater change in our schools through the passion and dedication of parents.

Five years ago, I would have wanted to speak up and speak out, but backed down in fear of offending others. Now I feel compelled to speak out with passion and compassion, sharing my thoughts and feelings, knowing that I too can make a difference with my voice. This journey transformed even me.

Little did I know that this small act of confronting the superintendent was preparing me for a larger and more visible role of activism that would happen days after emailing Superintendent Wagner and setting up our coffee date.

As I was returning home from hearing the Santa Barbara Junior College youth speak to our LifeWorks/Opportunities for Learning students, my phone pinged, signaling an email. The email came from our PFLAG Chapter President asking for members to support an Arcadia Council Meeting that evening to speak out against the mayor's decision to invite a Focus on the Family speaker to his Community Breakfast.

My husband, who had driven me to the L.A. Gay & Lesbian Center, was tired. I felt equally tired and unprepared to stand up in front of the city council to deliver a speech about something I knew very little about. I decided to go home, read up a little on the seemingly controversial speaker, and then send the mayor and city council members an email later that night. I knew I could not bury my head in the sand on this one. This was happening in my own city.

Here's what I learned in my quick research: Focus on the Family (FOF) was founded by Dr. James Dobson, who lived in Arcadia for many years. According to the Southern Poverty Law Center (SPLC), "No one has spread the anti-gay gospel as widely, or with as much political impact, as James Dobson. ... Among the scores of anti-gay commentaries, stories and products on FOF's website is a Dobson essay that strikes a typical note: 'Moms and Dads, are you listening? This movement is the greatest threat to your children. It is of particular danger to your wide-eyed boys, who have no idea what demoralization is planned for them.'"[1] A conservative organization, which in some circles is considered a "hate" group, Focus on the Family believes that marriage is between a man and a woman, your gender of birth should not be altered, and reparative therapy will help cure unwanted attractions to someone of your own sex. The invited speaker was a vice president of this organization, and city funds were being used to bring this organization to Arcadia to speak.

I felt sick to my stomach, outraged, then anxious. My stomach churned over how Aiden would feel about council members from his own city bringing in someone with these views. After all he had been through, now to have the mayor and the city council of Arcadia allow this individual to speak as if representing our city views appalled me. My heart sank as I mulled over who would attend this breakfast: parents who had served with me on the PTA, people who ran businesses in Arcadia that I patronized, ministers whose churches I attended.

That's when the mother bear in me rose up. My blood began to bubble. On his webpage, the Mayor wrote, "Public safety is the number one responsibility of local government." Why was he bringing in someone who would not make the city safer for my son? Aiden already had two violent incidences in Arcadia. Bringing in an organization that was intolerant of LGBT individuals would not make our city safer. I sent the Mayor an email voicing my displeasure and asked him to invite another, more accepting speaker. I also sent copies to the council members along with some advocate groups and two local newspapers.

The Mayor skirted my issue of bringing in a more accepting speaker and he focused in on getting the police to take a report in response to the physical violence I described Aiden experiencing. In reply, I indicated to the Mayor that these were past incidences and I wished to focus on the safety of my son and all LGBT youth now and in the future. Would he please consider another speaker that was more accepting of people or at least add another speaker that would provide a message more supportive to LGBT families?

His reply completely ignored my request and continued to focus on the distraction of prior violent incidents and wanting to have the police contact us.

I reached out to others about this situation. Stephen Jimenez said that discussing this issue by email would probably not make much progress. What politician would want to put something controversial in writing for all to read? I asked for a face-to-face meeting with the Mayor, since it appeared we were not getting anywhere. He never responded to that email. I wasn't surprised.

I did hear from one council member who seemed sympathetic to our situation and indicated that he had no idea that Focus on the Family had any position on homosexuality. He said he would do some research on the organization, but asked me to consider the whole organization and not just one issue, as misguided as that issue might be. This unsettled me; like ignoring the deeds of a pedophile because he donated millions of dollars to a good cause.

Later I found out this very same councilman was an active supporter of the Boy Scouts of America, a group that would not allow homosexual leaders, volunteers, or avowed homosexual youth into their organization because it goes against their Scout Oath to be "morally straight," which the Scout Law defined to mean "to live your life with honesty, to be clean in your speech and actions, and to be a person of strong character." I shudder when I read their point of view.

Another council member left a voice message with an Arcadia family, saying he tried to convince the Mayor to consider other alternatives. The Mayor was not going to change his position and it seemed to be the Mayor's prerogative, since it was his breakfast.

At the Arcadia City Council Meeting I didn't attend, I heard that two speakers stood up and spoke out against the speaker, H.B. London, Jr., and Focus on the Family. One Arcadia resident, Gary Searer, and one individual, Brian Ngyuen from the Asian Pacific Islanders Equality-LA (APIELA), bravely voiced their opinions. Gary didn't want city funds spent on bringing in such a speaker; he was appalled that the city of Arcadia would select such an anti-gay organization. And with Arcadia having 57% of their residents being Asian, Brian spoke for APIELA and any Asian family who believed in equality.

Other LGBT and equality groups picked up the controversy brewing in Arcadia. Patti, the PFLAG president for my chapter, asked in an email if individuals, especially Arcadia residents, would be willing to support this growing concern. The PFLAG regional director sent a letter to the Mayor voicing his feelings. Gary Searer, became the leader of us all. I meekly volunteered to speak at the next council meeting, since I lived in Arcadia. I did it for Aiden, but rolling around in my head I wondered, *What am I getting myself into? This is not a comfortable place for me—and there are talks about counter events and protests.*

I was beginning to wish I had never sent the email to the Mayor. I wanted to dig a hole and climb in, not re-surfacing until after the Mayor's Breakfast. I was so uncomfortable. There were days I daydreamed of ways to get out of this situation. Maybe I could turn into an ostrich for a month. Aiden would say to me, "You have to be comfortable being uncomfortable, Momma." *Fine for you to say,* I thought. *You are not going to have to speak.* Attempting to be his normal, encouraging self, Tad would say, "This is wonderful—more information for your book!" Fine for him to say; maybe he could speak in my place—he was an Arcadia resident and Aiden's father. I imagined eggs being thrown at my house, something painted on the side of my home, or shots being fired through my front window. Thank goodness none of those things happened.

On the night of the council meeting, Tad, my brother Marty, my personal assistant Melissa, and I walked from the parking lot to groups of people gathered on the walkway. Many of us who had become friends on Facebook or participated in the conference calls Gary set up met for the first time, exchanged greetings, and a few hugs. The Gay-Straight Alliance (GSA) student speakers huddled nervously together. Speech in hand, I tried to be calm, but the butterflies inside of me flew in an out-of-control frenzy.

I walked into the lobby of the City Council Chambers with my family. I filled out a card that announced my wish to speak, identifying the issue and our home address. We walked into the chambers and took a seat, along with approximately thirty others who showed up for this cause, either to speak or be of support. Aiden called and said he was caught in traffic and running late, but would be there with Mary. He decided not to speak, because he no longer lived in Arcadia. I also sensed a reluctance to relive those isolating and terrible years in front of the city where they occurred. There were nine speakers—plenty of voices already.

I prayed that I would not be the first speaker to be called to the podium. I was shaking and stuffed some tissue in my pocket, knowing I might cry. The first two speakers were called: one to take the podium and the second to be ready to speak when the first had finished. One of these young women began to cry on the stand, demonstrating the depth of her hurt and unhappiness with the Mayor's choice in speakers. They were the young GSA students from Arcadia High School and a neighboring district. Speakers three and four then got up and spoke.

I was fifth to speak. I walked up and placed my three-page speech on the podium. The speech was actually less than a page, but I used a large font so I wouldn't have to read with my reading glasses. I decided if I cried, having to deal with glasses and tissue was too much.

I faced the council members and began to read my speech. Before I finished my first paragraph, my voice was shaking from emotion. When I talked about "LGBT individuals only strive to live a life of integrity and alignment," tears began trickling down my cheeks as I thought of my son. I continued on. "By promoting an anti-gay group such as Focus on the Family, the city will be endorsing the message that LGBT people are inferior, that they are sick, that they need to be cured, and that bullying and discrimination of LGBT individuals are okay. My son is neither inferior nor does he need to be cured, bullied, or discriminated against."

By this time, tears streamed down my face as I tried to compose myself. I glanced up to make eye contact with the council. Some members leaned toward me compassionately, intent on hearing my words. However, one member sat erect with a scowl of contempt on his face. I didn't care. Tonight I spoke up for my son and all the families that loved their children, regardless of what Focus on the Family said about them.

When I finished, I returned to my seat. My husband, brother, and personal assistant gave me an encouraging smile or a whispered "good job." As I settled into my seat, Aiden, who was seated directly behind me, leaned forward and without a word wrapped his arms around my neck, resting his head on my shoulder. In that momentary hug, I felt his love, pride, and gratitude for my courage to get up and speak to the Arcadia City Council. It is one of those moments that I will remember forever. Those few seconds made it worth all the hours of doubt and anxiety that led up to this event.

The following day, Aiden, Mary, and I flew to Minneapolis, Minnesota, to attend the National Gay and Lesbian Task Force's Creating Change Conference. We had been looking forward to this event for months and it seemed so timely that it was coming on the heels of this brewing controversy in Arcadia. Creating Change draws thousands each year and for over twenty years had been supporting LGBT grassroots movements across the nation with this gathering.

The conference was created to provide information and support for those that wanted to "create change" in their communities. People came from all over the United States and included parents, young people, members from LGBT organizations, businesses, churches, and schools. I originally heard about the conference in 2010 because Aiden received a youth leadership award there.

Most of the workshops I attended pertained to making schools safer. That was my passion, so I wanted to learn how I could be a better advocate for this cause. Aiden, Mary, and I shared a room, but saw very little of each other as each of us attended different workshops. Besides safe schools, I wanted to learn more about social networking and media. With a Facebook page, blog and website, I needed to expand my exposure into this area not only for *Two Spirits, One Heart,* but for the high school diploma program I wanted to see grow.

I was learning how to be a more effective activist, and I suddenly discovered that I was networking every moment that I could. This Japanese mother unexpectedly and without much effort was moving into a more conspicuous role. I see now that I didn't consciously choose to be this activist, but I slid into this role by virtue of my desire to help the LGBT community. Thrust into the role, I would have fought it every step of the way; following my passions and dreams, I woke up one morning and realized I was now this person I thought I could never be.

On the evening before we flew home, I attended my final workshop about media. It was presented by two very enthusiastic men who ran MN Progressive Project, a community blogging and political activism online site. Joe Bodell and Eric Pusey shared how they used their site to get their messages out to the public and effect change. Intrigued, I hung on to every word, took plenty of notes and later shared what was occurring in Arcadia. Their ears perked up and they moved forward. This kind of situation piqued their interest. Others in the room seemed to gravitate towards my plight and it felt like many voices were talking at once.

"Well, I think you should shoot a video," one of the presenters said. "You have the perfect branding."

I threw up my hands in horror, as if to fend off danger and threat. "Oh no, that is not me," I replied. "I'm just a mother who is trying to do the right thing, but doing a video . . . I'm not sure that is right for me." And I thought to myself as I was speaking, *Perfect branding? What does that mean?*

"But you have the perfect branding: a fierce, but loving mother," the presenter continued. "It could go viral!"

"Let's go back to your room and shoot the video tonight," the workshop participant sitting next to me chimed in enthusiastically. Rebecca Long Lucas was the President of PFLAG Maryville in Tennessee.

"I wouldn't know what to say," I answered. I felt like I was being led to the edge of a cliff and asked to fly. How could I fly when I had no wings? I would crash and burn, humiliating my family and myself as I plummeted downward. Everyone in the room could feel my reluctance.

"Well, if you decide to do the video, then let us know," one of the presenters said. "We'll put it on our blog."

After seeing my withered reaction, they must have certainly thought the video would never be produced. I know I did not present a picture of fierceness, but this idea rested gently in my heart. *Could I be fierce enough to be that visible?* After the workshop was over, a couple of people came up to me to offer their help. I connected instantly with a gentleman from Chicago whose last name appropriately enough was Love. I exchanged business cards with a number of individuals while still weighing the possibility of doing a video. Coming back to California, I could not stop thinking about this idea.

When I returned home, I learned a counter event was planned for the weekend before the Mayor's Breakfast. A minister in Pasadena offered to host a lunch with some speakers who would "focus on" accepting all families. This event would make a statement to Arcadia and surrounding communities that the messages of Focus on the Family did not reflect the messages of all San Gabriel Valley residents. Gary Searer, another Arcadia young man named Alan and I were asked to speak. A visiting minister and Assemblyman, Anthony Portantino, were added to the program. Assemblyman Portantino had a gay brother who had recently taken his own life and this assemblyman was a strong advocate for the LGBT community. I humbly agreed to speak as long as a box of tissue was sitting on the podium.

However, the nagging feeling launched in Minnesota kept coming up. Could I produce a video that would convince others to write to the Mayor and city council members asking for a speaker that accepted all families? Could I put together something that would infuse more love and acceptance into this breakfast, so even if the Mayor did not change his mind, those in the community would know they were not alone?

Was this possible? I didn't know, but I decided I had to try.

I shared the video idea with my personal assistant, who said that she could shoot the video and have it edited. I emailed my new friend from Chicago and asked for his ideas. "Be short, to the point, and come from your heart" was his response. After numerous takes and some editing, the video was posted on YouTube for all to see. You can view it online at http://www.youtube.com/watch?v=1flMX0jyb0o. The video lasts three minutes, longer than I wanted, but it comes from my heart. Although it did not go viral, about 2,600 people have viewed the video as of this writing.

Once the video was posted, the next step was to get people to see and share it. I posted it on Facebook and then wrote a blog post. I sent personal messages to influential individuals and those who had encouraged me to tape the video. My MN Progressive Project friends posted it, talked about meeting me in their workshop, and encouraged their readers to share it with others, "Amongst the attendees was Marsha Aizumi," they wrote. "She's from Arcadia, CA. She came to MN on a horridly frigid weekend in support of her son who is transgender." Rebecca Long Lucas who wanted to shoot the video immediately, shared the completed video and this comment with her Facebook friends: "I am so proud to call Marsha Aizumi my friend. Your video is everything I knew it would be - honest, loving, and very moving. This is a beautiful gift to families everywhere...ALL families. Thank you for finding the courage to create this beautiful message."

The video was posted on the PFLAG National website and the National Gay and Lesbian Task Force website. One of my dear friends, who lives in a conservative small town in Illinois, shared it on her Facebook page. She got mixed reactions: some of her friends applauded me and talked about love and acceptance, but one Facebook friend condemned my actions to speak out for homosexuals, so Traci deleted her post and then deleted this person as her friend. It touched me so deeply that Traci would risk the anger and judgment of others for my son and me. It represented both her courage and unwavering love for Aiden and me.

I began to get messages from individuals across the nation and even in foreign countries, such as England, Australia, and Uganda. Despite my early uncertainty in producing the video, I could feel the video infusing more love and acceptance into an event that was formerly capable of hurting the LGBT families in our community. I believed I had made a difference in the community, broken through personal fears of being too visible, and allowed my voice to be heard. I felt proud.

Six days before the Mayor's Breakfast, about 100 people gathered for lunch to celebrate all families. For me, this was not only a time to thank the community and organizations that were putting in time and effort to speak out with us in Arcadia, but I thought it was the perfect time to talk about my wonderful family. Here is an excerpt from my speech:

Today, as I look over at Stefen, who stands by his transgender brother as an ally and says, "It doesn't matter who Aiden is, we get along," I think to myself how special is that love. Or my husband who loved his daughter for twenty years, but today loves his new son even more. I see my son, Aiden, who chooses each day to live life courageously as the man who always was inside of him. And finally, I see Aiden's beautiful fiancée, Mary, my future daughter who brought love into Aiden's life, when for years he thought love would never find him. What a gift our family has been given . . . to understand the true meaning of unconditional love and acceptance.

I wanted to look into the eyes of my family as I spoke about each of them, but I could only glance up briefly. Tears welled up inside of me. I knew if I gazed into their beautiful faces, I would begin to weep uncontrollably.

As I scanned the audience, I saw others wiping away tears, feeling the love that filled the room. Perhaps those tears reflected their empathy for me, or perhaps for the love they possessed or didn't possess in their lives. Whatever the case, I wanted my speech to give them hope. I always want to give people hope. I remember what life was like without it.

When I finished my speech, the minister asked for my family to come up front to be introduced. Aiden walked up first and gave me a huge hug. Tad and Stefen strode up and stood at the front of the room. I waved Mary forward, but she shook her head and remained at the table with my personal assistant. I loved sharing this moment with my family, especially Stefen, who often sat so quietly and watched his older brother from afar.

While I sit here writing about Stefen's quiet support of his brother, I remember a moment that defined how much Stefen admired his older sibling. He was about nine and Aiden twelve. Both of them golfed in a church tournament. Since Aiden identified as female at the time, he received endless compliments and praise for his skill and accuracy. Stefen received an occasional "nice shot," but none of the hoopla that surrounded Aiden. When they golfed together, this seemed to be a repeating pattern. On this day, I wanted to make sure that Stefen knew that he had as much talent and value as Aiden. So amidst all this fanfare, I checked in with how Stefen felt.

"Did you feel bad about all the attention that Aiden got today?" I asked.

Stefen turned to me with a quizzical look on his face. "No."

"Did you feel jealous?"

"No"

"Did you feel anything?"

"Yes"

I braced myself for a negative feeling. "What did you feel, honey?"

"I felt proud."

This statement of pride summed up Stefen's relationship with his older brother. Ironic how this is the same word the LGBT community embraces. Stefen shared recently that he never felt like he had to compete with Aiden. Part of this was his loving personality, but the other part was by parental design. Among the many parenting books I read as the kids were growing up, Siblings Without Rivalry by Faber and Mazlish was one of my favorites. Tad and I tried to do whatever we could to foster a relationship filled with respect and acceptance between the two siblings. Even today, with all the attention Aiden garners, Stefen says that he never felt like he had to compete for our love and attention. Thank you, parenting books!!

A couple of weeks later, a protest was planned for the Mayor's Breakfast since the Mayor hadn't brought in a different speaker or invited a second speaker to offset the concerns of those in the LGBT community. Oh, no, I thought. Here I go again. What am I getting myself into? At previous phone meetings with Arcadia protestors, I could sense there were people coming into the city to lend their voices—their loud, angry voices. I cringed, thinking that I would be standing with these radical individuals – or should I say, cowering behind these "anarchists," wondering how I got myself into this situation? But this was my city and my son, so I wanted to be there. I knew

I didn't want to walk away feeling ashamed. I'd be uncomfortable, perhaps, but not ashamed.

Phone conferences and emails flew back and forth, with the majority of the people voicing emphasis on a peaceful demonstration. When others emailed that "peaceful" did not always lead to change, I wrote that I lived in this city and when everyone left, the people living in Arcadia, like my family, would still live in Arcadia. I asked for all protestors to be respectful and participate in an event that I would be proud of. I know that some people disagreed with my message, but I also knew that I could not stand by quietly. I had found my voice, and I had to speak up.

As Tad and I began to talk about making our signs, my reserved husband did not appear uncomfortable at all. That surprised me. Tad wanted to carry a big sign on a stick. His first thought was to write the wording "Have a great breakfast!!" on one side—then flip it around to reveal the words "Have a gay day!!" We weren't sure if that would be offensive, so we changed it to "Have a great LGBT day!!" On the other hand, I wrote a whole page of ideas. I didn't want a stick, which would make my sign too visible. I finally decided to create a sign on bright yellow foam board that said "LGBT Love (using a rainbow heart as a symbol) and Accept All Families." I liked the message, poetic rhyme, and loving feel.

On the day of the Mayor's Breakfast, Tad, my brother, Melissa, Aiden, Mary, and I represented our family. The breakfast started at 7:30, but they wanted us arriving early, especially Arcadia residents who would be speaking to the press.

As we drove by the gathering area at 6:30, a dozen people were already assembled. I felt encouraged. Tad dropped us off, and then drove home to get the video camera, which he'd forgotten. Walking up to the protest area, I noticed one of the students who spoke at the council meeting. She came right up to me and shared that she had been invited to the White House that following week to be part of a meeting on bullying in school. She didn't know how the White House got her name, but she was thrilled. I also heard from others that her father had given her permission to miss part of school to participate in this protest. I thought how fortunate she was to have a father who supported her so completely.

As we waited for guests to arrive, I wandered through the growing crowd and talked with people. A couple of individuals came up to me and said they saw my video. In fact, one young man said he saw the video the night before, and decided he was going to attend—and here he was. His sign included a picture of his partner and their two beautiful children. He came to ask that all families, including his own, be accepted. Our leader, Gary, brought his daughter, who was about six years old. She carried a sign that said "Different is Good!!" with two Dr. Seuss characters, Sneetches—one with a pink triangle on his belly and one without. Aiden and Mary brought along their handmade signs.

We originally estimated that fifty people would attend the protest. A light guess, as it turned out: one newspaper reported a crowd of 150, another 100. Whatever the number, people demonstrated peacefully with police standing guard and an ominous black SWAT vehicle parked in plain sight nearby. Local reporters and photographers captured the event.

As the breakfast guests arrived, protestors chanted and raised their signs up high for all to see. One protestor kept yelling out, "Jesus was no bigot!" That made me uncomfortable. But another protestor who flew down from San Francisco broke the tension with, "I want some breakfast, too!" or "I'll take a latte, too!" We all laughed. Aside from the one angry protestor, the others were all well behaved and polite, per the request of the Arcadia residents.

There were about six individuals from the clergy who protested with us. One came all the way from Oregon. However, it didn't seem like there were that many breakfast guests arriving. At least not the 300 reported ticket purchasers. We found out later that many of the guests were ushered through a back door, away from the protestors. This upset Aiden, and I am sure others. However, we knew that the people attending the breakfast were people who would be supportive of Focus on the Family. Our protest would not sway them. Our goal was to influence the so-called "moveable middle": the moderate voters and citizens who might not be so familiar with LGBT issues.

In the end, I believe we accomplished our goal. We received newspaper coverage from local papers and also write-ups in at least three neighboring papers. We attracted families and individuals from nearby communities. Gary said that he hoped that the Mayor would think twice about whom to invite for the next Mayor's Community Breakfast and using city funds to bring in such a speaker. However, the most important goal for me was that LGBT individuals and families knew that the beliefs of Focus on the Family were not the beliefs supported by all in the community or around the nation. I left the protest feeling like I stood up for equality and acceptance. It felt good.

As the adrenaline from the protest died down, our lives settled back into a more normal routine. The following week, Aiden and I were asked to speak at an Asian Pacific Islander (API) Equality-LA meeting. This group was originally formed to fight for marriage equality in the API community, but later expanded their focus to other areas such as immigration, safe schools, as well as supporting families and LGBT youth through their coming out process. I met the director of this organization while at the Creating Change Conference in Minneapolis. Rev. Dr. Jonipher Kwong was a caring and kind individual who I instantly liked. He reasoned that inviting some Asian residents of Arcadia to share their experiences at the monthly meeting could be very timely, given the protest at the Mayor's Breakfast and since one of their staff, Brian, spoke out against Focus on the Family at one of the Arcadia council meetings. Since this was my first event with mainly Asian Pacific Islanders, I thought it would be interesting to meet other Asians, some of whom came to the protest, and begin to spend a portion of my time supporting the Asian Pacific Islander LGBT community. I knew how hard it was for me to overcome some of the discomfort when Aiden came out. We could be an example of a family that had made it through this "coming out" process. We were also a family willing to share both the joy and heartbreak of our journey.

As usual, I spent a few days writing out a speech and practicing it. Preparation always made me more comfortable. And, as usual, Aiden showed up ready to "wing" it. Sigh . . . .I wish I had that talent! My husband offered to take me to the meeting and I saw two benefits that thrilled me. First, I wouldn't have to maneuver the dark streets of Los Angeles alone at night. Second, Tad could see Aiden speak.

What I didn't anticipate was how the evening unfolded.

After dinner and updates, Aiden and I began our speeches. Tad, Aiden, and I sat together at one end of tables set up in a "U" shape. I turned to my husband and invited him to chime in with any thoughts. He smiled and nodded his head, but I knew he probably wouldn't say a word. Twenty minutes later, our speeches over, the floor opened up for questions. One member directed a curious question to both my husband and me regarding our feelings about Aiden's transition. I don't recall a word I said, because Tad's words burned into my memory. In a voice trembling with emotion, he said, "I loved my daughter so much . . . but I love my son even more. And I am so proud of my son."

My eyes filled with tears, and my heart felt as if it would burst open with love. Aiden's father, reserved and ever so private, publicly declared his love and admiration for his son in front of twenty-five people he barely knew. In spite of the challenging times our family has faced, moments such as this symbolize and typify the extraordinary love that has defined our journey.

Following the meeting at API Equality-LA, I was asked to speak at a "coming out" workshop the following month, designed specifically to reach API youth. The workshop featured three speakers: a young gay man, a young lesbian, and a mother—me. Two health care professionals facilitated the afternoon event. Someone told me very few youth would attend, but in the end, almost thirty young people bravely showed up, wanting to know how they could tell their parents who they really were.

I'm not sure if I can accurately describe how the next four hours opened my eyes to the anguish, fear, and conflict that rips at the heart of those who contemplate revealing their true selves. *Will my parents disown me? Will I lose my job? Will my friends abandon me or make fun of me?* On top of that, I heard about the religious and cultural layers that further threaten to shame and ostracize LGBT individuals from family, friends, churches, and co-workers ~ communities that we all need to belong to, so we do not feel alienated and alone.

In my speech, I couldn't help but cry when I shared my story. Youth in the audience cried or seemed as if they struggled to hold back tears. I knew that the fear and uncertainty gripping them was the same Aiden faced daily until he was able to ask me to accept and love him as the man he was meant to be.

At the end of the workshop, I understood more fully the torment

LGBT individuals face. In the past I had heard stories, but not truly felt the pain. As I glanced around the room, I saw the anguish many had hidden for years. I heard about the lying that undermined their worthiness when their parents asked their lesbian daughter, "Why don't you have a boyfriend?" or asked their gay son, "Why don't you ever have a girlfriend?" Many times these young people have to lie, because lesbians have girlfriends that they can't bring home, or gay boys have boyfriends that they hide from their parents. I saw strong, proud faces break down with suffering. They struggled to be themselves, yet agonize over how sharing their true self can change their world, not for the better, but in a way that creates greater alienation and despair. Meanwhile, I envisioned a world guided less by fear and shame and more by love and acceptance. Perhaps this is why I became driven to write this book. I wanted to change the world—their world—one heart at a time.

As a result of this "coming out" workshop, I began to think of creating a support group for Asian Pacific Islander families. In April 2012, we opened the first San Gabriel Valley Asian Pacific Islander PFLAG satellite group. At our first meeting we had over twenty-five individuals attending: LGBT youth, parents of LGBT children, and many allies from the community who wanted to lend their support to this effort. Believing in this vision were Harold and Ellen Kameya, who actively worked for twenty years to bring a voice to the Asian Pacific Islander community, and now supported me with their wisdom, resources, and network of people. Also working alongside of me were Andre Ting, John and Minsook Brady, Terrenz Vong, Alan Chan, Eric Arimoto, and Bill and Carol Mannion. I would love to see PFLAG support groups across the country providing encouragement, education, and resources for API families. One step at a time I tell myself, even as my mind races ahead to see the next place we can bring support.

On the heels of this "coming out" workshop, I also received a surprising invitation to participate in a White House roundtable on LGBT and Asian Pacific Islander issues. Someone had mentioned to me a few months back that my name had been recommended as a mother of a transgender son. They said Aiden had also been suggested as a possible attendee. Aiden had been contacted; and he decided to decline. I encouraged him to ask for the time off, but found out he and his class had just been given a stern lecture on commitment and failing responsibility to their work. The timing didn't feel right for him to ask that an exception be made, even if it was a White House invitation. In the end only a few young people were given the opportunity to speak, so in retrospect, I believe he felt good about his choice.

Although my name was suggested, I heard nothing and after a couple of months, I thought the event passed without me getting an invitation. I wasn't disappointed, but still thought it would have been a wonderful experience. Perhaps the timing wasn't right for me and another opportunity would arise.

A few days after releasing the possibility, I received an email invitation.

Tad saw the invitation exactly for what it was: the chance of a lifetime. Although I wanted to go with Aiden, I decided I couldn't pass up this opportunity. Aiden had years of activism ahead of him and I sat on the other end of the age spectrum, anticipating retirement. I may never again get a chance like this, so I decided with Aiden or without, I would be at the Roundtable.

A few weeks later, I entered the Eisenhower Executive Office Building (EEOB), located next door to the West Wing. The EEOB houses the majority of the White House staff. I loved the old architecture, and it made me wonder who had walked down the halls earlier that day. I took an elevator and was ushered into a room carpeted in deep red with a familiar rich blue backdrop. Feeling like I entered the set of television's *The West Wing*, I sat in awe with the many Obama Administration staff members who came from the LGBT community.

When I accepted this invitation, I didn't realize what a historic event this would be. But listening to President Obama's Directors, Deputy Directors, and various other staff who work for the Departments of Education, Justice, Health and Human Services, as well as Defense and State, the common thread that I heard was what a milestone they considered this day to be, intersecting both LGBT and Asian Pacific Islander concerns and issues.

The two and a half hour meeting flew by. Five youth shared their moving stories. LGBT staff serving the President shared their personal stories and updates on what was being done to support the LGBT/API community. I brought up issues of alternative safe schools in the form of charters and was able to make connections with a Deputy Director from the Department of Education and a Senior Adviser on White House Initiatives. I wanted to continue discussion on how to create more safe places for youth to obtain their high school diploma, like the program we have in place at the L.A. Gay & Lesbian Center.

My enduring takeaway from the White House meeting emerged clear and strong. Each of us who are standing up for equality, whether LGBT, straight ally, or Asian Pacific Islander brings hope not only to those in our nation, but around the world. That especially rings true for each LGBT individual courageously living their life as their true selves. Today, I understand how much our voices and our presence truly matter. We can never be silent—I can never be silent.

I have learned so much through all of my activism. I found that when passion drives my actions, I find courage I never thought I possessed. I have discovered a love of speaking to groups, sharing my story, and all that I have learned. As a natural introvert, I never thought I would enjoy this visibility. However, when I can speak from my heart and share a story that I believe makes a difference to others, I find a voice that speaks from love and fearlessness.

Most of all, I found that my voice matters. We all come from varied backgrounds and bring our own unique experiences into our daily lives, vocations, and passions. The anger, frustration, and disappointment that others may harshly vocalize, often makes me uncomfortable, but I have tried to understand and empathize with their feelings. I also try to bring my own feelings of love and acceptance into situations, because I believe people will fight less and want to support more when they don't have to defend their point of view against attack. I know I can't change how people think. I can only bring awareness to a situation. By shining a light of love and acceptance, perhaps this will illuminate a dark corner for others to see. In that dark corner, an answer may appear that will provide more understanding, and raise consciousness. That is how I want to change the world.

And yes, Joe and Eric from Minnesota, you were correct. I am a fierce and loving mother. And I can be both brave and bold.

CHAPTER ELEVEN

My Son Finds His Voice

In the midst of all the turmoil we suffered, Aiden frequently felt he would never find his place in the world. I, on the other hand, believed that, with his personality, spirit, and desire to help others, he would find his life's work if he followed his heart. It would only be a matter of time. "Let's concentrate on one thing at a time," I said. "First, you need to get yourself in alignment, then you can find out what you are meant to do."

That's exactly what we did.

By the end of 2009, with Aiden's top surgery behind us and hormone replacement therapy a regular part of his weekly routine, he blossomed into the person he dreamed he could be. As a transgender individual who had chosen not to blend into society as a man, but instead share his experience as a young FTM person, he became a "poster child" who was willing to go out and speak to others about his journey. He spoke on LGBT panels for colleges and high schools. He volunteered at LGBT events. He immersed himself into the LGBT community. The more he gave to the community, the more his self-esteem began to soar. "After transitioning, I didn't identify as a heterosexual male. I identified as an FTM," he said. "I didn't intend to be visible as a transgender individual. People just began asking me to speak and I would say okay. I started to feel like sharing my story meant something to others, so I kept doing it."

Suddenly and miraculously, signs began to appear confirming that he was travelling down the right path. Aiden was sponsored to march in Washington, D.C., asked to be one of the speakers at the opening ceremony for Models of Pride, shared his story at a candlelight vigil, and was selected as a youth leader recipient.

I remember the moment he told me about his leadership award like it was yesterday. I was in my office when Aiden stopped by unexpectedly. A huge grin covered his face. "Hey, Mom! I got a call today that The Trevor Project nominated me for an award at the National Gay and Lesbian Task Force Creating Change Conference. It's in Dallas, Texas!"

"Oh, really, that is nice," I responded, wanting to humbly acknowledge this honor in front of co-workers. The Asian mother in me didn't want to overdo the praise.

"And they picked me for the award!"

"Oh my gosh, Aiden, that is wonderful!" My attention now shifted wholeheartedly into this news. I could not restrain my excitement and I ran up to give him a big hug. I tossed my humble Asian persona to the side and replaced it with that of a mother who wanted to applaud this wonderful news and acknowledge how important this honor was for my son.

We didn't know many details about the award. The only thing we did know was the Paul A. Anderson Award would be handed out at the Creating Change Conference in Dallas; we assumed Aiden would be asked to make some type of acceptance speech. We also did not know much about this conference. In fact, this was the first time I even heard about The Task Force. I quickly learned that the National Gay and Lesbian Task Force had been around for over thirty years and its mission is to build the grassroots power of the LGBT community. I wasn't sure what "building grassroots power" meant, but I wanted to see my son get this award as a youth leader. I didn't want it to seem like I had to tag along wherever he went, but I also felt that an honor this prestigious deserved a family presence to celebrate the occasion with him. I thought if I didn't force myself on him, things would work out.

Without any pressure from me, Aiden asked if I would like to go. I tried not to show my overwhelming joy when I responded "Yes." We asked Papa if he wanted to attend, but Tad, who was not into conventions, begged off, saying that he would stay home with Stefen, who was a senior in high school. Papa would make sure things were being handled on the homefront. That seemed like a good idea.

On February 2, 2010, the day after the open house for the high school diploma program, Aiden and I flew to Dallas, Texas, to attend our first LGBT conference. Not knowing what to expect, we were both anxious and excited. Aiden continued to experience panic attacks that, while less frequent than before, still made him leery of venturing too far from familiar surroundings. However, the fact he was receiving this award among all the nominees across the United States paralleled the hypnotic nature of our Bali trip. Uncertain at times, Aiden pushed through his fear, knowing that the prize at the end would be worth his investment of courage.

At the airport, we saw some of The Trevor Project staff. One of the staff, Phoenix Schneider, was Aiden's mentor through the LifeWorks Mentoring Program and Aiden also served on The Trevor Project Youth Advisory Council. Aiden spent time with the staff from Trevor as I sat and waited for the announcement to board. Thankfully, the flight was uneventful. With Aiden's agoraphobia and panic attacks, I tried to relax, but always felt an underlying uneasiness. I lightened up once we landed in Dallas.

At baggage claim, a group of us met up to share a ride to the hotel. One of the transgender individuals needed to use the restroom. Aiden commented how much anxiety accompanies this simple biological function. Will someone find out that you identify as a man, but still possess parts of you that are female—or vice versa? Will a humiliating confrontation ensue? Worse, will physical violence erupt? I understand this anxiety at a very deep level, but from a mother's perspective. Even today, when I am with Aiden, I worry every time he goes to the restroom. I am aware of the time he is gone. I picture myself running into the restroom to check on my son's safety and hold back the urge to do so, fearing I will just embarrass him. For Aiden is not only a man, but also an adult. I can't protect him every minute nor can I hover over him like a mother hen. But that doesn't stop me from worrying about his safety. So now I wait and count the minutes and watch for his return. I only breathe a sigh of relief when I see him walking back unharmed.

Once I shared my unease with Mary, who always seemed so calm and nonchalant. She said she knows Aiden is careful, so he has to take his time. He must use a stall, which often involves waiting for one to be available, since there are more urinals. Apart from Aiden being hyper vigilant when using the restrooms, he also shared that he must be equally watchful while in the privacy of the stall. There are also differences in sounds between men and women urinating, so he often waits for others to flush the toilet to mask the differences. Anything that may give him away could result in unwanted attention and generate possible confrontation. I don't obsess over the risks that Aiden must face, but when these thoughts rise up to my consciousness, a part of me vows to work harder to make the world more loving and accepting of all human beings, especially the LGBT community.

At the hotel, I registered and received a pleasant surprise: we were upgraded to an executive suite, which meant a bedroom and separate living room and dining room awaited us. How perfect! If Aiden wanted to bring friends to hang out in this suite, as I nestled in my bedroom at night, he'd be free to do so. Many of the young people possessed very little funds, so they crammed themselves into a single room to save money. I imagined that this could be a place where they hung out and had space to relax before returning to sardine-like quarters to sleep.

Aiden and I went down to register for the conference. I attend my share of educational conferences, so I didn't feel like a "newbie." However, walking into this registration area, I became slightly overwhelmed by the enormous space in which the registration was taking place. It was unlike any of the other conferences I attended. It was simply huge. It felt like the size of a football field, although I'm sure it was smaller. And with ceilings that seemed two stories high, I rode down the escalator overlooking this expanse wondering how I would find my way around and wishing I had brought some low-heeled shoes.

The 100-page program booklet confirmed the enormity of this event. I realized that I needed to "study" the booklet to determine which workshop or event I wanted to attend. With about twenty workshops being held in each time slot and five designated time slots per day, I had to choose five workshops per day that spoke to me out of approximately 100.

Naturally, my interest gravitated toward workshops about the transgender community. On the first day, I attended a daylong institute on transgender awareness. I sat and listened intently to everyone's comments, feeling like a sponge soaking up each drop of water available. When noon came, I boldly decided that I would ask someone to have lunch with me. This was so unlike me, but I decided that I needed to network and meet people who could help me open up more LGBT high school diploma programs. I selected a professional looking gentleman who came from a foundation. He already had plans for lunch. Not defeated, I turned around and saw another gentlemen who appeared equally as professionally dressed. I approached him. "Do you have plans for lunch?" Caught off guard, he stared at me momentarily, weighing whether to have lunch with me or not, and then said, "No."

My boldness succeeded in landing me a lunch date with Darrin Wilstead, a Mentoring and Alumni Program Director at the Point Foundation, which provides scholarships, mentorships, leadership training, and hope for students of merit who have been marginalized due to sexual orientation, gender identity, or gender expression.

Darrin and I made a heart-to-heart connection. He is an encouraging, enthusiastic, and warm human being. He suggested Aiden apply for the Point Foundation scholarship, which had a rapidly approaching deadline. Aiden applied, but due to his less than stellar academic background, he did not move forward during the initial process. When I talked to Darrin about Aiden's scholarship application, he encouraged Aiden to apply again the following year and to focus on his grade point average for a year, since his leadership and LGBT involvement were excellent. Aiden brought up his GPA the following year, but another opportunity became available to work at Public Allies; following his heart, he tried out for one of the thirty slots offered. Out of an estimated 650 applicants, Aiden became one of the individuals selected. We took it as a sign that this one-year paid apprenticeship could be a valuable experience working in a career field he wanted to enter. Aiden returned to college in Fall 2011 following graduation from Public Allies.

Coming from the High School Diploma Program Open House, I talked up this project with everyone I met at Creating Change. Even though it was unlike me to reach out to strangers, I found an inner courage to meet with as many people who would help me with this program. Here were individuals who worked in the community. They had resources, knowledge, and connections that I didn't possess. Could they be the next person who would help me open another high school diploma program?

I set up a few meetings between workshops. One such meeting was with Terry Stone, the Executive Director of Centerlink, a non-profit founded in 1994 as a member-based coalition to support the development of strong, sustainable LGBT community centers. Jody Huckaby, Executive Director of PFLAG National, introduced me to him. Terry was a tall, affable individual who listened to my story and the reasons behind my passion to help high school students obtain their high school diplomas. When I shared parts of our journey his eyes teared up. Since he also had a supportive mother who loved and accepted him, my story became personal to him. I liked his vulnerability and sincere kindness immediately. We agreed to meet in a couple of months, so he could see a model of the program at the Los Angeles Gay & Lesbian Center.

After his visit to Los Angeles, he contacted a few local gay and lesbian centers to introduce the program and me. Terry and I met again in 2011 at the same conference to catch up on what each of us was doing. I consider him to be a lifelong friend working together for the LGBT community.

The spotlight and unforgettable memories of the conference culminated with Aiden's acceptance of the Paul A. Anderson Youth Leadership Award. In honor of The Trevor Project staff that nominated him, Aiden was going to wear an orange tie (Trevor's signature color) with a black suit and black shirt. After top surgery, we had shopped for the perfect suit for the new man.

In typical Aiden Aizumi form, prior to arriving at the conference, he had no acceptance speech written. "No worries!" he said. After watching him speak at other events, I knew he spoke best when he didn't overly rehearse. His charismatic personality revealed himself at those times and he was comfortable with the last-minute scramble to prepare and speak on LGBT topics. On the day of the award ceremony, he had not yet written his speech nor even written notes. In the past, I would have been on him to get something down on paper, but he said that he was going to prepare this time, so I trusted that would be the case. I attended my carefully selected morning workshops and returned to the room, finding Aiden hunched over the table, papers strewn around, and an intense focus in his gaze.

As he finished writing a short, two to three-minute acceptance speech, he asked if I would listen to it and give him my impressions. He began to read what he had written and I realized quickly how far he had come and what a magical journey this had been for him, for me, and for our family as he spoke about his depressing, withdrawn world years ago and the man that lived in him today. I wiped away a few tears as he completed his speech, however a swell of emotions stayed within me: mostly pride, but immeasurable gratitude as well.

I gave Aiden a few thoughts about his speech and he incorporated them. But I kept any changes to a minimum. He didn't need his speech rewritten an hour before his presentation. And his speech was really perfect: vulnerable, to the point, and written from his heart.

Aiden said that he wanted some private time to practice his speech and get ready. I decided to go down early, find the room where the plenary session and awards were to be handed out, and hoped to capture the perfect seat to witness this special moment. I walked down the corridors of the hotel and entered the elevator with pure emotion still quivering gently throughout my body. *Thank goodness I know what Aiden is going to say, so I won't be a blubbering mess at the awards ceremony,* I thought as I stepped off the elevator and headed toward the main ballroom.

As I arrived at the ballroom, I noticed that the doors were closed. I started towards the door anyway, thinking they may be closed but not locked. A woman stepped in front of me and indicated the room wasn't open yet.

Still picturing a front row seat, I paced in front of the area and finally said something shyly to the woman guarding the door so she wouldn't think I had nowhere to go and nothing important to do but wait for these doors to open. "I'm kind of excited to get a front row seat."

The woman just stared at me.

"My son is getting an award and I want to be sure I can take pictures of the moment."

The woman perked up. "Are you Aiden Aizumi's mother?"

"Yes," I said warily, wondering from where this newfound enthusiasm in her voice came.

Whipping out her walkie-talkie, she said in an official voice, "I have Aiden Aizumi's mother here at the door waiting to enter. May I let her in?"

"Yes," crackled through the walkie-talkie and she escorted me to the doors.

Not having attended any of the previous plenary sessions, I walked into the ballroom and almost inhaled audibly. The room was massive, set up for somewhere in the neighborhood of 1,000 people. The stage spanned almost half of the front of the room, with multiple huge screens as a backdrop. The screens enabled those in the back rows to see what was happening on stage. There was a crew inside the room playing with the lighting of pink and purple, official colors of The Task Force, testing sound and moving multiple cameras around, not only by hand, but by large robotic arms. While being escorted to my seat, I imagined this was what the Academy Awards felt like and what a Best Actor or Actress nominee experienced.

I chose a seat a little bit to the left of the podium. Some Task Force board members approached me, introduced themselves, and thanked me for coming to the conference to support my son. Even though I know there are many LGBT parents who do not support their children, it still felt strange to be appreciated for something that I think is a normal part of being a mother. I wouldn't have missed this for anything.

About ten minutes later, the doors officially opened and the crowds poured in. The Trevor staff took front row seats next to me and we began to converse lightly. Then the awards program began. They announced the recipients one by one. Each recipient came up, gave a speech, received their award, and exited. I waited anxiously, wondering how Aiden was doing backstage, knowing that he still suffered from anxiety attacks. I turned around and saw the hundreds of faces that Aiden would see in the audience and brushed away any thoughts of him fleeing the ballroom due to his agoraphobia. *He will be fine.*

And then it was time to announce the Paul A. Anderson Award for Youth Leader. Darlene Nipper, Task Force Deputy Executive Director, began with a short bio on Aiden and then announced his name. I clapped harder than I thought possible. I'd never been prouder of my son. The emotions welled up inside me again. This time the feelings gained strength. *I can't cry yet,* I thought. *He hasn't said a word.* But inside I wanted to weep for happiness.

The applause died down and he started his speech.

"Actually before I get started, I did want to share someone really important to me who is here . . ."

Oh my gosh, is he going to introduce me? My hands instinctively flew up to my face, as if in disbelief.

"My mom."

The ballroom erupted in applause for me. As I stood to be acknowledged, I could see out of the corner of my eyes that Aiden had his arms wide open, waving them upward, urging the audience to clap louder. I cried as I waved to the crowd. When I turned around to be seated, Aiden and I made eye contact. With a shrug of his shoulders and eyes that said, "This moment is for you," Aiden gave me the warmest, most loving smile I had ever seen on his face.

That moment, that smile, and that twinkle in his eyes have been etched in my heart ever since. I have replayed that look on his face more times than I can count. In that second, I saw that all my love, worry, and thoughts about "am I doing the right thing, saying the right words, following the right paths" were answered. My fears and my guilt melted away. My son would always have this memory to tell him who he was and that his life mattered ～ he was being acknowledged and celebrated for his courage, contribution, and leadership. I witnessed every step leading to this honor.

Below is a portion of Aiden's acceptance speech. I will never forget how proudly he stood and how confidently he spoke.

I wanted to tell you a little bit of where my passion, my motivation for what I do for the community comes from. It involves a little bit of a story. It's a story about this sixteen- year-old sophomore in high school who comes out of the closet in a relatively conservative high school. During the next couple of years, (he) goes through some physical and some verbal abuse. As those years go on (and) the senior year rolls around, he's diagnosed with agoraphobia and in addition to that panic disorder. And being so uncomfortable outside of the walls of his house, withdraws inward, becomes a cutter, and (is) severely depressed. And because of those problems, has a hard time graduating. The person in this story holds a place very special and close to my heart, because every time I think of that person... I see him in the mirror... that same sixteen-year-old was me.

I remember when I turned sixteen, I didn't think I would ever make it to see twenty-one. And it is why I feel especially close to the work that I do for Trevor and for what The Trevor Project stands for. But I stand before you now, twenty-one years old and many miles from my house in Los Angeles and I would not have been able to do that and overcome those problems without the support of the people in the community here. It's the work that we're doing here that is making this world a better place for us now and for future generations of LGBT youth.

As Aiden closed his speech, he turned to thank The Trevor Project for their nomination. His voice stalled momentarily as he attempted to hold back the emotion that was starting to build within. And then he gave a final thank you to The Task Force for his award and creating such an amazing conference. With those words, he walked off the stage to applause from the audience.

One or two other awards were given out and then the plenary closed with a youth panel presentation. After the plenary session, Aiden posed for photos with the Executive Director of The Task Force, Rea Carey. Rea exhibits grace and power, compassion and passion as a charismatic leader who began as Deputy Executive Director of the National Gay and Lesbian Task Force in 2004 and was promoted to Executive Director in 2008. Aiden took pictures with me, Lorri Jean of the Los Angeles Gay & Lesbian Center, and other Task Force staff and board members. Later, as we walked around the conference area, people came up and congratulated Aiden, while they thanked me for supporting my son. I received comments from young and old. One individual in his forties came up to me and said, "I wished my mom supported me like you support your son. He's lucky!" I reflect on that moment now and think, *No, I'm the lucky one.* Aiden is still alive. Through all my ignorance, avoidance, and fear, my son decided that life was worth living. I am blessed beyond words.

The rest of the conference felt like a blur as I spent the final days making my way through the remaining workshops. I attended an Asian Pacific Islander caucus, meeting new individuals. I sat around a table at the closing day breakfast and watched people congratulate Aiden for the award he received the day before. As the conference came to an end, I felt more certain that this was the place, the people, and the cause for which I wanted to dedicate the rest of my life. Aiden sparked the flame in me to get involved, but the flames of my activism were fanned by the gratitude that I carried toward all the individuals who so bravely carved this path for Aiden and me to follow. Today, I feel a passion I never thought existed within me. It continues to grow stronger and stronger each day. And where once I wondered if I could make a difference in my lifetime, I now know that I have found a place to leave my mark, as small and as humble as it may be.

Following the conference, our lives settled back to the everyday routine of working, continuing our activism, and Aiden returning to school. Three months later, I met with an editor, who sensed right away that *Two Spirits, One Heart* was a book that needed to be written. "You need to begin now," he said. And so I did.

Then, during the summer, an intriguing concept crept into Aiden's world. He began to pursue a paid apprenticeship with Public Allies, an organization whose mission is to advance new leadership to strengthen communities, nonprofits, and civic participation. The organization believes everyone can lead, and that lasting social change results when citizens of all backgrounds step up, take responsibility, and work together. Aiden knew the apprenticeship would amount to an intense ten months. Working forty-plus hours per week, going to school in the evening, and attending all the required meetings, trainings, and service projects definitely felt like a grueling commitment. As an added incentive, if Aiden completed the program, he would receive a five thousand five hundred dollar stipend to help pay off student loans or assist with future college expenses.

To apply for this program, though, Aiden would have to step out of his comfort zone big time. First, he would need to leave the safety of a position he had held for over five years with people who had seen him through panic attacks, agoraphobia, and transitioning from female to male. Secondly, he would need to compete against a large number of applicants for about thirty available positions. One of the organizations applying to be a placement non-profit with Public Allies was LifeWorks. LifeWorks is the organization that partnered with Opportunities for Learning Public Charter

School and matched Aiden with a mentor. This non-profit also provided a welcome place for LGBT youth to interact socially with other youth at the L.A. Gay & Lesbian Center. Aiden knew the program well, since previously he participated in many of their activities as a young person. Now he wanted to work for the program through Public Allies. LifeWorks definitely wanted to apprentice Aiden, but two things needed to happen. First, Aiden needed to make it through the application process and attend a "matching" fair. Second, LifeWorks needed to be selected as a placement non-profit.

Aiden's first hurdle was the interview panel: 150 candidates out of 650 applicants would be interviewed. Aiden hoped he did well enough to be chosen as one of the 150, which he was. However, the competition grew stronger and more intense. Aiden competed against many highly qualified individuals who already held college degrees. How could he be chosen over those with such outstanding educational backgrounds? He only had a high school diploma and a handful of college credits. Aiden wanted this opportunity, but feared that his qualifications would not measure up.

The field then narrowed to 75 after the interviews. The second hurdle was a group project where individuals were observed on their participation, interaction, and contribution.

"Momma, I made it to the second round!" Aiden informed me one day. "Next comes some kind of group project that they will observe us working together on. I am not sure what we are supposed to do, but I guess I'll find out."

"That sounds interesting. Just be yourself and I am sure things will work out fine." And I was sure they would.

The final hurdle was the matching fair. Only 45 finalists would be interviewed by the various non-profits chosen to be part of the Public Allies program for 2010-2011. The matching process was interview-based. Following the interviews, the organizations listed their top candidates, and the finalists listed the top non-profits for which they would like to work. If the organization's number one candidate matched the candidates' number one non-profit, it was a match. If there wasn't a number one to number one match, then they would go to number one to number two or number two to number two.

Aiden was selected to go to the matching interviews. He had made it to the final round!!

Since Aiden had not been informed that LifeWorks had been chosen as a sponsoring organization, he needed to attend the matching fair and hope he would be matched. Dressed in his suit, he sat opposite one non-profit organization answering questions. As he examined the room, he noticed that LifeWorks was not present at the matching event. How disappointing! He had hoped to be matched with this LGBT youth organization, and now they were not even selected to be a sponsoring organization. As he prepared to find out which non-profit would conduct his second interview, one of the Public Allies staff pulled him aside.

"Aiden, you don't have to go through this process."

"I don't?"

"No, you have already been matched with LifeWorks, so you are free to go."

Jumping for joy within, Aiden left the matching fair knowing that the organization with which he wanted to work felt the same about him. In the end, only 28 first-time candidates were matched out of 650 applicants. He was one of the 28 new Public Allies. What an accomplishment!

Aiden knew that the next ten months of his life were going to be challenging. He needed to work forty hours—or sometimes more—for LifeWorks to fulfill a 1,700-hour Public Allies requirement. On some days after work, he attended college classes at Los Angeles Trade Technical College. The group also broke down into smaller teams, and each team needed to complete a service project. Teams were committed to three service days throughout their apprenticeship. On top of all these requirements, there were mandatory trainings three times per month, often delving into deep vulnerable topics.

Listening to all of this, I knew it would be a demanding ten months, often pushing my son to the limits of what he thought himself capable of doing. However, if Aiden could be open and honest during this apprenticeship, I felt it could be a wonderfully growing and empowering experience as the workshops presented opportunities for deep self-reflection. In addition, many of the workshops provided a chance for his team members to give him direct feedback about how he showed up in the group and where he could show up more. Having participated in a number of seminars over the years, I knew that some concepts could change the way you saw yourself and the world when they were understood and digested. I hoped that would be the case for Aiden.

Throughout the months, I heard the good, bad, and very ugly from him. The hours demanded all of his time and energy. Sometimes he dragged himself to our house when invited for dinner, complaining about how hard it was to work so much without a break. Mary didn't see too much of Aiden, so she joined in with her displeasure. Once he wailed, "With all the hours I am putting in, I don't even make minimum wage!"

However, I noticed the continual growth. My son sounded ever more confident in the person he was becoming. Often intimidated in the past when faced with confrontation, Aiden now seemed to be more grounded in his direction and place in this world. He was more comfortable standing up for himself and speaking his truth, even working with those very close to him in age. I always saw him as wise, intuitive, and possessing an awareness far beyond his years. Now others were beginning to see that side of him as well, because he shared what he observed, felt, and believed. Tad and I would talk about this part of Aiden with amazement. Now certain of whom he was, a man living in a man's body, he could look around and decide where he wanted to fit in this world.

In the end, listening to what he learned about himself and others, I wished that I had had the opportunity to experience a program like this when I was younger.

One day, I went to visit him at his new apartment. "Hey Momma, do you want to see my POL (Presentation of Learning) DVD?" he asked.

"Sure."

As I sat down in front of the television to watch his POL DVD, I could only see the video, as the audio was poor. The acoustics in the room were terrible and Aiden had no microphone, so the combination of the echo and terrible audio made it difficult to understand his words. But watching my son smile shyly as he talked confidently to this group for ten minutes reiterated how much he had learned and grown in the past ten months.

At the end of the video, I asked, "What did you talk about during this presentation?"

"I talked about the ways I have grown over the past ten months."

"And what were those things?"

"Well, I have learned I have a voice," he said pensively. "And I discovered my self-worth,"

I wanted to know more, but Aiden's voice trailed off and his attention turned elsewhere.

I decided to file it away for future conversations.

About a week later, Aiden dropped by and seemed in a talkative mood.

"Remember last week, when you were talking about your POL?"

"Yes."

"What kind of voice did you discover you had?" I asked

"I think it is a powerful and passionate voice...one that is growing in confidence."

"What else did you learn from your Presentation of Learning?"

"Before transition, I didn't feel worthy of anything. Then I transitioned and my self-worth began to grow. Now with Public Allies, my self-worth has risen to the point where I see myself becoming a confident leader."

At the time of this writing, Aiden is twenty-three. I can't imagine what it would be like to be his age and understand what he has already learned.

The culmination of this ten-month experience was his graduation ceremony. Aiden was given five tickets, so Papa, Mary, Aiden's future in-laws, and I received invitations. Stefen said it was okay that he didn't have a ticket. However, Stefen's spirit was definitely represented through some unexpected circumstances that happened right before the event.

A casual remark made by Aiden caused me stop for a moment: "Since I didn't really have a graduation from high school, this will be kind of like my graduation." I realized what a big deal this event represented, much more than I had initially thought. Immediately, I began to think of the graduation that Aiden never had and started to plan how to make this evening special for him. First, he would need a lei. We had given Stefen one when he graduated from high school. Then we would order some balloons.

A post-graduation dinner would bring this evening to a nice end, so that became the plan.

The night before the PA graduation, as I got ready for bed, I stopped mid-step. *I forgot to order the lei and balloons! How could I forget?* The next day, I had a retirement luncheon, then my retirement party, then Aiden's graduation. How was I going to find a lei on such short notice?

Enter Stefen. Everything came together because his graduation gift to Aiden was his running around to pick up everything then delivering them to my office so that I could leave my retirement party and go directly to Aiden's graduation. A mother's personal disaster was averted with the support of her son.

When Tad and I arrived at the graduation, Aiden met us. "Can you hold this certificate that I received?" As I took it from him, I snuck a quick glance: "Most Inspirational."

"What is this for?" I asked him.

"My PA class voted for people and then we got these certificates."

"So your class voted you 'Most Inspirational'?"

"Yeah, me and one other person got this award."

"Wow, Aiden, that is quite an honor!"

"Uh huh." He walked away, responding in typical male form.

We took a front-row table. A nice tray of cheese, crackers, fruit, veggies and dip sat in the center of the table. I watched Aiden mingling with his classmates, smiling and so at ease. He came back to check in with us, but then he disappeared to get ready for the evening to begin.

The program started with some speeches and performances by graduating Public Allies...a skit, a poem, and a couple of songs. Sponsoring organizations received recognition. Finally, the moment we came for: the presentation of the graduates. Each graduate was announced individually, walked on stage, and received a plaque, water bottle, and embroidered bag with the Public Allies name and logo. Classmates, family, and sponsoring organizations cheered for each graduate. But when Aiden's name was called, an extra burst of energy filled the room. The extra energy probably came from me—Aiden finally got to graduate.

In some ways, Public Allies provided closure for Aiden and me. We could look back and know that, although he did not walk at his high school graduation or attend his all-night party five years before, he did graduate from Public Allies, a program that recognized and developed leaders. I am so grateful to Public Allies for giving Aiden this opportunity. I also believe the "Most Inspirational" award that he received was a statement on how far his journey had taken him. No longer a scared, confused, and depressed young person, he confronted fear, took risks, and found his voice as a leader.

Brene Brown, in her book, *The Gifts of Imperfection*, says, "Owning our story can be hard, but not nearly as difficult as spending our lives running from it. Embracing our vulnerabilities is risky, but not nearly as dangerous as giving up on love and belonging and joy...the experiences that make us the most vulnerable. Only when we are brave enough to explore the darkness will we discover the infinite power of light."[2]

I see my son today and notice the power of his light. In his walk, his smile, his attitude, and his dreams, an aura surrounds him as never before. He has found his voice. Oh, how wonderful that voice sounds to this mother.

CHAPTER TWELVE

Believing in Love Again

One of the moments that I will remember the rest of my life, is the day that Aiden confessed he would sacrifice finding love in favor of transitioning to be the man he felt lived inside him. When those words were spoken, I understood that at the core of his being, transitioning was not an option, but a crucial step for his future happiness. He would give up love to live a life of truth. At the same time, I believed with his wonderful spirit, he would find someone who adored him, saw his many gifts, and recognized the courage it took for him to live authentically.

At times, I would falter from this belief, replaying his past relationships and seeing how he'd faced discrimination from others who judged him from afar. I remembered the parents of girls he dated. Their rejection and disdain for him as a lesbian made me sad, projecting into the future a life where his wife would be caught in the middle of loving him and pleasing her parents. I didn't live in bleakness, but I also wanted to be realistic to the challenges he might face. I knew no transgender individuals in relationships, except some I had seen in movies or documentaries. Aiden even made a comment after watching one documentary which echoed my unspoken thoughts: "Gee, Momma, all those trans people are with people that are so much older, or seem to have problems." Many of the partners of transgender individuals interviewed were quite a bit older or seemed socially and emotionally damaged by their own struggles. I could see the wheels of Aiden's mind processing: *Will I have to settle for someone twenty years older than I am or someone who is so desperate for someone to love?* Since then, I have met countless transgender individuals in loving and healthy relationships. My fears vanished over time.

After Aiden's breakup with Julianna in 2008, he confided in me that he would not rebound into another relationship. He vowed not to be impetuous—his natural inclination. He promised himself that grasping at someone again and thinking she may be the only person in the world that could love him wouldn't happen. He seemed to be comfortable and confident in this decision. I supported him 100%.

During this period, Aiden seemed too busy and occupied with other matters to enter into a serious relationship.

However, prior to his breakup with Julianna, Aiden became friends with a girl named Mary. They met at a PFLAG Young Adult Group. Mary's first impression of Aiden was strong. "He seemed like such a genuine person with a wealth of experiences and wisdom...someone I could be friends with. I was looking for friends in the LGBT community." Aiden liked Mary's easygoing ways and playful attitude. Unlike Julianna, who seemed to be critical of Aiden and all he did, Mary enjoyed Aiden's sense of humor and childlike wonder. She laughed easily with him, empathized deeply when he worried or became anxious, and appreciated his caring heart. Although Aiden didn't think Mary liked him in the beginning, their friendship grew as they continued to attend the monthly PFLAG support group meetings, and then grabbed a bite to eat after each meeting. Following Aiden's breakup with Julianna, they began to hang out at our house every Sunday night to watch *The L Word*. They didn't see each other much during the week, except if a PFLAG meeting occurred, but when they were together on Sunday nights, they cuddled and enjoyed each other's company.

One day Aiden came to me and said, "I think Mary likes me, but I am not ready to get in a relationship. What do you think I should do?"

"Well, do you like spending time with her as a friend?"

"Yes."

"Does she know how you feel?"

"Kind of."

"Is she getting mixed signs because of the cuddling?"

"Maybe."

"Then, I feel you have to tell her the truth. You like to cuddle, but you are not ready to be in a serious relationship."

"Okay," he responded reluctantly.

I knew Aiden was thinking an honest conversation might change their relationship. Since he didn't have anyone special in his life, the thought of losing this friend wasn't appealing to him. But I also knew that he would do the right thing, and he did. Aiden remembers, "She told me she liked me and I was pretty sure I liked her, too, but I didn't want to confuse those feelings with just trying to fill the void of being alone." Mary recalls that she really liked Aiden, but the timing didn't seem right. What she needed at the time were friends and a support system, since she had recently come out to her parents as a lesbian. She found both of those things through PFLAG and Aiden. "Aiden was someone who I felt I could talk to, someone I found I could totally be myself around...there was not a single part of me that I felt I needed to hide."

I questioned the relationship privately in my head. If she was a lesbian and Aiden was transitioning to male, how would that work? Would she eventually turn away from Aiden as he became more and more male? Was she mistaking the comfort and ease of their relationship as something more than being just good friends? And was Aiden attracted to Mary because she accepted and felt so at ease with him now? Would things change as he became more masculine? I kept those questions to myself. Time would determine the direction, but for now Aiden had someone to spend time with and enjoy her company.

Like Aiden, Mary's life had amounted to an ongoing series of challenges. Starting at the age of nine months, she lost all of the hair on her head due to Alopecia Areata, an autoimmune disease, in which the immune systems attacks hair follicles. Soon afterwards, she lost her eyebrows and eyelashes, which eventually returned when she was seven. The first couple of years of elementary school, Mary's mother would go into her classes at the beginning of the year and talk to the class about Alopecia. In some ways, this shielded Mary from the harassment and taunting from her classmates, but she continued to endure the stares of others outside of her classes. This resulted in Mary being a more private individual, so she and Aiden shared a knowingness, an understanding about withdrawal and isolation. However similar to Aiden, Mary had an optimistic and accepting heart that would emerge in times of comfort and trust.

Another thing that Aiden and Mary shared was heartbreaking past relationships that raised their walls of mistrust. Like Aiden's relationship with Julianna's mother, Mary experienced more moments of discomfort and disapproval than feelings of positivity and acceptance with parents of girlfriends. However, Aiden and Mary each gathered strength and hope from those relationships, which was important at the time. Mary says that her problematic relationship played a large role in her coming out. In the end, both Aiden and Mary used their difficult relationships to springboard them into more healthy partnerships, learning and growing from them rather than letting the relationship defeat and define them.

Today, Mary still has no hair, except small patches that she shaves off. She has tried wearing wigs, but is not comfortable with them, especially since she is a swimmer. Her parents never forced wigs upon her. "I was allowed to be bald and proud of it. I haven't worn a wig since 1999." Initially, I was afraid I might say something wrong. With Tad owning a hair salon and beauty supply business, a comment about hair or hair products could likely come up, but we all laugh if a comment is made inadvertently about hair or lack of it. With our relationship growing in love and trust, a comfort has emerged between us all.

After Aiden's talk with Mary, he informed me that she recognized where he stood. I could tell he was relieved. He liked Mary, but he just needed time to see where the relationship headed without the baggage of his last breakup. I felt good that he considered her feelings, spoke directly to her about the relationship, and expressed his truth in spite of the possibility of losing her as a friend. This unselfish act showed that he cared a lot for Mary.

The Sunday night cuddling went on for about seven months. Mary was in a rigorous master's degree program in school psychology at a private university, so her week was occupied with studies, internship hours, and attending classes. She also squeezed in time to serve as a high school and college swim coach. Aiden seemed happy with this arrangement as well, since he was busy with school, work, and his activism.

During these months of being "friends," Mary would join our family occasionally. On the first Thanksgiving dinner to which Aiden brought her, she was slightly taken aback. After being introduced, my sister-in-law Leslie enthusiastically said, "Mary, oh, MARY, you remember Mary!" Leslie turned to my brother Marty for affirmation.

Marty appeared puzzled and said, "Mary?"

"Yes, Mary, you remember Mary?"

This banter went back and forth. Mary's name was repeated so many times that we all sat dumbfounded, our heads moving from Leslie to Marty and back again as we watched this scene unfold. I'm certain that Mary was even more overwhelmed, not knowing our family very well. Apparently, my niece Lindsay and Mary were in the same preschool class. Leslie said she always remembers Mary's smile and cheerful outlook in spite of her lack of hair and was struck by how resilient this little girl seemed to be. The "Mary" event became an icebreaker that threw Mary into our family. She became a welcomed guest at all our family events, even though she and Aiden hadn't moved beyond the friendship stage.

That changed a month before we traveled to San Francisco for top surgery. Aiden informed me that he wanted to take a step toward becoming boyfriend and girlfriend, since enough time had passed for him to know he liked her and she wasn't a rebound relationship from Julianna. He asked me how he should approach it.

I began to spout out what I thought would be a good approach to take. Aiden's eyes glazed over. My motherly approach plainly was not his style. He responded simply, "That doesn't sound like me." He added he would figure something out before the weekend, when he and Mary would hang out again. I planned to be out of town on an annual overnight "slumber party" with Joan and two other friends, so I told him I would envision a good outcome and we left it at that.

That weekend, my three girlfriends and I sat comfortably in our room, catching up on the past year's news. The subject turned to Aiden.

I shared what had been going on with him and his transition, the highs, lows, and everything in between. One of my girlfriends, Janet, turned to me and said, "Could Aiden have picked a better mom to see him through these challenges?" I wanted to throw my arms around her with appreciation. During all these years of struggle, being the best mom, the good mom, or the better mom had never been my self-image. So many days I considered myself the terrible mom, the ignorant mom, the mom who didn't care enough. And I felt so alone, as if no one else in the world was going through what I was experiencing, apart from Tad. I, like Aiden, suffered in silence for many years.

Janet's words meant so much to me. I don't remember saying anything in response. I think I feared a breakdown, complete with sobbing and hysterical tears. I smiled warmly and appreciatively. The conversation moved on.

I told my three friends that tonight was going to be very special for Aiden. I explained the reasoning behind Aiden and Mary just being friends and how the relationship had developed over the past months. Joan, almost a second mother to Aiden, Auntie Janet and Auntie Cheryl enthusiastically thought that Mary would say yes. I felt the same way. However, I still sat on pins and needles, knowing that if my intuition faltered, it would be devastating for Aiden. I hoped he would call me, his normal pattern, but also realized that with me being out of town with girlfriends, he might assume that I'd be preoccupied.

The hours ticked by. Finally at 11:00 P.M. I excused myself to give him a call. "Hey, Aiden, how did it go with Mary tonight?"

"Oh, hi, Mom," he answered with a tense voice, sounding very flustered and restrained at the same time. "I'm right in the middle of something here."

"Oh my gosh, are you asking her right now?"

"Yeeeessss."

"Okay, bye."

I waited up a little while longer, but Aiden never called me back. I fell asleep wondering, *Did Mary say yes?*

The next morning, as we dressed for breakfast, I couldn't wait another minute. I decided to call him. My girlfriends, also curious, continued getting themselves ready but kept their ears alert for the results of Aiden's big night.

"Hi, honey. Sorry about last night."

"Yeah, your timing was awful. I was just getting up the courage to ask Mary, when you called."

"Well, tell me what happened?"

"She said yes!"

I cupped my hand over the phone and turned to my friends, "Mary said yes!"

My girlfriends responded with cheers: "All right, Aiden," "Woo-hoo!" "That's great!"

Being the mother who liked details, I asked, "What did you say?"

"I just started talking about being single and that I didn't want to be single any more. Now I wanted to be in a relationship. Then I asked Mary, 'Do you not want to be single? Would you like to be a couple with me?' And she said yes!"

"That is so wonderful! I am so proud of the way you handled everything."

So on May 15, 2009, for the first time as a man, my son had a girlfriend who adored him. I was thrilled for him. He could believe in love again!

Still unsure of how the relationship would develop with Mary identifying as lesbian and Aiden soon to be declared a man (top surgery was scheduled for the following month), I cautiously broached the subject with both of them when we were hanging out one day.

"Can you explain something to me," I began very softly. "If Mary is a lesbian and Aiden, you are a man, how does that work?"

Both looked at each other and then Aiden replied, "Well, we don't get it either. All we know is that we like each other and it works."

"Okay" I replied. If it worked for them, then it was good enough for me. Today, Mary identifies as a queer individual, which means she believes she doesn't see herself fitting into a traditional heterosexual relationship. That works for Aiden, since he does not hide that he is a transgender person. And in the end, does it really matter? They have found each other and they love each other. Isn't that more important?

Mary was scheduled to graduate with her master's degree in May 2010, so they faced another year of busy schedules. I watched the relationship blossom as the months passed by. Mary says, "We built our relationship on a strong friendship. Being a couple has been amazing!" Aiden added, "It's kinda crazy. We were basically dating before without knowing it. We always just had fun."

The one significant difference in this relationship, which quickly became apparent, was how Mary's parents and family treated Aiden. Aiden talked about family events that he would attend or times he would visit Mary's parents. With a huge smile on his face he would say, "Mary's uncle says if we ever break up, I am still invited to their house." Or "Mary's mom and grandmother really like me and her dad is always joking with me, which Mary says he only does with people he likes."

At one PFLAG meeting where Mary's father and mother would attend, I encouraged Tad to come along with me. I had not met them yet, so some twinges of anticipation occupied my thoughts. I could tell they were good people with caring and accepting ways. What I observed most was how kindly they treated my son. Mary's mother hugged him as if he were family, and Mary's father had an easygoing way around Aiden. People were commenting, "Oh, the parents are meeting now... Hmmm... Is something serious developing between Aiden and Mary?"

In some ways, Mary and Aiden's relationship signaled a huge change in Aiden and my relationship. He was beginning to find his way without me and it felt bittersweet. I would miss the closeness we had always shared, but I also saw him starting to mature into his own person. With or without me, I knew he would be fine now. And then seeing Mary's mother and later grandmother pulling my son into a warm embrace, I could see him venturing out into the world and possibly building his own family. He was growing up and no longer needed his mother looking out for him. I could release him to the world and know he would now carve his own path. We would always be on a journey together, but perhaps now our paths would separate, converge, and then separate again. It was time for Aiden to soar.

With Mary and our family, things were different. There wasn't that easygoing flow that I saw with Aiden and Mary's parents. I sensed her reluctance to let her guard down with us. I didn't know where it came from. I suspected that with her Alopecia, she needed to protect herself from judgment, so I patiently allowed her to move slowly towards us. We were welcoming and inclusive, but tried not to overwhelm her. She remained at a slight distance for months—not rude or detached, just cautious and quiet, watching Aiden and following his lead on what was acceptable.

After Aiden and Mary were together for a year, we planned a trip to San Francisco. I imagined getting to know Mary better in the car travelling together and sharing stories. Aiden hoped we would go up together. But my ideal picture of this trip dissolved when Aiden said that they wanted to take their own car. I left the conversation disappointed and unsure why they didn't want to travel with Tad and me.

I decided this meant a mother and son heart-to-heart. "Aiden, have Papa and I done something to cause Mary not to trust us? Have we said something to hurt her feelings?"

"I don't think so, Momma. Why?"

"Well, why don't you and Mary want to ride with Papa and me up to San Francisco?"

"We want our own car to have the freedom to go visit friends and see the things we want to see."

"Papa and I can rent a car when we get up there. He was hoping you could drive part of the way, so he wouldn't have to do all the driving. I was hoping we could spend the time together and get to know Mary better. If you want to go on your own, that is fine, but I think Papa and I would rather stay home if that is the case." I tried to speak softly, so he wouldn't think it was an ultimatum. I wanted him to know that being together was my purpose for this trip."

"Let me talk with Mary and see what she thinks."

Aiden got back to me a couple of days later and said that he and Mary would go with us, so he could help Papa drive. I felt better, but a gnawing feeling remained in my stomach—a sure sign that I needed to communicate further. I decided to talk with Mary.

A few days later, I approached her gently. Asking if we could speak for a minute, I said, "I was wondering if Tad or I did something to make you feel uncomfortable with us. You seem unsure about travelling with us. Have we said anything that hurt your feelings? If we did, I am sorry."

"No, you haven't done anything," she replied directly, but with little emotion in her voice.

"Then can I ask why you didn't want to go in the same car with us to San Francisco?"

Mary explained that she had a very painful experience with a past relationship, and having her own transportation gave her a sense of security and a feeling of some control. She didn't go into much detail and left it at that. Months later, she shared a few more details.

At the age of nineteen or twenty, she was invited by a girlfriend to go on a family weekend trip to Catalina Island. The first day proved to be filled with unwelcoming and uncomfortable energy, but nothing prepared her for what occurred next. The mother told her daughter that Mary had to return home because the family no longer wanted her around. Feeling totally rejected, Mary boarded a boat the next morning alone, deeply humiliated. When she shared this story with me, I began to understand her reluctance to travel with us. I felt her embarrassment and I sensed the pain this incident brought up for her. I told her that Tad and I would never do anything like that to her. She answered softly, "I know you wouldn't."

As it turned out, we enjoyed a great trip to San Francisco. Following that trip, Mary was much more open and relaxed around us. "I think the trip to San Francisco was the final piece that I needed to experience to realize that I must put my past behind me," Mary told me later. "And that this family was accepting of me and my relationship with Aiden. It was hard to accept at first, because my instincts told me to be cautious. But I was always welcomed with open arms."

Two months after San Francisco, Aiden and Mary came over to the house with big smiles on their faces. Aiden said that he had made a DVD that he wanted us to watch. We all sat down in front of the television and saw pictures of them so happy together with music playing in the background. In the end, these words written in the sand flashed on the screen: "We are getting married"—and the final screen said, "In two years."

I was surprised, though I knew this might happen. Aiden had moved out to live with Mary, so their relationship had progressed further. On the other hand, Mary didn't have a stable job, and Aiden still faced two or three more years of college. Even the thought of marriage in two years did not seem like something they would be able to manage. However, upon seeing their announcement, Tad and I both congratulated them while concerned thoughts were streaming through my mind. I felt I presented a less than enthusiastic response to their wonderful news. Aiden didn't appear to notice, as he beamed with joy knowing that both sets of parents supported their announcement with well wishes and hugs.

After they left, I felt bad. We loved Mary, but perhaps she thought my tepid response had to do with Aiden marrying her. That was not the case. I only worried about their financial future and Aiden finishing college. How would they cope financially? How would they make ends meet with him in college? But they were waiting two years. Much could change over that period of time. I began to relax.

My mind jumped to my less than wholehearted response. I had a brilliant idea ~ I would announce it on Facebook, and they would know how happy I felt before they got home. I typed quickly and posted my happiness for them. Immediately comments started to flow back. Congratulations and excitement flew across the Facebook page.

Then I heard a familiar ding. It was a text from Aiden: "Shame on you Momma!! We haven't told anyone because we wanted our parents to be the first to know."

I literally felt sick to my stomach. Of course, they wouldn't have told people before the parents. What was I thinking? I just took away an important moment for them. What could I do to fix this?

Another brilliant idea: I will delete the post. It had only been up for ten minutes, so I rushed to the computer and clicked to delete the post. Now I had to call Aiden and clean up my huge faux pas. "I am so sorry I posted that comment on Facebook, Aiden." I explained to him that my intention was to show the world my happiness that Mary would be my daughter-in-law. I also told him I felt like I had not responded as joyfully when they originally broke the news to us.

"I know, Momma. We hadn't told anybody yet and people were texting me and I was thinking, *What's going on?*"

"I am so sorry, honey, I was trying to do something good, and I really messed up. But I deleted the post, so now you and Mary can post it, because I only had it up ten minutes."

"Oh, no, Momma! There were some beautiful comments and you deleted them?"

I felt sick again. Another brilliant idea that fell completely flat. "Yes, I did, but I want you and Mary to receive all the congratulations."

Feeling like I had really messed things up royally, I returned to the computer and noticed that Aiden and Mary had posted their announcement. Congratulations began rolling in ~ congratulations that may have come to my post instead of theirs if I hadn't deleted my announcement. The sinking feeling in my stomach began to evaporate. I made the right decision to delete the post. *Finally* I did something right.

The next day, I decided that cleaning up the situation with Aiden wasn't enough. I needed to clean up with Mary as well. I called her and left a message. She didn't call me right back. *Was she furious with me? What a way to start a relationship with my future daughter-in-law.* Later in the day, she called and apologized for taking so long to return my call. She had been tied up all morning on a project and this was her first opportunity to return my call. I breathed a sigh of relief.

I apologized about making the announcement and explained to her why I did so. I told her I was so happy that she and Aiden were engaged, but I didn't realize that my post would be taking away the attention that should be theirs. I just didn't take the time to think things through because I wanted to post something before they got home.

With an accepting voice Mary said, "We all make mistakes. I won't hold it against you. And I knew it was done with good intentions in mind." I think it was in that moment that I fell more in love with my future daughter-in-law. Sometimes, mistakes show you the essence of a person. It certainly did that for me with Mary, and it instantly imbedded her more deeply in my heart.

Since the announcement of their engagement, Aiden's relationship with Mary continues to grow. I asked Mary what the future holds. "A dog, a wedding, and a lifetime spent having fun, laughing and supporting each other's hopes and dreams." Aiden says the future for them is two dogs, two children (gender not important!), and a nice home in which to raise his family.

In the beginning, Aiden thought he would have to give up love to live as a man. But as he grew into a more confident man after transitioning, he vowed to find someone worthy of his love, someone who saw his greatness, and believed in the loving, kind, and respectful human being that he is. He does not view himself as a second-class citizen who must settle or compromise. In fact, his journey has lifted him up to another level of responsibility, visibility, and purpose.

I have watched Aiden and Mary's love for one another develop and deepen. What I have noticed about each of them is their kindness to each other and their acceptance of the other's ups and downs. They don't cling to each other out of desperation and a feeling of "I'll just settle," but have grown together respecting what the other has endured and overcome. They trust each other implicitly, sharing some of their greatest fears and disappointments. Mary certainly fulfills everything I have wished for Aiden—a person who adores him with her whole heart, embracing who he is, has been and will be. And when Mary is troubled, I see my son comfort and console her in the most loving way.

I know life holds no guarantees, but if I had to bet on a relationship, I would absolutely put my money on theirs.

CHAPTER THIRTEEN

The Wolf I Choose to Feed

At the start of this whole journey, I could only see the terrifying possibilities, feel the dread, and think about all the negative things that might happen. However, I faced fear over and over again. I called upon my greatest courage and as a result grew more courageous. I became what I practiced over and over again. What I practiced the most was courage, acceptance, gratitude, and love. I stopped taking life for granted and chose to live with my whole heart.

What does it mean to live with my whole heart? It means that I am willing to face fear, risk the unknown, and trust the direction where my heart leads me. It means saying things that are uncomfortable, often feeling so vulnerable that I fear being judged. It also means that when I am not doing something that makes things better, then I must be willing to look at myself, take responsibility for what I have done or not done, and move boldly in the direction I have been resisting. This may require that I open my heart wider and dig deeper to speak my truth, the whole truth, with compassion and honesty. It may require finding the courage to do something that has been holding me back. The change must come from within me.

One of these moments that exemplified living with my whole heart had to do with Aiden not being able to tell me he loved me. I would say, "I love you, Aiden," and he would sometimes acknowledge it with a simple "okay." At other times, he seemed unmoved by my words. In the beginning, I understood his reluctance, because he told me he had given up on love after losing Julianna. He needed space. Then when he fell in love with Mary, I thought things would change. I hoped that when I said, "I love you," he would now be able to tell me he loved me, too. That wasn't the case.

When Aiden got engaged, I thought finally he would say, "I love you, Momma." But my words of love for him were still met with a blank stare and a deaf ear. Every time I expressed my love for him with no response, I felt deeply hurt. And every time I failed to get Aiden to say I love you, I felt like a bad mother. I had stood by his side every step of his extraordinary journey and I did so because I loved him, but he couldn't say the words to me. I had at least six discussions with him over the years about this subject, all to no avail. Finally, I knew I had to change something: the way I explained to him how his inability to tell me he loved me was affecting me. I decided to do it with my whole heart—no holding back—and tell him the whole truth.

"Aiden, I have been telling you for the past few years how much it means for you to tell me you love me and still you can't do it. Are you mad at me?"

"No." He seemed genuinely confused by my question.

"Have I done something to hurt you so bad that you don't love me?"

"No."

"Is it hard for you to love Mary and then say to your mom that you love me?"

"No."

"Then I don't understand why it is so hard for you to say I love you to me. Every time I tell you I love you and you say nothing, I feel like you are mad at me, or I have said or done something bad." My voice began trembling with emotion now. "I feel like you think I am a terrible mother. And when I close the door as you leave I want to cry because I am so hurt. I don't expect you to say that you love me every time I tell you I love you. But even if you say it once in a while, that would mean so much to me. Do you think you can do that?" I asked with tears in my eyes.

"Yes, Momma," he replied very quietly, his eyes averting mine.

Later that night, as Aiden left our house to return to his apartment, I thought to myself, *Shall I say "I love you, Aiden?" or should I wait until the next time?* My heart answered, *Just say the words and have no expectations.* And that is what I did. I gave him my usual hug goodbye, took a deep breath, looked at him softly, and said, "I love you, honey."

Without hesitation, Aiden answered, "I love you more, Momma." *He loves me more, He loves me more. . . .* the words rang in my head. After all these years, I opened my heart, told him my truth, and he said, "I love you more, Momma."

As he drove off, I stood in the doorway and waved to my son, smiling from ear to ear. Closing the door, I felt the tears begin to trickle down my cheeks. My son loves me more. After more than two years, he finally said the words. How beautiful this lesson had been for me. I finally told Aiden with my whole heart how I felt ~ and with his whole heart he answered.

Opening up my whole heart was not an easy thing to do as I traveled down this road. It made me feel like a mother with no protective shell. Around every corner stood the possibility that someone would shoot me some disapproving look, pierce me verbally with judgment or disdain, or respond in a way that made me feel inadequate and worthless. When that happened, I would want to wither away in shame. Fortunately, it happened very infrequently. When it did, my resolve increased and it challenged me to find my worth within. It made me stronger.

Operating through life with an open heart was absolutely necessary for me. Rather than numb or shield myself from the shame, hurt, guilt, and fear, I allowed those feelings to wash through me. I didn't welcome them with open arms, but I didn't try to run and hide from the negative feelings, either. That course of action would have also robbed me of some incredible moments, like Aiden's proud announcement that his mother would be marching with him in Washington D.C. I could not shield myself from the negative and allow the positive to flow through me without both feelings being deadened. This journey has been amazing because I allowed both the negative and positive to become part of my experience. I learned and grew from the negative, I appreciated the positive, and I embraced both as part of my journey. It was frightening at times, but that's how I chose to handle things. Consequently, this fearless and bold mother blossomed and became visible. The activist in me that dreams of a different world for my son and all LGBT individuals would never have emerged without an open heart. It became an essential part of my growth.

With moments such as Aiden telling me he loves me and countless other etched memories, I appreciate life so much more, the people in my life so much more, and the experiences that helped me to be a better wife, mother, and human being so much more. I would be lying if I said that I would eagerly return to the horrifying, painful, and guilt-filled moments. But I know that I would go back and do it again in a heartbeat just to have the depth of courage, love, and appreciation that exists in my life today. That is how life changing this journey has been for me.

I would encourage every parent to open his or her whole heart to this challenging yet rewarding passage and allow your child to be your guide through parts of it. No matter what the passage may be, no matter how harrowing the journey, we as parents have the ability to communicate to our children that they deserve to live a life of love, acceptance, and belonging. Sometimes this may be hard for us when we see them moving down a different path than the one we imagined or believed was best for them. We as parents tell our children what to do in hopes of preparing them for a successful and fulfilling life. But sometimes we empower our children most by listening to them and learning from their pure and straightforward perspective. Children can be wonderful teachers, and they can also possess wisdom far beyond their years. In this way, my respect for Aiden has grown tremendously. By following his lead, I have also earned greater respect from him. I received what I gave. I loved, appreciated, and respected the person he was and is. That love, appreciation, and respect was returned to me tenfold.

My knowledge about the LGBT community and my connection to this community that I consider an extension of my family has also been part of this incredible journey. Prior to Aiden coming out, I knew the words "gay" and "lesbian," but really did not understand them, as I had had no close experiences with any gay or lesbian individuals. The terms "bisexuality" and "transgender" were even more foreign. My newfound awareness of this community has opened my eyes to a whole world of extraordinary discoveries, and this community has lovingly held me close and supported me as a mother. I have found encouragement and support, which I needed so desperately as I searched blindly for the right paths to take with Aiden's transition. I wasn't told what to do, but brought into a circle of new consciousness so that I could make those decisions that were right for my family and me. I fell in love with the LGBT community out of appreciation and admiration. And that love revealed an exciting and meaningful life purpose for me as well.

I want to spend the rest of my years making schools safer for LGBT youth and helping to render discrimination and cruelty a thing of the past. I want to work with school districts and public school leaders to change the culture of schools to be accepting, open, and respectful of differences. I also want to find alternative ways to serve students who cannot endure another day of harassment and torment while we are transforming school culture. Until the schools are safer, we need to find alternative ways to help our youth so they do not drop out of school—or worse—decide that life is not worth living. I may never have discovered my life's purpose without Aiden's courage to live a life of truth. I followed my heart with my son, and my heart has led me here.

I also believe ongoing communication has been vital for our family to achieve the level of success that we've created up to this point. Our ability to keep lines of communication unclogged with ego and hurt kept us talking to one other. If we severed open and loving dialogue within our family, the result would have been closed hearts and the building of walls. We could not continue to grow in understanding without talking and listening. Sometimes, my ego got in the way and I wanted to blame others. As a mother, I wanted my children to respect and honor my decisions, so I never wanted to be wrong. But making mistakes and admitting them showed my children that it was okay for them to make mistakes as well. I continued to grow and develop, and gave them permission to do the same.

When Aiden came out as a lesbian, then as a transgender individual, I said and did things I wish I'd never said or did. Sometimes it felt humiliating to apologize again and again. My defensive ego waited at every turn to cast off responsibility for my misstep. However, I realized that I had made the best possible decisions with the knowledge and awareness

I possessed at the time. I was a good mother who was getting better. After each mistake, I became a better mother. We were all working without an instruction manual, and when we focused on loving each other, accepting each other, and being responsible for having a good relationship, we took the steps necessary to make that happen.

Unless one person makes a commitment to open communication, those who don't know what to say or how to say it may wait for someone else to take charge. At times, my husband took the lead. Without my husband reaching out to Aiden that Christmas Eve Day after fear overcame me and I jumped to conclusions about Aiden killing himself, our Christmas and perhaps much more would have been ruined. Then there were the times when my children reached out to us first. Aiden told me that it took him years to figure out who he was, so he wisely recognized that he needed to give us time to figure it out as well. Aiden took the lead on being patient and gave his dad and mom space to process all the new information coming our way. Aiden communicated that patience so Tad and I could focus more on doing what we needed to do to love our child while maneuvering through unfamiliar waters.

And Stefen's love of Aiden never wavered, so he often took the lead on unconditional love—not so much in words, but in actions. He became my role model for flowing with situations, not getting ruffled, and loving without drama. I worried that he might face exclusion from circles of friends because he had a transgender brother, but he never seemed to fret about such things. When I asked about those concerns, he would just respond that there was no problem. I can proudly say that I raised two wonderful sons.

In the end, I decided to ensure that communication in our family was ongoing and our hearts continued to stay open. I was fortunate that others in the family picked up the slack when I faltered or needed support.

I have heard many stories from LGBT individuals who "came out" to their parents with rocky results. However, these LGBT individuals took a step back to gather courage and then moved forward again and again to help their parents understand and grow in knowledge. Those parents are lucky to have children so wise and resilient. Sometimes parents are so afraid, they need their children to help them push through this journey.

If you are an LGBT individual who is struggling with your parents, please don't give up on them if they can't move past their fear quite yet. Sometimes, fear masquerades as anger. The screaming fit I threw with Aiden was just that. I was so afraid—and fortunately, I recognized how fearful I was. Remember a time when you were unable to move past your fear, but you finally took the steps? Your parents may be at that same place; they need your help to step up their courage. Give them time, give them encouragement, and let them know that you understand where they're coming from. Direct them to support groups like PFLAG or your local LGBT Center, if you have one, for resources and people with whom they can talk about their feelings. Get support yourself from friends who have successfully worked things out with their parents, or from parents who have successfully moved past their fear. Find people who have walked this path you want to walk and live the results you want to realize. Our family needed support, patience with each other, and ongoing communication to travel this difficult road. Please search for the tools you need to support your journey.

As much as you want others to see the greatness and good in you, please do the same for your parents, children, spouse, family, or friends. Believe that people have the ability to change, because we all do. I'm not referring to changing characteristics that are an inherent part of who we are— our sexual orientation, gender identity, or race. Our family had to change the way we thought in order to embrace our new son, nephew, and brother. Many of our extended family and friends chose to change their viewpoints on sexuality and gender identity to support Aiden. They were growing and learning along with us. We all attended Aiden's "LGBT 101" class with no official book to guide us except for the book of real life itself: our day-to-day experiences and our open hearts. There were multiple teachers and lots of homework.

There were some people in our lives who needed more time or needed to feel our love and acceptance as they made their way. Tad and I vowed that we would do everything to bring as many people along with us on this journey. We did not give up on them because we didn't want them to give up on Aiden. His physical appearance would change, but not his personality, heart, or wonderful spirit. We hoped people would recognize Aiden as the same person inside, but if they didn't, we worked to bridge that gap in knowledge. I tried not to take people's negative comments and reactions personally. They were in a different place and on a different path. But I strove to give them every opportunity to understand. Sometimes it was easy, while at other times it felt so difficult that I couldn't imagine anything harder.

I could not be the same person, think the same thoughts, and do the same things while still hoping to see different results. I had to be willing to take risks and think and act differently in order to achieve the relationships that I wanted with Aiden, my family, and our friends. It wasn't always simple. There were times when I was so afraid to open my mouth and say what I felt, but I persevered. There were times I didn't speak up at all because I was so scared of being rejected and humiliated. Along the way, I found my voice, developed courage, and asked those I love and respect for support and understanding. It truly has been a journey. It did not happen overnight.

But what about individuals who do not want to change? There were those people and situations where I was required to invest more time and effort than I was willing to. In those cases, I needed to accept them from afar. This took practice. When physical violence was part of our lives, I could not even find a place of acceptance in the beginning. When that visiting minister rejected Aiden, I lived for months with disappointment and resentment directed against the church. In both of these instances, rather than spending my energy feeling victimized or railing against the injustice of the situation, I needed to change. It took time.

Along the way, it got easier. First, I had to let go of my negative feelings and accept that these individuals were on their own paths, just as we were on ours. We could not change them. That would be their choice. My anger and judgment towards them would not make them more open to my feelings. In fact, if they even knew my feelings, they would have dug deeper into the belief systems they currently held. In my heart, I tried to wish them well, which sometimes felt impossible. With time, I got better at it, and then accepted them to the best of my ability so I could move on with my life.

One of my friends, Eric, is a gay man who just received a scholarship to work on his master's degree at Duke University. He comes from a conservative religious background and his mother believes that he will go to hell with "the lifestyle he has chosen." She can't see that Eric is not choosing a "lifestyle." Eric is simply a man who happens to be gay. As I got to know Eric better, I was drawn to his wisdom, openness, and the wonderful way he seemed to accept his situation with his mother. I told him that I wanted to bring hope to the LGBT community. He cautioned me not to give individuals false hope, but realistic hope. That thought intrigued me. I always believed hope was a positive thing. We made plans to meet again to talk about this further.

The next time we met, I began to ask him questions about hope, his mother, and the resilience he possessed. Every single day, he told me, he wrote down not only the things he wanted to accomplish, but also three things for which he was grateful. This sense of appreciation and completion allowed him to have hope within himself, the life he could create, and the value he'd bring to those around him.

He also came to a place where he tried to accept his mother, because "in order for my mother to accept me, I have to accept her for who she is," he said to me. "I recognize that for her to embrace me would mean completely changing everything and abandoning everything she's believed for the last forty to fifty years. I know that it's going to take a very long time and it may never happen. If it doesn't happen, it's not going to impact my own sanity or my own love or my own happiness."

Eric is finding ways to accept his mother, while not letting her viewpoints diminish his light or character. He works at it every day through goals and gratitude. He counts each day as a blessing, and though he admits some days are more difficult than others, he finds a way to get along with his mother while seeing himself as worthy. His strength and depth of love astound me.

I believe that individuals must discover their own worthiness and find people who will support them while parents and others make their way. Parents can be afraid for their children and themselves. I was one of those parents. If your parents never find their way to totally accepting you, love them anyway and find people who believe in who you are.

As important as parents are to the success of their LGBT children, the most important person is the LGBT individual himself or herself. I began to formulate these thoughts as I discovered the work of Brene Brown.

In her Technology, Entertainment, Design (TED) Talk video, "The Power of Vulnerability" on YouTube, I was struck by her words. She talked about the concept of worthiness; that being worthy meant you are enough at this moment—who you are and what you have, you are enough. Goals and dreams could be things you still aspired to, but whether you reached those goals and dreams did not determine your worthiness.

I remembered how difficult life was for Aiden before he transitioned. Even with our love and support, he seemed sad and lost. When he transitioned, his life began to turn around. He started to believe that he deserved to be happy, he deserved to find love, and he deserved to live a life where he is respected. As he believed, so his life began to change. Aiden's opinion was the only one that would create his future; his world would become a reflection of what he believed. If he believed he was born to do great things, then the world would accommodate his thoughts and feelings and lay before him unimagined opportunities. And when Aiden manifested his hopes and dreams, I hoped that he would take a moment to say "thank you" to the people who helped make those dreams come true.

I know it is not always easy to find worthiness and gratitude from within, especially when the world tells you that your differences make you unworthy of love and acceptance. I remember hearing a true story about a young boy who lived in the back of a truck with his family. Every day at school, he bounded into class ready to learn after brushing his teeth and washing up in the school restroom before the bell rang. After a time, the teacher pulled him aside and asked him how he could be so happy and eager to learn each day when his living conditions were so difficult. In a small, humble voice he replied, "But I am with my whole family. We are together. And so I have a lot to be thankful for, even though I am living in the back of a truck."

Like Eric, this boy found purpose and gratitude even though his circumstances were less than perfect. Aiden and I found that same worthiness in the work we did and by appreciating all that was in our lives.

When I am feeling low, I write in my Gratitude Journal at least five things for which I am grateful. When I am feeling unworthy, I go out and do something for someone else or find someone who will support me as I shift from this negative state. Helping others requires me to snap out of feeling sorry for myself. Asking for support moves me from the negative to the positive as well.

To parents of LGBT youth reading this book, I believe the most important things I told my child through my actions and words were that he was loved and he deserved to live a life of truth. Can you imagine waking up each day knowing you could not be your true self? To be compelled to lie about whom you are and how you feel to those that you love? When our child "comes out," we as parents "come out" with that child. Through this coming-out process, we must deal with the same feelings and questions of integrity, worthiness, and love: Will my brothers still love me when they find out that my child is transgender? What will my friends think? Will others judge me as being a bad mother? What will my employees or employer think?

Aiden and I walked a similar path of fear, possible rejection, and confusion over how to tell the truth. I also know that at times Aiden walked a different path because he changed his body to live his truth. Aiden's journey required much more courage than I ever had to face. Yet at the end of the day, both Aiden and I wanted to say that we were proud of the words we spoke and the person who showed up in the world. I also wanted to look in the mirror and say, "Today, I loved my child with my whole heart—I did the best I could and I am a good mother." Even if others judged me to be a terrible mother – and I know some may see me in that way – only I knew if I did the best that I could. Did I love my child? Did I face fear and choose love? Did I take time to appreciate myself for my courage and appreciate others for their support? Like my son, I am worthy of love and acceptance.

My primary compass to know whether I am on the right track each day rests in how I feel. Do I have a sick feeling in my stomach? Am I angry, afraid, or filled with guilt? Do I feel defensive? If I don't feel good, I take time to reflect on why. Is it the way I handled something? Is it the way my child communicated with me? Am I afraid inside and don't know what to do? Once I know why I don't feel good, then I can find the solutions that make me feel like a good mother again.

If I handled things in a way that didn't leave me feeling very good, I went back and "cleaned up" the situation with the child involved, whether it was Aiden or Stefen. To me, cleaning up consists of an apology, a discussion to clarify something that didn't feel right, or how I could do it better next time. Many times it required me to ask for what I needed. Each time I cleaned up with my sons, I felt respectful and felt I was a good mother. If my child seemed distant or unhappy with me, I would gently talk with him. Sometimes it took only one discussion. Many times it took multiple conversations. The number of times we talked did not matter. What mattered most was that we were communicating in a compassionate, honest, and respectful way. I had to confront my fears again and again and decide I was worthy of whatever result I sought.

If I can't find the answers within myself, because many times I don't have them, I reach out for support. Whenever I try to figure out something when I don't have the answers, I spin in circles. It takes me into a downward spiral of inadequacy and hopelessness. Finding a support group or friend who I trust brings back hope and possibilities into my life or allows me to release situations I believe I need to control. As a result, I feel lighter and happier, not heavy with worry. I begin to feel good again. I believe in the law of attraction. I continually want to attract all that is good and positive to my life and to the lives of those I love. I can only do that if my heart is in a good and positive place. And then the answers appear—like a miracle.

All of this took time, but Aiden was worth every minute. And so was I.

Today, I still face fear, judgment, and other negative feelings. My approach is always the same—step back, decide what I can do to feel better, and then take the steps to act with courage *and* love. One of my friends told me love without power is weak, but power without love is harsh. I want to be loving and strong, so I strive to balance my courage with my compassion.

My journey is not over. I want to grow in awareness so that I become even more courageous, accepting, and loving. I am still learning and that is how I want it to be. If I think I have arrived, I will not be open to ways I can improve. And I most certainly can be better.

There is a Native American story that Aiden had posted online for years. It goes like this:

> An elderly Cherokee Native American was teaching his grandchildren about life.

He said to them, "A fight is going on inside me, it is a terrible fight and it is between two wolves. One wolf is evil—he is fear, anger, envy, sorrow, regret, greed, arrogance, self-pity, guilt, resentment, inferiority, lies, false pride, competition, superiority, and ego. The other is good—he is joy, peace, love, hope, sharing, serenity, humility, kindness, benevolence, friendship, empathy, generosity, truth, compassion and faith. This same fight is going on inside you, and inside every other person, too."

They thought about it for a minute, and then one child asked his grandfather, "Which wolf will win, Grandfather?"

The Elder simply replied, "The one I feed."

When I read this story, I knew this was the struggle I faced daily as my son sought to find his truth and I searched for mine as well. In the beginning of our journey, the evil wolf won many of my struggles. As that wolf dominated my life, things did not get better. I did not feel better about myself. But as time went on, I found the courage to feed the good wolf. The more I fed the good wolf, the stronger she became. She grew in courage because she practiced being courageous. She grew in acceptance because she practiced acceptance. Most importantly, she grew in love, because she filled her life with as much love as she could.

Today, I believe the good wolf is the wolf that I nurture. However, there are still times the evil wolf appears. When she does so, I appreciate and accept her. Without her, I would have never grown as strong as I am, so in a sense she wasn't really evil, but rather the side of me that was afraid and unaware. She taught me so much, and I love her as much as the good wolf.

Each of you reading this book may be facing your own struggles. If I could leave you with the most important lessons that I learned along the way, here is my list:

• Commitment to the Relationship: This commitment can be from children to parents, parents to children, spouse to spouse, sibling to sibling, and so forth. Our family never gave up on our relationship to each other because we knew the answer to this question—Why? In the end only one answer stood out for me: I loved my son and my love did not have conditions.

• Communication Kept Us Connected: Honest, vulnerable, and loving communication kept our hearts open. With open hearts, our understanding expanded and our connection to each other grew stronger out of respect for one another and respect for ourselves as well. We spoke our truth and listened with our hearts. We apologized when we did or said something that did not strengthen our relationship. We reached out and asked how we could do things better, if we sensed any distance between each other.

• Staying Objective: Taking things personally clouded my objectivity and resulted in reaction and judgment. Staying objective attracted calmness, clear thinking, and more positive results.

• Reaching Out for Support: In the midst of my struggle, it was so critical to have someone or a group of someones (if you are lucky) who remained by my side to keep me optimistic, encourage positive action, and applaud my efforts and successes. I found people who held my best interests in mind. These trusted friends listened to the things I said and didn't say. They saw the greatness and good in me, sharing their thoughts in the most unselfish, loving ways.

• Take Responsibility: The one thing I could control was my ability to change. It was never easy, but it was always what I needed to do to arrive at the results I wanted. Feeling like a victim or blaming others never helped me to change situations to be better. I had to find ways within me to "be the change I wished to see in the world."

• Courage and Compassion: When I balanced the two, I found my greatest power. When they were out of balance, I found myself ineffective either because I came across too weak or too harsh. The extraordinary appeared with equal parts of both.

• Gratitude: Looking for things that were great in my life and saying thank you, kept me from getting stuck in the negative and those things I still needed to work on. When I was grateful, I attracted more things to be grateful for.

• I Deserve: This was always where I ended up so I could progress to the places I wanted to go. I had to see myself worthy of having a good relationship with my son. This allowed me to take action, course correct when the relationship moved sideways, and communicate to keep my bond with my son strong and loving. I had to see myself worthy of being viewed as a good mother. This required me to see myself on a journey, rather than having arrived. I made mistakes, I asked for forgiveness, but within me a mother existed who made every effort to do the right thing.

I see the world changing rapidly to be more accepting of those who are perceived as different. Over the past year, New York, Washington, and Maryland legalized same sex marriage, California signed the FAIR Education Act to include LGBT curriculum in our schools, and "Don't Ask, Don't Tell" has been repealed. Unfortunately, the world will never change fast enough for those of us who want it to be safer for our children, more kind to those we love, and more respectful to ways that are neither a choice nor an option. But we are moving in the right direction.

Yes, this world was filled with some difficult times for our family, but it was also filled with amazing, extraordinary, and unforgettable moments of triumph, connection, joy, and love. Your journey will be different than ours, yet in some ways the same. Your decisions will match what you believe is best for your family. As we faced whatever challenges we encountered with compassion, courage, and love, I believe things improved—ideas came to us and people rushed to support. Almost magically, solutions appeared. Like our family, you will create your own incredible journey.

Aiden and I sincerely wish you the most amazing life filled with all that will bring you peace and joy. We hope that our paths cross somewhere along the way and you can share with us some of the wonderful moments that you have been able to create. We believe that you deserve this kind of life. And we hope you believe it as well. Because in the end, your belief is the only thing that truly matters.

Epilogue

When I reflect back on our journey, I'm so grateful for all the wonderful experiences I have had. Since the original publication of Two Spirits, One Heart in 2012, Aiden and I have traveled the United States speaking at conferences and events where we've been received with open arms again and again. We've continued exploring new ways to reach out to others, hoping to bring greater understanding of what a family goes through when their child transitions from one gender to another. And we marvel at how amazing this journey continues to be for all of us.

One of the most incredible experiences for Aiden and me came in the most unexpected way. In fact, I almost missed the opportunity. Scanning through my unread emails one morning, I noticed an email address that I didn't recognize. Thinking that it might be a scam or a virus, I almost deleted it, but somehow I got distracted and so it sat in my inbox the whole day.

That night I saw posts from Facebook friends with comments like "I almost deleted an invitation from the White House!" and "Boy, am I glad I opened that note from the strange email address. It was a White House invitation." Curious, I went back to my inbox and opened that unread email—and what should I see but an invitation to come to the White House for an LGBT Pride reception! I later heard that only 300 individuals were invited to this special event. Could it actually be that I'd been invited? Yes, it turned out that I had. I was going to the White House and would get to see President Obama in person!

Since the invitation included one guest, it only seemed appropriate that my husband should accompany me, as he had been my strongest supporter. But in his usual unselfish fashion, Tad said, "No, you should take Aiden."

"Are you sure, honey?" I replied, feeling uncertain.

"Yes," he answered. "You and Aiden should go."

In a way, that seemed appropriate, because my involvement with the LGBT community happened only because of Aiden. He had weathered so many negative experiences and fought so hard not to succumb to the dark days that this trip would be one of those affirming moments that told him—told us— it was all worth the struggle. My son and I were going on another incredible adventure, all because of his courage, his resilience, but mostly his love and faith in me.

So we booked the airline tickets, our hotel room, and all through our preparations I felt like pinching myself, thinking I was only imagining that we would soon walk into that historic building that I never dreamed I would ever gain access to.

Because I'd been told that other PFLAG staff and members had received an invitation to the LGBT reception, I notified PFLAG that I'd received one too. I was told that the organization wanted to bring together those PFLAG individuals who'd also received an invitation and gather everyone for lunch at their national office. We would then all travel to the White House together after lunch. PFLAG Executive Director Jody Huckaby told me that while all invitees would attend the reception, a very small group of people would actually get to meet the President. If I was chosen, he said, I would probably be notified the week before. I tingled inside, feeling strangely certain I would be among those selected. I don't know what possessed me to believe that out of 300 people I would be among the select few, but somehow I just felt it inside.

During the week before the event, I checked my email all day. No special invite. I was told by PFLAG that if I didn't get an invitation by Tuesday, it probably would not happen. Tuesday came and went.
Still no invitation. Well, maybe, they were behind one day, I thought. But Wednesday came and went and no special invitation. On Thursday, Aiden and I flew to Washington D.C. with still no email. It was then that I decided that my intuition must have been wrong. I wanted to enjoy the White House reception and not be disappointed that I didn't get a personal invitation to have a more intimate moment with the President. I gratefully settled into the fact that I would be able to walk inside the White House and actually be in the same room as him. Wasn't that an honor enough? Yes, yes, yes, I thought, and without a bit of disappointment I moved on.

On the morning of the reception, I got myself ready and then decided to check my email as Aiden readied himself. Hope springs eternal!

And there in my inbox was an email from Gautam Raghavan, a member of President Obama's staff. The note simply asked me to be in touch with him by email or to give him a call. I did both. When Gautam answered his phone, he said a small group of reception guests would be invited to take a photo with President Obama, and I WAS ON THAT SHORT LIST! He asked whether I was in Washington D.C. and if I would be interested. Without hesitation, I said I would.

Thrilled beyond words, I hung up the phone and rushed over to Aiden with the news. I then texted my husband, who was naturally excited for me. I paced the hotel room—I just couldn't sit still!—while jabbering on and on to Aiden. Finally my son said, "Momma, you have to calm yourself down, now." I couldn't help myself. "Well, it isn't every day that you get to shake hands with the President," I replied and tried to compose myself. But how do you quiet yourself down when faced with a once in a lifetime moment like this? I did my best.

Our first stop the day of the reception was the PFLAG national office for lunch, where I pulled aside Jody and told him the good news. He was elated for me and handed me some PFLAG pins to put on my jacket and another to give to the President should the opportunity arise. There were other PFLAG individuals going to the reception but not meeting the President, so I didn't want to spoil their moment. Aiden and I had some wonderful conversations with them about how excited we were to be invited to the White House, but we made no mention of our special time with the President. Then we were all whisked away by taxis to the White House.

After passing three security checkpoints we were finally inside the White House. It was so awe-inspiring, unlike anything I had ever seen. I walked from room to room, taking pictures of portraits of First Ladies Jackie Kennedy, Mamie Eisenhower, and Eleanor Roosevelt. I especially loved seeing the china that belonged to George Washington and artifacts that had belonged to so many others that I had read about in history books.

Aiden and I walked up to the next floor, which overlooked Pennsylvania Avenue. As we peered out the White House windows, we saw people taking photographs of the White House from the street. I wondered if they could see us and if they thought, Who are those people looking back as us from inside the President's home?

On this floor we were greeted by a military band playing rousing marching music. They looked so sharp in their uniforms. Aiden and I walked around noticing the staircase leading up to the President and First Family's residence. We were directed to the room where the President would be addressing all the guests. Already a crowd had formed ten rows deep in preparation for his appearance. But Aiden and I were too anxious to stay in one place and decided to explore a little more. We walked into the White House dining room, where food and drinks were being served to guests. Aiden and I decided to forego the food until after we had met the President. We were both too nervous and excited to eat.

At the designated time, Aiden and I appeared at the door to the Red Room where Gautam had told us we would be checked in. Our nervousness was heightening. From the Red Room we were ushered through the Blue Room and on to the Green Room, where we waited with about forty other guests. We saw a few people we recognized from our work in the LGBT community, talked to people that we'd waited in line with, but mainly we just savored the moment.

Then it was time. The President was here! All the invited guests had a card with their name typed on it and the name of the guest they had chosen to bring. As the line began to move and we inched closer to the door of the Blue Room, where President Obama stood, I could hear people's names being read off of the white note cards. We were going to be announced to the President! And as we stepped closer, guided by others to keep moving forward, suddenly we were at the front of the line and only a few feet from the President. I turned to Aiden and said, "I think I am going to cry!" Aiden looked at me and in his honest and comical way he said, "You better not cry, Momma! Your face is going to be all ugly when they take the picture of you with the President." I didn't want to have an ugly face on this momentous occasion, so I held back my tears.

And then it was our turn. A strong, booming voice announced, "Marsha and Aiden Aizumi." We walked forward with great excitement. I shook the President's hand but didn't say a word. I was still sucking in my tears so I wouldn't have an ugly face, and I knew if I spoke I would cry. So Aiden said, "Mr. President, it is an honor" as he held out his hand to shake President Obama's hand. President Obama looked so handsome and so natural in person, as if he'd known us for years. Both Aiden and I, despite our nerves, felt relaxed immediately. Then it was time for the photo. We weren't allowed to take any pictures of our own, so we stood on each side of the President, his arms around us, and smiled as the White House photographer snapped our picture.

Before I turned to leave, I handed the President a PFLAG pin and thanked him for the work he was doing to make the world safer for my transgender son and others. President Obama said in his kind but commanding voice, "We like to make moms happy." And then the moment was over.

We were ushered out of the Blue Room, through the Red Room, and guided out to the State Dining Room. By now we were ready to sample all the different food that we had seen. Aiden grabbed a handful of White House napkins, some to use and some to keep as a souvenir, as we sat down to enjoy the wonderful food. Beth Kohm, the Deputy Executive Director of PFLAG, found us and wanted to know the details, and Jody shared our news with PFLAG's social media. But Aiden and I sat absorbed in all that was happening around us and tried to capture every detail of this day as people moved around us.

When it came time for President Obama to speak, Aiden and I watched on monitors positioned in the State Dining Room. The room where the President was to speak was now packed, and we had no chance of finding a place to stand where we could see the President. So we watched from the monitors and tried to concentrate on his message. But truthfully, I can't remember a word he said that day because I was in such a daze.

Not all of our days are this glamorous needless to say, as Aiden and I continue to travel this journey together with our family. Following the original publication of Two Spirits, One Heart, we have spoken at colleges, universities, high schools, and both LGBT and non-LGBT organizations that are interested in bringing the stories of the transgender community to the forefront. We have spoken at the LGBT Creating Change Conference in Baltimore and Atlanta and also at the Philadelphia Transgender Health Conference. Due to Aiden's college schedule and my work schedule, we have also had to speak separately. No matter where we go, we walk away hoping that we have touched a few hearts, because we have been touched by these wonderful LGBT families, LGBT young people, and straight allies who have come to hear us speak. We have many friends around the country now and feel blessed to have met so many individuals who share in our work and our dream of greater understanding, compassion and respect for all.

Another area where Aiden and I have begun to speak at is churches. I have met so many young people around the country where the religious community has created much hurt and separation within our LGBT families. With religious institutions interpreting the Bible so strictly, parents in fear of the souls of their children and wanting the best for their children try to "change" them into being "straight." What initially seemed like parents being very closed minded and unloving to their children, I now see as a huge amount of fear for their children's future and happiness. What parent would not fight hard to secure the happiness of their children because they loved them so fiercely?

But as churches are evolving, so are parents. One story I heard recently that broke my heart was an evangelical Christian mother, who said, "If my gay son is going to hell, then I am going with him." Why did this mother feel she had to make that choice to love her son, I asked myself? I'm hearing more stories of families challenging their churches to embrace the LGBT community, so that the church is "walking their talk" about love. This is often an uphill battle that seems almost insurmountable, but voices are no longer being silent. Yes, we have a long way to go with the church, but we are moving in the right direction. And I am proud to say that Aiden and I are slowly moving our way into the faith community with our story.

As far as Aiden's life today, he is now at the University of La Verne focused on getting a degree in education. He wants to be a person who can be a role model as a teacher and create a safe space for young people. I think he will be both an asset and an inspiration to any school district that is lucky to have him on their staff.

In addition, Aiden is serving on the PFLAG National Transgender and Gender Non-Conforming Advisory Council and was recently honored with the Alexis Rivera Trailblazer Award during 2013 Trans Pride Los Angeles. He continues to be a positive role model for the transgender community and for me.

But the biggest thing that has happened in the past twelve months is that Aiden and Mary have set their wedding date. They will be married on November 8, 2013 in front of a small group of family and friends. Their wedding has a whimsical feeling that reflects both their personalities and their dreams for the future. It will be a magical day filled with many surprises, both for Aiden and Mary and their guests. I'm bringing a whole box of Kleenex because I know that I will be moved by every part of the day; a culmination of all the dreams I have had for my son to find love and discover that he can be loved, cherished, and respected for the man that he is.

As for me, I am continuing my advocacy work, focusing mainly on the Asian Pacific Islander community and making connections around the United States in hopes of finding courageous API parents who stand up for their LGBT children. The PFLAG San Gabriel Valley Asian Pacific Islander program, a group I co-founded in 2012, is now a chapter of PFLAG and growing under the leadership of president Carol Mannion. New York City now has an API program founded by Clara Yoon that is a satellite program out of PFLAG New York City. PFLAG Bellevue is working with the Japanese American Citizens League (JACL) to bring more visibility to the API LGBT community in the Seattle area. And I am looking to Chicago as the next city for us to bring more support to API LGBT families.

My work in safe schools also continues. The high school diploma program at the Los Angeles Gay & Lesbian Center is still in operation and I helped to co-found in 2012 a coalition to work on bringing courageous conversations to school districts in our area.

There is much work left to do, but there is so much that has been accomplished, even just since the first publication of this book one year ago. Same-sex marriage has been approved in Washington, Minnesota, Maryland, and Maine. Proposition 8 was overturned, allowing same-sex marriages to resume in my home state of California, along with the Defense of Marriage Act (DOMA) being struck down. Same-sex marriage has been approved in France, the United Kingdom, and other countries around the world.

The momentum is on our side. But it doesn't mean I can just sit back and wait for things to improve further. I still have to stay as focused and unwavering in my determination and my love as an activist. This is the world I am helping to create for my son and all LGBT individuals: a safer, more accepting world. It is a place where people are respected for who they are and allowed to love who they love. It is a different world than the one I grew up in or even imagined could exist one day, but it is the world I dream my children and all of us will live in.

Notes

Chapter Ten: Inspired to Activism

[1] Southern Poverty Law Center's Intelligence Report magazine, "A Dozen Major Groups Help Drive the Religious Right's Anti-Gay Crusade," published Spring 2005, issue 117, http://www.splcenter.org/get-informed/intelligence-report/browse-all-issues/2005/spring/a-mighty-army#10 (accessed August 19, 2012)

Chapter Eleven: My Son Finds His Voice

[2] Brené Brown, *The Gifts of Imperfection: Let Go of Who You Think You're Supposed to Be and Embrace Who You Are* (Center City, MN: Hazelden Publishing 2010), 6.

Resources

The following resource list includes the names of organizations you may find helpful on your journey. It is by no means comprehensive and not all of them may be of interest or a fit for you. However, I offer the list as a good starting point for anyone on the path Aiden and I took.

ADVOCATES FOR YOUTH
2000 M Street, NW, Suite 750
Washington, DC 20036
T (202) 419-3420
F (202) 419-1448
www.advocatesforyouth.org
www.youthresource.com
info@advocatesforyouth.org

Advocates for Youth is dedicated to creating programs and advocating for policies that help young people make informed and responsible decisions about their reproductive and sexual health. Advocates provides information, training, and strategic assistance to youth-serving organizations, policy makers, youth activists, and the media in the United States and the developing world.

Youth Resource, a project of Advocates for Youth, is a website created by and for LGBT youth thirteen to twenty-four years old, which offers support, community, resources, and peer-to-peer education about issues of concern.

AMERICAN CIVIL LIBERTIES UNION FOUNDATION LGBT &
AIDS PROJECT
125 Broad Street, 18th Floor
New York, NY 10004-2400
T (212) 549-2627
www.aclu.org/getequal
getequal@aclu.org

Founded in 1986, the Lesbian & Gay Rights and AIDS Projects are a special
division of the American Civil Liberties Union. The "Get Equal" website
provides, among other things, a step-by-step guide showing how to get an
anti-harassment policy in your school district and tools for a gay-straight
alliance at your school.

ASIAN PACIFIC ISLANDER EQUALITY - LOS ANGELES
(API EQUALITY - LA)
1137 Wilshire Boulevard
Los Angeles, CA 90017-1900
T (213) 580-1800
www.apiequalityla.org
Online Contact Form: http://apiequalityla.org/contact-form

Founded in 2005, API Equality-LA has been a tireless advocate in the
Greater Los Angeles Asian and Pacific Islander (API) communities for fair
treatment of LGBT people and marriage equality for same-sex couples.

ASIAN & PACIFIC ISLANDER FAMILY PRIDE
P.O. Box 473
Fremont, CA 94537
T (510) 818-0887
www.apifamilypride.org
info@apifamilypride.org

Asian and Pacific Islander Family Pride is a volunteer organization that
offers support and information to lesbian, gay, bisexual, and transgendered

APIs and their families. Their volunteers provide a safe space to talk, and offer their own stories to help promote understanding and acceptance within families and communities.

BISEXUAL RESOURCE CENTER
P.O. Box 170796
Boston, MA 02117
T (617) 424-9595
www.biresource.net
brc@biresource.net

The Center educates the public and organizations about bisexuality and provides an information and support network.

CENTERLINK
P.O. Box 24490
Fort Lauderdale, FL 33307
T (954) 765-6024
F (954) 765-6593
www.lgbtcenters.org
CenterLink@lgbtcenters.org

A fundamental goal of CenterLink's mission is to help build the capacity of LGBT community centers to meet the social, cultural, health, and political advocacy needs of LGBT community members across the country. CenterLink also acts as a voice for LGBT centers in national grassroots organizing, coalition building, and social activism in order to strengthen and build a unified center movement.

COLAGE
PEOPLE WITH A LESBIAN GAY BISEXUAL TRANSGENDER OR
QUEER PARENT
1550 Bryant Street, Suite 830
San Francisco, CA 94103
T (855) 4-COLAGE
www.colage.org
colage@colage.org

COLAGE is a national and international organization that supports young
people with LGBT parents through education and community building.

FAMILY EQUALITY COUNCIL
P.O. Box 206
Boston, MA 02133
T (617) 502-8700
F (617) 502-8701
info@familyequality.org
www.familyequality.org

The Family Equality Council works to ensure equality for LGBT families
by building community, changing hearts and minds, and advancing social
justice for all families.

THE GAY AND LESBIAN NATIONAL HOTLINE (GLNH)
2261 Market Street PMB #296
San Francisco, CA 94114
GLBT National Hotline (888) THE-GLNH
GLBT National Youth Talkline (800) 246-7743
www.glnh.org
info@GLBTNationalHelpCenter.org

GLNH provides nationwide toll-free peer counseling, information and
referrals to the LGBT community. Peer counselors are available Monday-
Friday, 4pm to midnight EST, and Saturday, noon to 5pm EST.

THE GAY, LESBIAN, AND STRAIGHT EDUCATION NETWORK
(GLSEN)
90 Broad Street, 2nd Floor
New York, NY 10004
T (212) 727-0135
F (212) 727-0254
www.glsen.org
glsen@glsen.org

GLSEN strives to assure that each member of every school community is valued and respected regardless of sexual orientation or gender identity/expression. It provides safe school tools and guides, and is an official sponsor of the Day of Silence (www.dayofsilence.org), an annual event to raise schools' awareness and protest discrimination against LGBT students.

GAY - STRAIGHT ALLIANCE NETWORK
1550 Bryant Street, Suite 800
San Francisco, CA 94103
T (415) 552-4229
F (415) 552-4729
www.gsanetwork.org
info@gsanetwork.org

GSA Network is a youth leadership organization that connects school-based GSAs to each other and community resources.

GENDER SPECTRUM EDUCATION AND TRAINING
1271 Washington Avenue #834
San Leandro, CA 94577
T (510) 567-3977
www.genderspectrum.org
info@genderspectrum.org

An organization that provides education, resources, and training to help create a more gender sensitive and supportive environment for all people, including gender variant and transgender youth.

HUMAN RIGHTS CAMPAIGN (HRC)
1640 Rhode Island Avenue, NW
Washington, DC 20036-3278
T (202) 628-4160
F (202) 347-5323
TTY (202) 216-1572
www.hrc.org

HRC is a nonpartisan organization that works to advance equality based on sexual orientation and gender expression and identity, to ensure that LGBT Americans can be open, honest, and safe at home, at work, and in the community.

LAMBDA LEGAL DEFENSE AND EDUCATION FUND
www.lambdalegal.org
legalhelpdesk@lambdalegal.org
Help Desk (866) 542-8336

National Headquarters
120 Wall Street, 19th Floor
New York, NY 10005-3919
T (212) 809-8585
F (212) 809-0055
www.lambdalegal.org/nhq

Lambda Legal is a national organization committed to achieving full recognition of the civil rights of LGBT people and those with HIV through impact litigation, education, and public policy work. The organization provides legal assistance and representation to students and school professionals facing discrimination, harassment and censorship based on sexual orientation or gender identity.

LIFEWORKS
L.A. Gay & Lesbian Center
The Village at Ed Gould Plaza
1125 N. McCadden Place
Los Angeles, CA 90038
T (323) 860-7373
F (323) 308-4152
www.modelsofpride.org
lifeworks@lagaycenter.org

LifeWorks is the youth development and mentoring program of the L.A. Gay & Lesbian Center. It offers one-on-one, peer, and group mentoring opportunities for lesbian, gay, bisexual, transgender, queer, and questioning youth ages twelve to twenty-four. Their goal is to help LGBTQ youth to realize their goals and dreams with a safe space, positive and affirming role models, and workshops and activities that are fun and educational.

LOS ANGELES GAY & LESBIAN CENTER
McDonald/Wright Building
1625 N. Schrader Boulevard
Los Angeles, CA 90028-6213
T (323) 993-7400
healthservices@lagaycenter.org
www.lagaycenter.org

The L.A. Gay & Lesbian Center provides a broad array of services for the LGBT community, welcoming nearly a quarter-million client visits from ethnically diverse youth and adults each year. Through its Jeffrey Goodman Special Care Clinic and on-site pharmacy, the Center offers free and low-cost health, mental health, HIV/AIDS medical care, and HIV/STD testing and prevention. The Center also offers legal, social, cultural, and educational services, with unique programs for seniors, families and youth, including a twenty-four-bed transitional living program for homeless youth.

NATIONAL CENTER FOR LESBIAN RIGHTS (NCLR)
870 Market Street, Suite 370
San Francisco, CA 94102
Legal Help Line (800) 528-6257
T (415) 392-6257
F (415) 392-8442
www.nclrights.org
info@nclrights.org

The National Center for Lesbian Rights is a national legal organization committed to advancing the civil and human rights of lesbian, gay, bisexual, and transgender people and their families through litigation, public policy advocacy, and public education.

NATIONAL GAY AND LESBIAN TASK FORCE (NGLTF)
1325 Massachusetts Avenue NW, Suite 600
Washington, DC 20005
T (202) 393-5177
F (202) 393-2241
TTY (202) 393-2284
www.thetaskforce.org
info@thetaskforce.org

The Task Force is a national progressive organization working for the civil rights of LGBT people. Its website provides reports and guides for activists, including a report on making schools safe. At its annual "Creating Change" conference NGLTF offers sessions and panels to develop skills and strategize for LGBT equality.

NATIONAL RUNAWAY SWITCHBOARD
3080 N. Lincoln Avenue
Chicago, IL 60657
Hotline (800) RUNAWAY
Agency and Information Line (800) 344-2785
T (773) 880-9860
F (773) 929-5150
www.1800runaway.org

The National Runaway Switchboard provides crisis intervention and local and national referrals to youth and their families, training materials and resources for communities and schools and is the federally designated national communication system for runaway and homeless youth.

NATIONAL CENTER FOR TRANSGENDER EQUALITY
1325 Massachusetts Avenue NW, Suite 700
Washington, DC 20005
T (202) 903-0112
F (202) 393-2241
www.transequality.org
ncte@transequality.org

NCTE is a social justice organization dedicated to advancing the equality
of transgender people through advocacy, collaboration, and empowerment.

NATIONAL QUEER ASIAN PACIFIC ISLANDER ALLIANCE
(NQAPIA)
1322 18th Street, NW
Washington, DC 20036
(202) 422-4909
www.nqapia.org
nqapia@gmail.com

The National Queer Asian Pacific Islander Alliance (NQAPIA) is a
federation of LGBT Asian American, South Asian, Southeast Asian, and
Pacific Islander (AAPI) organizations. They seek to build the organizational
capacity of local LGBT AAPI groups, develop leadership, promote
visibility, educate the community, enhance grassroots organizing, expand
collaborations, and challenge homophobia and racism. NQAPIA is a
project of the Tides Center in San Francisco, CA.

OPPORTUNITIES FOR LEARNING
PUBLIC CHARTER SCHOOLS
320 N. Halstead Street, Suite 220
Pasadena, CA 91107
T (818) 952-1790
F (818) 952-1795
www.emsofl.com

Opportunities For Learning is dedicated to its mission of being the best independent study public charter school, empowering underserved students by unlocking their passions and dreams and moving them daily towards graduation.

PARENTS, FAMILIES, AND FRIENDS OF LESBIANS AND GAYS (PFLAG)
1828 L Street, NW, Suite 660
Washington, DC 20036
T (202) 467-8180
F (202) 349-0788
www.pflag.org
info@pflag.org

PFLAG promotes the health and well-being of LGBT persons, their families, and friends through: support to cope with an adverse society; education to enlighten an ill-informed public; and advocacy to end discrimination and to secure equal civil rights. PFLAG provides opportunity for dialogue about sexual orientation and gender identity, and acts to create a society that is healthy and respectful of human diversity.

POINT FOUNDATION
5757 Wilshire Boulevard, Suite 370
Los Angeles, CA 90060-0108
T (866) 337-6468
F (866) 397-6468
www.pointfoundation.org
info@pointfoundation.org

Point Foundation provides financial support, mentoring, leadership training, and hope to meritorious students who are marginalized due to sexual orientation, gender identity, or gender expression.

THE SAFE SCHOOLS COALITION
11401 East Jefferson Street, Suite 401
Seattle, WA 98122
24-Hour Crisis Line (877) 723-3723
T (206) 451-7233
www.safeschoolscoalition.org

The Safe Schools Coalition offers a variety of resources to help youth, educators, administrators, parents, and guardians end bullying and create safe school environments for LGBT youth. Resources include hotlines for LGBT youth experiencing harassment.

TRANSGENDER LAW CENTER
870 Market Street, Room 400
San Francisco, CA 94102
T (415) 865-0176
F (877) 847-1278
www.transgenderlawcenter.org
info@transgenderlawcenter.org

A civil rights organization advocating for transgender communities.

TRANSYOUTH FAMILY ALLIES
PO Box 1471
Holland, MI 49422-1471
T (888) 462-8932
www.imatyfa.org
info@imatyfa.org

Partners with educators, service providers, and communities to develop supportive environments in which gender may be expressed and respected.

THE TREVOR PROJECT
8704 Santa Monica Boulevard, Suite 200
West Hollywood, CA 90069
Toll-Free Hotline (866) 4U-TREVOR
T (310) 271-8845
F (310) 271-8846
www.thetrevorproject.org
support@thetrevorproject.org

The Trevor Project provides a national twenty-four-hour toll-free suicide prevention hotline aimed at LGBT and questioning youth and offers an educational package and other resources to raise acceptance for LGBT youth in school and institutional settings.

YOUTH GUARDIAN SERVICES
101 E. State Street, #299
Ithaca, NY 14850
T (877) 270-5152
F (703) 783-0525
www.youth-guard.org

Youth Guardian Services is a youth-run, nonprofit organization that provides support and services on the Internet to LGBT and straight, supportive youth.

Acknowledgements

This is a book about love and family. We thank these people who have stood by us and said, "We love you no matter what."

Uncle Marty Ogino, Auntie Leslie, Lindsay, Jonathan and Ryan Fiske. Uncle Paul Ogino, Auntie Arlene, Stephanie, Matthew and Dan Hopkinson. Uncle Bert Tanaka, Auntie Ailene, Uncle Gordon Chang, Auntie Cheryl, Auntie Janet Henze, Auntie Karen Tanaka, Patrick and Jamie, Uncle Drew Tamaki, Auntie Sachi, Joy, Uncle Wayne Kamiya, Auntie Kathy, Karrie, Brett and Jamie Haagsma, Uncle Bob Shimasaki, Auntie Bonnie, Auntie Grandma Mitsue Tanaka, and Auntie Susan Aizumi. Ross Manzo, Cathy, Ross W. and Grandma Mary Wallace, the Sam Salazar Family, Janice Hurtado, Jeanne Takatani, Judy Asazawa, and Susie Arii.

This book is about hope. We thank these people and organizations that supported, nurtured, and showed us that our lives could be even richer and filled with more purpose:

PFLAG National, especially Jody Huckaby, who always believed in my dreams; Elizabeth Kohm, who is helping me realize them one by one; Liz Owen, who shares my stories and often cries when I tell them; and Jean-Marie Navetta, who motivated me to think outside the box.

Pasadena PFLAG, especially Patti Loitz, Betsy Hanger, the Torres-Rangels, and Adam LaRue.

Rea Carey, Darlene Nipper, Russell Roybal, and Sue Hyde at The National Gay and Lesbian Task Force, who recognized the leader in my son and unlocked our passion to create change.

The L.A. Gay & Lesbian Center, especially Lorri Jean, Michael Ferrera, and the entire staff at LifeWorks who provided us with invaluable resources and a place to call home.

This book is about discovering your greatness. Aiden would like to thank these individuals for believing that he, too, could make a difference:

The Trevor Project, especially my mentor, Phoenix Schneider, for showing me that I am never alone.

Public Allies Los Angeles, Class of 2010-2011: Eko Canillas, Carlos Arceo, and Vanessa Vela-Lovelace for supporting me in finding my voice and giving me the tools to become a leader in my community.

This book is about dreams. We thank these individuals who helped us to make our dreams come true:

Dana Newman, our agent, who fell in love with our story and believed this story needed to be shared with other families.

Don Weise, Magnus Books, who lovingly edited Two Spirits, One Heart, and Don Weise and Lori Perkins from Riverdale Avenue/Magnus Books who finally gave our book a place to call home.

Bob Yehling from Word Journeys, who told a mother it is time to write this book and navigated me through the uncertain waters of writing.

Melissa Tanaka, my personal assistant who did whatever needed to be done, whenever it needed to be done, with a beautiful spirit and loving heart.

The Hall Family: John, Joan, Jamie, Jennifer, John Jr., and Jodi whose lives revolve around dreams and making them come true for themselves, others, and especially me.

Bill Toomey, a man who is my role model for speaking the truth in such a wonderful way.

Mike Canney, my foxhole buddy and a dear friend.

Jim Davis, a sacred leader and respected friend.

Stephen Jimenez, who felt our passion, believed we could make a difference, and with his faith and trust opened up doors for us.

Harold and Ellen Kameya, who for twenty years have dedicated their lives to being the Asian American parent voice, giving Asian LGBT youth hope that their parents will one day accept them.

Helen Oyakawa, who bought me my first subscription to Writer's Digest and planted the seed that I could be a writer.

Gwenyth Searer, who read through our manuscript, helped polish it, and made it better.

And to the countless others who were a part of our dreams, we are so grateful for each and every one of you.

But in the end, this book has been about an amazing journey to acceptance and love. And for that we have to thank Papa, Stefen, and Mary for showing us what those words truly mean.

About the Authors

Marsha Aizumi is an educational consultant, spokesperson, and advocate for the LGBT community. She has been married for forty years to Tad and has two sons, Aiden and Stefen. Her greatest passions are creating safer, more accepting schools, bringing healing and hope to families by sharing her story, and spending time with her family. You can visit Marsha online at www.marshaaizumi.com.

Aiden Aizumi is a transman, storyteller, and activist for the LGBT community. He is currently a college student majoring in social work. In his free time, Aiden loves to listen to music, connect with friends, and spend time with Mary and their dog, Kuma.

Made in the USA
San Bernardino, CA
17 June 2017